Hollywood or History?

A volume in
Hollywood or History?
Scott L. Roberts and Charles J. Elfer, *Series Editors*

Hollywood or History?

Scott L. Roberts and Charles J. Elfer, *Series Editors*

Hollywood or History? An Inquiry-Based Strategy for Using Film to Acknowledge Trauma in Social Studies (2022)
    Paul J. Yoder and Aaron Johnson

Hollywood or History? An Inquiry-Based Strategy for Using Film to Teach About Inequality and Inequity Throughout History (2022)
    Sarah J. Kaka

Hollywood or History? An Inquiry-Based Strategy for Using Film to Teach World History (2021)
    Scott L. Roberts and Charles J. Elfer

Hollywood or History? An Inquiry-Based Strategy for Using Film to Teach United States History (2018)
    Scott L. Roberts and Charles J. Elfer

Hollywood or History?
An Inquiry-Based Strategy for Using Film to Teach World Religions

edited by
Thomas E. Malewitz
Spalding University

Adam P. Zoeller
Saint Xavier High School

INFORMATION AGE PUBLISHING, INC.
Charlotte, NC • www.infoagepub.com

Library of Congress Cataloging-in-Publication Data

A CIP record for this book is available from the Library of Congress
http://www.loc.gov

ISBN: 979-8-88730-151-8 (Paperback)
       979-8-88730-152-5 (Hardcover)
       979-8-88730-153-2 (E-Book)

Copyright © 2023 Information Age Publishing Inc.

All rights reserved. No part of this publication may be reproduced, stored in a retrieval system, or transmitted, in any form or by any means, electronic, mechanical, photocopying, microfilming, recording or otherwise, without written permission from the publisher.

Printed in the United States of America

Contents

Preface vii

Introduction to Hollywood or History? World Religions Edition ix

1   Faith in Action 1

Unity and Community: *Big Hero 6* and Paul of Tarsus's Vision of the Body of Christ 3
Thomas E. Malewitz

The Death and Resurrection of the Dark Knight 13
Adam P. Zoeller

The Hero's Journey of Frodo Baggins 25
Adam P. Zoeller

The Nature of the 10 Plagues Against Egypt and the Egyptian Gods 35
Thomas E. Malewitz

2   Historical Contexts 43

Catholic Social Teachings and Eunice Kennedy Shriver's Catholic Faith 45
Daniel E. Martin

Henri Dauman and Telling the Untold Stories 54
Stephanie Garrone-Shufran and Rory Tannebaum

Understanding the Effects of Residential Schools and Initial Steps of Reconciliation 63
Thomas E. Malewitz

In the Face of Martyrdom: Testing the Bedrock of Faith 72
Thomas E. Malewitz

3   Religious Figures 81

Guidance on Non-Violence: *Gandhi*, Living for Change Through Faith 83
Thomas E. Malewitz

The Legacy of Authentic Discipleship 93
Adam P. Zoeller

Through the Eyes of Dr. King and Malcolm X: The Intersection of Civil Rights and Religion 102
Colleen Fitzpatrick and Ariel Cornett

Of Gods and Men: On Hospitality and Interreligious Dialogue 115
Thomas E. Malewitz

4   Rituals 123

The Relationship Between Music and Traditional African Religion 125
Miguel David Hernandez Paz

Exorcism, Healings, and Mercy: The Role of the Holy Fool and Prophet in *The Island* 140
Thomas E. Malewitz

Exploring the Egyptian Book of the Dead: Weighing of the Heart Ceremony 147
Thomas E. Malewitz

The Camino de Santiago: Pilgrimage as a Devotion of Cultural Awareness and Personal Renewal 156
Thomas E. Malewitz

5   Wisdom Literature 167

The Truth of Salvation Is Reconciliation 169
Adam P. Zoeller

Escaping the Cycle of Groundhog Day 179
Adam P. Zoeller

Wisdom Literature and the Power of the Poetic Word 189
Thomas Malewitz

About the Contributors 197

Preface

Hollywood tells the same story, right? Over and over again there is a young hero in the making who has to deal with adversity and train to be able to save the world. Over and over again this hero is guided by a father figure. Over and over there is a seemingly all-powerful enemy trying to stop the protagonist. And, most importantly, over and over again, the hero puts himself on the line to save everybody else. *Harry Potter. Lord of the Rings. Percy Jackson.* Avenger's movies. *Star Wars.* (Sample Student Work)

Recently, students in my secondary school theology class were given the choice to select project-based assessments to evaluate how Christopher Nolan's (2012) *The Dark Knight Rises* is a contemporary Christian allegory. This assessment strategy matches the Center for American Progress (CAP) article titled, "Elevating Student Voice in Education," which states, "Teachers and schools can give students a voice in what and how they learn through personalizing instruction. Personalized learning tailors at least some of the learning experience based on a students' individual need, skills, and interests" (Benner et al., 2019, p. 19). Two popular assessment choices by the students were to (a) read Isaiah 52:13–53:12 from the Hebrew Scriptures and create a homily/sermon that compares and contrasts Bruce Wayne/Batman and Jesus Christ in light of the theological concept of the suffering servant or (b) write a letter to the school administration expressing the value of media literacy as a necessary 21st century skill for theology class.

Upon successful completion of these assessments, students would be able to express their creativity in light of scriptural exegesis and/or knowledge of media literacy. Students were provided the definition of media literacy which according to the National Association of Media Literacy Education:

> To become a successful student, responsible citizen, productive worker, or competent and conscientious consumer, individuals need to develop expertise with the increasingly sophisticated information and entertainment media that address us on a multi-sensory level, affecting the way we think, feel, and behave. (Center for Media Literacy, 2001, para. 4)

Below is a selection of sample student work that demonstrates the importance of creating student-centered project-based learning where choice is paramount and modern media is utilized.

- "While they should not be used as a primary teaching tool, they are imperative reinforcing ideas through a pathway in which students can be engaged and attentive."
- "It also helps us to analyze media on a deeper level and truly understand the message it is trying to convey."
- "Media should continue to be used in the classroom and is crucial to a successful learning environment."
- "The skill of media literacy can help us explore allegorical aspects of the entertainment media that we consume today. A prime example of such aspects is *The Dark Knight Rises* and its subdued symbolism of the Paschal mystery and many other Christian theological concepts."
- "Modern media gives students something to relate to and understand more clearly instead of only reading the Bible. The Bible is an amazing source to learn the history and details of Jesus' life, death, and resurrection. However, many students cannot connect with the messages and themes within the Bible because of the language used, the age of the scriptures, etc. Not everyone learns best from reading ancient texts, so having alternative forms of learning allows for a variety of students' academic needs to be met."
- "Jesus perfectly fits the description of the suffering servant. Just like this servant, Jesus was 'wounded for our transgressions'" (Isaiah 53:5). "The "suffering servant" description of Jesus from Isaiah can also be applied to Batman in *The Dark Knight Rises* because he doesn't care about his misfortunes if it means that he can help other people."

These selections demonstrate the ability to synthesize information from various sources and complete a project that showcases a student's individual skills or interest. These types of learning experiences represent transferable critical thinking skills necessary for students in the 21st century.

REFERENCES

Benner, M., Brown, C., & Jeffrey, A. (2019). *Elevating student voice in education.* Center for American Progress. https://www.americanprogress.org/wp-content/uploads/2019/08/StudentVoice-report.pdf

Center for Media Literacy. (2001). *What is media literacy? NAMLE's short answer and a longer thought.* National Association for Media Literacy Education. http://www.medialit.org/reading-room/what-media-literacy-namles-short-answer-and-longer-thought

Nolan, C. (Director). (2012). *The Dark Knight Rises* [Film]. Warner Brothers, Legendary Pictures, Syncopy, DC Entertainment.

Introduction to Hollywood or History?

World Religions Edition

In response to the limitation associated with teaching through film, we sought to develop practical lesson ideas that might bridge gaps between theory and practice and assist teachers endeavoring to make effective use of film in the classrooms. We believe that film can serve as a powerful tool in the social studies classroom and if appropriately utilized can foster critical thinking and civic mindedness. The college, career, and civic life (C3) framework, adopted by the National Council for the Social Studies in 2013, represents a renewed and formalized emphasis on the perennial social studies goals of deep thinking, reading, and writing. The C3 is comprehensive and ambitious. Moreover, we believe that as teachers endeavor to digest and implement the platform in schools and classrooms across the country, the desire for access to structured strategies that lead to more active and rigorous investigation in the social studies classroom will grow increasingly acute. Our hope is that the present text might play a small role in the larger project of supporting practitioners, specifically teachers of history and world religions, by offering a collection of classroom-ready tools designed to foster historical inquiry through the careful use of theologically-themed motion pictures and documentaries (Roberts & Elfer, 2021, p. xiii)

The Hollywood or History? method is a unique educational strategy and to adhere to its expectations the following method section is included to offer a consistent and clear series introduction for reader ease and clear implementation throughout each of the volume editions within the Hollywood or History? series. The following Hollywood or History? method section below, acknowledges and adapts the outline for the step-by-step method that was established for this educational strategy (see Roberts & Elfer, 2021, pp. xiii–xx).

THE HOLLYWOOD OR HISTORY? METHOD

Through our collaborative work with both new and experienced teachers, we have developed and refined a classroom strategy that provides a structured and inquiry-based approach for viewing Hollywood feature films in the social studies classroom. This strategy—which we refer to as Hollywood or History?—bridges components of the C3 framework, especially, deep reading, deep writing, and deep thinking, through a guided analysis of historical materials and historically themed films. The strategy challenges teachers and students to evaluate competing claims, detect bias, and measure evidence from multiple sources with the goal of developing reasoned perspectives regarding the relative accuracy of commercially produced motion pictures. By the end of the Hollywood or History? exercise, students are positioned to express those self-generated assessments—orally and in writing—by making claims about whether a film selection is 100% history (all fact), 100% Hollywood (all fiction), or somewhere in between. The Hollywood or History? approach is fundamentally a platform for historical inquiry and analytical-skill building (Roberts & Elfer, 2021, pp. xiii–xiv).

As a practicing middle grades teacher of state history, Scott Roberts originally developed this strategy through his efforts to implement historical thinking in his classroom in a way that was approachable and engaging. Informed by well-known inquiry focused work of Sam Wineburg as well as his appreciation for the television series Hollywood or History? Roberts was able to make effective use of both topically relevant historical films and historical material (primary and secondary sources) in a way that was developmentally appropriate for eighth grade students of state history. In designing and implementing several Hollywood or History? lessons in his own teaching space, he saw firsthand how well the strategy was received with his middle grades students and was encouraged by the motivation that went on to share the strategy at regional and state conferences and in staff development sessions. As he moved into teacher education and the role of social studies methods instructor, Roberts introduced the approach to his preservice education students as a means of modeling effective approaches for using traditional pedagogical tools (e.g., textbooks, films, worksheets, lecture, etc.) in the social studies classroom. In an effort to show how these traditional tools can assist in teaching through C3, Roberts asked his students to participate in a hands-on Hollywood or History? lesson based on a clip from the movie *Gone With the Wind* ([Fleming, 1939]; Roberts, 2014; Roberts & Elfer, 2021, p. xiv; Roberts & Wellereiter, 2015).

Encouraged by his early successes as a K–12 practitioner and teacher education, Roberts later shared his experiences with long-time colleague, Charles Elfer, who was also interested in best practices for using film in the social studies classroom. Since that time, their collaborative work on the subject has grown tremendously. Together, Roberts and Elfer have worked to share the Hollywood or History? framework throughout the United States at professional venues. Additionally, Roberts and Elfer have elaborated on illustrations of the approach and its effectiveness in a variety of professional journals, books, and as published lesson plans (Elfer et al., 2017; Roberts, 2014; Roberts & Elfer, 2017). The feedback received has been generous and overwhelmingly positive and provides the impetus for the Hollywood or History? manuscript series (Roberts & Elfer, 2021, xiv–xv).

The Hollywood or History? approach represents a structured plan for the evaluation of film which incorporates the use of primary and secondary historical materials. Lesson materials themselves will necessarily vary from one lesson to the next as a function of topical differences and student readiness; however, the procedures are largely consistent across applications. A detailed outline of those procedures is offered below in a step-by-step format for clarity. The procedures outlined here are incorporated throughout the text in each of the exercises included (Roberts & Elfer, 2021, p. xv).

Step 1: Film Selection

The list of potential useful films for the world history or world religion classroom is expansive and forever growing. To provide an exhaustive accounting is beyond the scope of the present text. The included plans offer a variety of themes and potential topics that are addressed throughout the secondary curriculum, as indicated at the beginning of each lesson plan (Roberts & Elfer, 2021, p. xv).

The first step in Hollywood or History? lesson plan development is generally to make the film selection. In the present text, we have drawn on the experiences of educators from a wide variety of contexts. Within those examples, readers will find that contributors have paid attention to ratings, availability, and practicality of the lesson topic. Ratings are especially important, and while they will vary from one school context to another, we offer our sincere caution to practitioners to ensure that the films incorporated into the classroom contain content that is consistent with the norms and expectations of the wider community served (Roberts & Elfer, 2021, p. xv).

The lesson plans offered throughout this volume offer a unique combination of social studies and global awareness, through a focus on topics directly connected to world religions. Although the desire in the Hollywood or History? method is to rely primarily on film clips and not use films in their entirety (Roberts & Elfer, 2021, p. xvi), due to the nature of a particular religious theme, or in the need to complete a story arc, some of the lesson plans included in this volume have allowed the option of utilizing film clips or the entire film as an option for lesson plan as the need of the teacher warrants. Please be aware of the context of the topic and read the lesson plan thoroughly to have a complete context of the expectations of the activities and assessments.

Step 2: Develop the Inquiry

Once the film selection has been made, the second step in a Hollywood or History? exercise is to develop an interesting question or set of questions. As the showcased lessons demonstrate, a narrative describing the scene, the film, and/or context of world religion under review often guides the students into inquiry. In a Hollywood or History? lesson, the fundamental question that students must answer is: "Is the material depicted in the film 100% Hollywood (fiction), 100% history (fact), or somewhere in between?" In several instances, that essential question will suffice as an overarching task for the inquiry. In other cases, teachers may develop additional questions to guide the exercise. Additional questions may be especially useful for beginners who may not have a great deal of experience with analytical exercises like these and/or where the level of rigor is so high as to require additional scaffolds for students (Roberts & Elfer, 2021, pp. xvi–xvii).

Step 3: Selection of Sources

As the series title suggests, the crux of the Hollywood or History? strategy begins with film. Equally important is the careful selection of accompanying documents that serve to compliment, verify, and/or challenge the film under review. As the lessons presented below will demonstrate, we often suggest bookending the film selection with primary and secondary sources. In our experience in working with students and preservice teachers in a variety of classroom contexts, we find that this approach (a) provides for an inquiry exercise that is suitable to a single classroom session, (b) reinforces primary and secondary materials as the core of historical work, and (c) is developmentally appropriate for a wide range of student audiences. As is true of many of the recommendations for practice provided in the present text, we invite teachers to scale-up their Hollywood or History? lessons in a way that is suitable to their student populations (Roberts & Elfer, 2021, p. xvii).

Step 4: Develop Student Supports

Some of the Hollywood or History? exercises provide a graphic organizer which follows a template developed by Roberts (2014). Our intention is to provide classroom-ready materials that are accessible for both teachers and students. With that in mind, and in anticipation of the fact that many teachers may want to make the Hollywood or History? strategy a regular part of their practice, we endeavored to standardize the student supports to some degree. The supports have been field-tested and enjoy a demonstrated level of effectiveness. Our objective is not to provide a rigid set of prescriptions and tools, and readers should note that the accompanying worksheets and graphic organizers are highly flexible. Once students learn the strategy it can be applied to multiple topics with ease. As with other suggested practices, the exact format of the student support is completely flexible (Roberts & Elfer, 2021, p. xviii).

Step 5: Show the Film and Review the Resources

With documents and film clips carefully selected, the next step in the Hollywood or History? approach is to carefully have students review the collection of materials. In most cases, we recommend showing the film clip first. Much of the gravity, or hook, in the strategy centers on the medium of film, which has the unique capacity to capture student attention and generate interest. In our ongoing collaboration with a community of practitioners, it is worth noting that a number of educators have suggested a flipped protocol, whereby the sources are examined first and then the film clips are reviewed by the students. Traditionally, we have organized our classes into small groups, but this exercise could also be treated as an individual activity. Similarly, readers may find benefit in a whole class arrangement as a way of modeling the expected behavior and process (Roberts & Elfer, 2021, p. xix).

Step 6: Hollywood or History?

Once students have had an opportunity to view the film and document collection, they should be invited to deliberate and prepare their evaluations regarding the relative accuracy of the clip. This portion of the exercise is straightforward, but students should be instructed to support their conclusions with evidence from the texts and film. There is no right or wrong, per se, as the primary goal is to mobilize the evidence in support of conclusions. We encourage the reader to use the included worksheets and/or graphic organizers to assist with the students forming and supporting their conclusions (Roberts & Elfer, 2021, p. xix).

Step 7: Debriefing Activity and Extensions

After students have had the opportunity to draft their evidence-based determinations regarding the historical accuracy of the film clip, we suggest that teachers unpack the conclusions as a whole class. Throughout this manuscript contributing authors have offered a wide variety of methods to assist in debriefing the student conclusions. Readers may find that in some instances, authors have suggested an individual writing assignment, whereby students are asked to write an essay for homework, or authors have suggested group research projects to further investigate the historical contexts presented in the film and sources. We also invite teachers to introduce additional documents that further challenge or confirm the film and resources encountered. Students can work to make sense of these new documents in class if time permits, or as part of a homework assignment (Roberts & Elfer, 2021, p. xx).

LAYOUT OF THE BOOK

Chapter 1

The topical focus for the first chapter in the World Religions volume explores what motivates a character to conduct virtuous actions in light of their respective worldview and conditions. The title for Chapter 1 is "Faith in Action" which introduces the genre of action films while expanding on the primary characters and their development towards working for the common good as understood in Judaism and Christianity. Thomas Malewitz bookends the chapter (Lessons 1 and 4) using the animated films of *Big Hero 6* (Hall & Williams, 2014) and *Prince of Egypt* (Chapman et al., 1998) as they relate to obstacles to faith through the lens of mythology and history. Along with *Prince of Egypt* (Chapman et al., 1998), Malewitz uses *Exodus: Gods and Kings* (Scott, 2014) to invite adolescents to a greater understanding of order and disorder within the story of the plagues of Egypt and how the deeper purpose of the story can still have bearing on their personal choices and lives.

In Lesson 2, Adam Zoeller studies death and resurrection through events of DC superhero Batman in Christopher Nolan's (2012) *The Dark Knight Rises*. Based loosely on *Batman: Knightfall* (Moench, 1993), Zoeller provides the opportunity for secondary school students to understand the film as a Christian allegory that encapsulates the Paschal mystery in Christianity. In addition to action films, Zoeller introduces the genre of fantasy in Lesson 3. This lesson features protagonist Frodo Baggins from Peter Jackson's (2001) *The Lord of the Rings: The Fellowship of the Ring* as he embarks on a journey to save Middle Earth. This saving mission strategically analyzes how Frodo reflects the first six stages of the hero's journey popularized by 20th century author, Joseph Campbell (2012). Please note that additional stages of the hero's journey motif for Frodo Baggins are included throughout Peter Jackson's Lord of the Rings trilogy.

Chapter 2

The topical focus for Chapter 2 explores historical contexts surrounding the lives of individuals or events that are defined by, or influenced by, religion firmly rooted in history. The first lesson by Daniel Martin uses the life of Eunice Kennedy Shriver and the creation of the Special Olympics as an exemplar of the Catholic social teachings. Through the ESPN short film *Brave in the Attempt* (Mitchell, 2015), Shiver's life bears witness as a lifelong fierce advocate for recognizing the dignity of others, especially individuals with disabilities. The second lesson of this chapter, by Stephanie Garrone-Shufran and Rory Tannebaum, offer a captivating account of the life and work of photojournalist Henri Dauman. *Henri Dauman: Looking Up* (Jones, 2020), offers a concrete experience of a holocaust survivor capturing life in a posh world. The documentary and lesson offers a tangible example of the juxtaposition between acceptance and isolation, citizenship and refugeeism, and searching for one's identity.

Lesson 3 explores a contemporary wound from a witness testimony from residential school life of children of the First Nations unearthed at the Canadian Truth and Reconciliation Commission. Thomas Malewitz uses the short film *Holy Angels* (Villeneuve, 2017) to spark secondary students to start a dialogue from listening to understanding as well as challenge the students to think about what initial steps of authentic advocacy would look like for future generations. The final lesson in the historical contexts chapter challenges students to explore Martin Scorsese's adaptation of *Silence* (Scorsese, 2016). This lesson by Malewitz examines the limits of an individual's faith and witness through the lens of the stories of Christian martyrdom during 16th century Japanese nationalism.

Chapter 3

The topical focus for Chapter 3 explores religious figures whose example of perseverance amidst adversity continues to inspire those who seek change albeit social, political, or economic. Authored by Thomas Malewitz, the first lesson in Chapter 3 is written using the Academy award-winning film *Gandhi* (Attenborough, 1982) and has students research and compare how Gandhi's nonviolent resistance influenced later leaders in their movements of social change. Adam Zoeller introduces the incomparable American social advocate Dorothy Day for the second lesson through the Journey Films documentary, *Revolution of the Heart: The Dorothy Day Story* (Doblmeier, 2020). Her extreme activism for the poor and marginalized gained recognition and concern within the Catholic church as well as the U.S. Government. Likewise, authors Colleen Fitzpatrick and Ariel Cornett compare and contrast the civil rights activists, Malcolm X and Dr. Martin Luther King Jr. This third lesson uses the films *Selma* (DuVernay, 2014) and *Malcolm X* (Lee, 1992) to discuss the impact of the American civil rights movement and how a civil or political leader's faith directly and indirectly can influence their actions. The final lesson in Chapter 3 features the French drama of the final days of the Trappist monks of Tibhirine, during the Algerian Civil War, in *Of Gods and Men* (Beauvois, 2011). Thomas Malewitz provides the primary question for his students in this lesson. This question is quintessential to the main theme of Chapter 3, "Why do you think some people are willing to become a witness and sacrifice their time and lives for the betterment of others?"

Chapter 4

The topical focus for Chapter 4 explores the role of rituals and devotions in religious belief systems. The first lesson by Miguel Hernanadez Paz explores the Spanish film *Calle 54* (Trueba, 2000). This lesson explores the importance and embodiment that the history of jazz and Gospel music has played in developing a cultural identity within the American ethos, especially in Latino and African communities, rituals and traditions. The second lesson uses the Russian film *The Island* (Lungin, 2006) to explore the role of prophets, exorcisms, and healings from an Othrodox lens. Thomas Malewitz explores how this simple and mysterious ritual aims at a wholeness and for an individual through dedicated prayer rather than focusing on the power of demonic possession as often portrayed in Hollywood horror films.

The third lesson challenges the students to investigate the ancient historical record of Egyptian rituals through the Egyptian *Book of the Dead* and the weighing of the heart ceremony to better understand the plague narrative from Exodus. Using *The Ten Commandments* (DeMille, 1956) Thomas Malewitz explores the deeper meaning that lay in the narrative of the story and how that is subtly displayed through the timeless masterpiece of Cecil B. DeMille. Finally, Malewitz also explores the importance of the ritual devotion of pilgrimage in Christian and islam through a research project about the Hajj and The Camino de Santiago. Through video clips from *The Way* (Estevez, 2010) Malewitz explores the devotion of pilgrimage through aspects of personal change and cultural awareness.

Chapter 5

The topical focus for Chapter 5 explores wisdom and its attainment. Merriam-Webster (n.d.) identifies the essential meaning of wisdom in the following: "knowledge that is gained by having many experiences in life and the natural ability to understand things that most other people cannot understand." These definitions are reflected perfectly in the selected choices for this chapter. Lesson 1 by Adam Zoeller used the short film *Admissions* (Kakatsakis, 2011) in order for his students to discover the importance of conflict resolution and interreligious dialogue, especially among Christians, Jews, and Muslims. The wisdom necessary to witness and appreciate the beauty of the human condition regardless of religion is paramount in order to foster a more peaceful world. Zoeller also explores the wisdom and peace of Buddhism in Lesson 2. Although *Groundhog Day* (Ramis, 1993) is classified as a comedy, there are many aspects of the plot and character development that are in fact quite Buddhist. This film playfully invites the audience into seeing the world through a person trapped in a cycle of his own making through inaction and selfishness. Thomas Malewitz concludes Chapter 5 with the power of poetic word in a short film titled, *Thursday Appointment* (Kheradmandan, 2019). The study of this Sufi poem examines not only how poetry can offer wisdom to everyday life but also how digital media brings ancient sacred poetic writings new meaning and connection to life in the digital age.

REFERENCES

Attenborough, R. (Director). (1982). *Gandhi* [Film]. Columbia Pictures.
Beauvois, X. (Director). (2011). *Of gods and men* [Film]. Mars Distribution.
Campbell, J. (2012). *Hero with a thousand faces*. New World Library.
Chapman, B., Hickner, S., & Wells, S. (Directors). (1998). *The prince of Egypt* [Film]. DreamWorks Pictures.
DeMille, C. B. (Director). (1956). *The ten commandments* [Film]. Paramount.
Doblmeier, M. (Director). (2020). *Revolution of the heart: The Dorothy Day story* [Film]. Journey Films.
DuVernay, A. (Director). (2014). *Selma* [Film]. Paramount Pictures.
Elfer, C. J., Roberts, S. L., & Fahey, B. (2017). "They're not just for Fridays anymore:" Historical inquiry, media literacy, and Hollywood films. *Teaching History, 42*(2), 83–96. https://doi.org/10.33043/TH.42.2.83-96
Estevez, E. (Director). (2010). *The Way* [Film]. Filmax Entertainment.
Fleming, V. (Director). (1939). *Gone with the wind* [Film]. Selznick International Pictures; Metro-Goldwyn-Mayer.
Hall, D., & Williams, C. (Directors). (2014). *Big Hero 6* [Film]. Walt Disney Studios.
Jackson, P. (Director). (2001). *The Lord of the rings: The fellowship of the ring* [Film]. New Line Productions.
Jones, P. K. (Director). (2020). *Henri Dauman: Looking up* [Film]. Nocturnal Media.
Kakatsakis, H. (Director). (2011). *Admissions* [Film]. One Film Company. http://www.admissionsfilm.com/

Kheradmandan, M. R. (Director). (2019). *Thursday Appointment* [Film]. Soureh. (Available at https://www.youtube.com/watch?v=XXx_Hw34V-Q)

Lee, S. (Director). (1992). *Malcolm X* [Film]. Warner Brothers.

Lungin, P. (Director). (2006). *The Island* [Film]. Pavel Lungin's Studio. [Russia]

Merriam-Webster. (n.d.). *Wisdom.* https://www.merriam-webster.com/dictionary/wisdom

Mitchell, F. (Director). (2015). *ESPN 30-for-30 shorts: Brave in the attempt* [Film]. ESPN.

Moench, D. (1993). *Batman: Knightfall.* DC Comics.

Nolan, C. (Director). (2012). *The Dark Knight Rises* [Film]. Warner Bros., Legendary Pictures, Syncopy, DC Entertainment.

Ramis, H. (Director). (1993). *Groundhog Day* [Film]. Columbia Pictures.

Roberts, S. L. (2014). Effectively using social studies textbooks in historical inquiry. *Social Studies Research and Practice, 9*(1), 119–128. https://doi.org/10.1108/SSRP-01-2014-B0006

Roberts, S. L., & Elfer, C. (2017). Hollywood or history?: Inquiring about U.S. slavery through film. In W. Russell & S. Waters (Eds.), *Cinematic social studies* (pp. 255–283). Information Age Publishing.

Roberts, S. L., & Elfer, C. (2021). Introduction to Hollywood or History? In S. Roberts & C. Elfer (Eds.), *Hollywood or history?: An inquiry-based strategy for using film to teach world history* (pp. ix–xx). Information Age Publishing.

Roberts, S. L., & Wellereiter, B. (2015). *Teaching middle school level social studies: A practical guide for 4th–8th grades* (2nd ed.). Digital Textbooks.

Scorsese, M. (Director). (2016). *Silence* [Film]. Paramount Pictures.

Scott, R. (2014). *Exodus: Gods and kings* [Film]. Chernin Entertainment; Scott Free Production; Babieka Volcano Films; TSG Entertainment.

Trueba, F. (Director). (2000). *Calle 54* [Film]. Buena Vista International.

Villeneuve, J. C. (Director). (2017). *Holy Angels* [Film]. National Film Board of Canada.

CHAPTER 1

Faith in Action

What makes someone a hero, or an action heroic? Merriam-Webster (n.d.) defines hero in the following ways: "a mythological or legendary figure often of divine descent endowed with great strength or ability; an illustrious warrior; a person admired for achievements and noble qualities; or one who shows great courage." The stories of heroes are present in literature as well as in film. These heroic storylines include themes of discernment, discovery, and dedication to a cause greater than one's self interest. Heroic characters or characteristics are also present in ancient religious texts such as the *Torah* (Moses), *New Testament* (Jesus), the *Qu'ran* (Muhammad), or the *Bhagavad-Gita* (Krishna). What makes these people heroic is their ability to put their faith into action. This chapter of *Hollywood or History? An Inquiry-Based Strategy for Teaching World Religions* will examine heroic characters in the genre of action films, in light of religious beliefs or traditions.

The National Council for Social Studies (NCSS, n.d.) recommends that state departments of education work to ensure inclusion of the study of religion in all social studies programs including stand-alone world religions courses. Engaging students in the 21st century classroom requires strategies familiar to an adolescent from their secular society; thus, to use media to relate the sacred stories of the major world religions. With the rise in popularity of the superhero film genre, movies that explore the heroic actions of pop culture icons is a great avenue to bridge the gap between faith and action. Christopher Nolan's (2012) *The Dark Knight Rises*, which grossed over one billion dollars at the box office, is based on Batman, a legendary figure with great ability. The themes of redemption and sacrifice most notably aligned to the Christian faith are present in the film with emphasis on the Paschal mystery of Jesus Christ. Peter Jackson's (2001) adaptation of Catholic author, J. R. R. Tolkien's (1954) classic *The Lord of the Rings: The Fellowship of the Ring* highlights the value of myths as the protagonist, Frodo Baggins, demonstrates great strength and shows great courage. Frodo as the sacrificial priest archetype enters into a quest to save Middle Earth. The characteristics of sacrifice along with the concept of salvation are seen in faith tradition.

DreamWorks Pictures *The Prince of Egypt* (Chapman et al., 1998) and Ridley Scott's (2014) *Exodus: Gods and Kings* use creative license to depict the story of Moses from the Torah. The truths of the epic from Exodus demand a critical mind in order to analyze the culture and time period, specifically the nature of the 10 plagues against Egypt and the Egyptian gods. Lastly, the noble qualities of gentleness and kindness are evident in the character of Baymax from Walt Disney's *Big Hero 6* (Hall & Williams, 2014). Although Baymax is part of a team of illustrious warriors where his physical abilities are apparent, his true strength is his caring nature. The characters in this chapter, "Faith in Action," each uniquely reflect the qualities that epitomize what it means to be a hero or what it takes to possess heroic qualities along life's journey.

REFERENCES

Chapman, B., Hickner, S., & Wells, S. (Directors). (1998). *The prince of Egypt* [Film]. DreamWorks Pictures.
Hall, D., & Williams, C. (Directors). (2014). *Big hero 6* [Film]. Walt Disney.
Jackson, P. (Director). (2001). *The lord of the rings: The fellowship of the ring* [Film]. New Line Productions.
Merriam-Webster. (n.d.). Hero. In *Merriam-Webster.com dictionary*. Retrieved January 26, 2022, from https://www.merriam-webster.com/dictionary/hero
National Council for the Social Studies. (n.d.). *The study of religion in the social studies curriculum.* https://www.socialstudies.org/position-statements/study-of-religion-in-social-studies
Nolan, C. (Director). (2012). *The dark knight rises* [Film]. Warner Bros., Legendary Pictures, Syncopy, DC Entertainment.
Scott, R. (Director). (2014). *Exodus: Gods and kings* [Film]. Chernin Entertainment; Scott Free Production; Babieka Volcano Films; TSG Entertainment.
Tolkien, J. R. R. (1954). *The fellowship of the ring.* George Alen & Unwin.

Unity and Community: *Big Hero 6* and Paul of Tarsus's Vision of the Body of Christ

Thomas E. Malewitz

FILMS: *Big Hero 6* (2014)

Grade	Subject	Topic
9–12	Christianity	Understanding the concept of the Body of Christ

Chapter Theme	Estimated Time Needed for Lesson
Faith in Action; Community; Origin Story	Three 45-minute class periods

National Association for Media Literacy Education

Standard Number	Detailed Description of Each Standard You Are Discussing
Core Principles of Media Literacy Education in the United States	2. Media Literacy Education (MLE) expands the concept of literacy (i.e., reading and writing) to include all forms of media. *Implications for Practice* 　2.2 MLE enables students to express their own ideas through multiple forms of media (e.g., traditional print, electronic, digital, user-generated, and wireless) and helps students make connections between comprehension and inference-making in print, visual, and audio media. 　2.5 MLE welcomes the use of a broad range of media "texts," including popular media. 　2.6 MLE recognizes that evolving media forms, societal changes, and institutional structures require ever new instructional approaches and practices. 3. MLE builds and reinforces skills for learners of all ages. Like print literacy, those skills necessitate integrated, interactive, and repeated practice. *Implications for Practice* 　3.3 MLE engages students with varied learning styles. 　3.4 MLE is most effective when used with co-learning pedagogies, in which teachers learn from students and students learn from teachers and from classmates.

4 ■ Hollywood or History?

State and USCCB Standard Description

State	Detailed Description of Each Standard You Are Discussing
Illinois Communicating Conclusions and Taking informed Action	**SS.IS.6.9-12.** Construct and evaluate explanations and arguments using multiple sources and relevant, verified information. **SS.IS.7.9-12.** Articulate explanations and arguments to a targeted audience in diverse settings.
New York Civics	**12.G2e.** Rights are not absolute; they vary with legal status, with location (as in schools and workplaces), and with circumstance. The different statuses of United States residency bring with them specific protections, rights, and responsibilities. Minors have specific rights in school, in the workplace, in the community, and in the family. The extension of rights across location, circumstance, age, and legal status is a subject of civic discourse.
United States Conference of Catholic Bishops (USCCB) Curriculum Framework	**Doctrinal Elements of a Curriculum Framework for the Development of Catechetical Materials for Young People of High School Age** (USCCB, 2008b)
USCCB.IV The Church— II.B.1, 6	The Body of Christ (USCCB, 2000a, nos. 787–795), The Family of God (USCCB, 2000a, nos. 791, 1655–1658, 2204–2685)
The Church— V.A.2	We receive Christ's redemption as members of his body the Church.
USCCB.Option C Social Justice— I.B.3a-e	Mystical Body of Christ (USCCB, 2000a, nos. 774–779, 787–796, 805–807, 872, 1123, 1396, 1548, 2003), Family of God (USCCB, 2000a, no. 2790), Community of Sanctified Believes (USCCB, 2000a, no. 824)

NCSS C3 Framework

Dimension	Detailed Description of Each NCSS Dimension You Are Incorporating (should have all four).
D1.2.9-12	Explain points of agreement and disagreement experts have about interpretations and applications of disciplinary concepts and ideas associated with a compelling question.
D2.His.5.9-12.	Analyze how historical contexts shaped and continue to shape people's perspectives.

D3.3.9-12	Identify evidence that draws information directly and substantively from multiple sources to detect inconsistencies in evidence in order to revise or strengthen claims.
D4.1.9-12	Construct arguments using precise and knowledgeable claims, with evidence from multiple sources, while acknowledging counterclaims and evidentiary weaknesses.

NCSS Core Themes and Description

Theme Number	Detailed Description of Each Aligned NCSS Theme
I Culture	The study of culture examines the socially transmitted beliefs, values, institutions, behaviors, traditions, and way of life of a group of people; it also encompasses other cultural attributes and products, such as language, literature, music, arts and artifacts, and foods. Students come to understand that human cultures exhibit both similarities and differences, and they learn to see themselves both as individuals and as members of a particular culture that shares similarities with other cultural groups, but is also distinctive. In a multicultural, democratic society and globally connected world, students need to understand the multiple perspectives that derive from different cultural vantage points.
IV Individual Development and Identity	The study of individual development and identity will help students to describe factors important to the development of personal identity. They will explore the influence of peoples, places, and environments on personal development. Students will hone personal skills such as demonstrating self-direction when working towards and accomplishing personal goals, and making an effort to understand others and their beliefs, feelings, and convictions.
VIII Science, Technology, and Society	Science, and its practical application, technology, have had a major influence on social and cultural change, and on the ways people interact with the world. Scientific advances and technology have influenced life over the centuries, and modern life, as we know it, would be impossible without technology and the science that supports it.

Handouts/Materials/Web Links

Handout/Materials:
- "Hollywood or History?" graphic organizer
- "Hollywood or History?" character notes worksheet
- "Hollywood or History?" essay directions worksheet

Web Links:

A. Link to Film Clip(s):
- *Big Hero 6* (Hall & Williams, 2014)
  https://itunes.apple.com/us/movie/big-hero-6/id929423754
B. Primary Source(s):
- 1 Corinthians 12:12–31
C. Secondary Source(s):
- "The Four Oxen and the Lion" (DaBoss, 2013)
  https://fablesofaesop.com/the-four-oxen-and-the-lion.html

Guiding Questions

What should students know or understand at the completion of the unit or lesson?

Primary Questions:
- What does the analogy "Body of Christ" by Paul of Tarsus' mean?
- Why is it important to include a diverse set of talents/skills in a community?
- How can the old adage "united we stand, divided we fall" apply to a family, neighborhood, or team?

Important Vocabulary

List all of the important indicators of achievement (important people, places, and events) and vocabulary that students will need to know at the conclusion of the lesson.

Aesop Fable: A collection of oral amusing, humorous, and moral stories from ancient Greece 620–564 BCE.

Body of Christ: Allegory used by Paul of Tarsus to describe the dynamic of the Church, where Jesus is the head and the body, the Church, is composed of parts of the body each playing an essential role to the whole.

Assessment Strategies

Describe the assessments that will be used during the unit.

Formative Assessment: compare/contrasting, analysis/discussion

Summative Assessment: class discussion/participation, "Hollywood or History?" character notes worksheet

Teaching Strategies

10 min	Warm-up activity	10 min	Read/discuss: 1 Corinthians 12:12–31	**Additional 2 days/ HMWK**	Watch: *Big Hero 6* (Hall & Williams, 2014) while having students take notes for paper assessment
10 min	Read/discuss: Aesop's "The Four Oxen and the Lion" (DaBoss, 2013)	10 min	Hollywood or History?: Graphic Organizer		

Times are highly flexible and should be adjusted according to the number of sources used, length of introduction, period/block schedule, etc.

Sparking Strategy/Warm-Up

Sparking Strategy (Lesson introduction)

Lead the students in a brief discussion to explore the importance of the role of athletes on a team (baseball, basketball, football, soccer, etc.). Write on the board some of the positions within a team and how the roles connect together to support the whole. Encourage the students to offer their experiences of being on a team and the interaction of how it was successful or not successful based on the unity between the players on the team.

Lesson Procedures

In a numerical list, provide a step by step outline of what you plan to do in the lesson. Include questions you will ask the students and materials you will use.

1. Hand out copies of Aesop's "The Four Oxen and the Lion" (DaBoss, 2013). Invite a student to read out loud. Have the students discuss the story in groups, using questions such as: "What was the moral of the story?" and "How did this relate to the earlier discussion of teams and teamwork?" Have the student representative from the group share from the group discussion.
2. Project or hand out copies of 1 Corinthians 12:12–31 (NRSV). Break this reading into parts for several students to read out loud. Within the same groups, have the students explore the allegory of the "Body of Christ" using questions such as: "Explain how Paul of Tarsus and Aesop's fable compare and contrast"; "What does the analogy 'Body of Christ' by Paul of Tarsus' mean?" Verbally discuss or have the students turn in a written account of their discussion.
3. Handout copies of "Hollywood or History?" character notes worksheet as a character guide for notes throughout the film.
4. Watch the film. The teacher has the option to stop the film and discuss important aspects of characters, character actions, or decisions made by the characters throughout the film as a guide of analysis for younger students.
5. After the film, introduce the essay assignment for the students so that they can compare and contrast characters in *Big Hero 6* (Hall & Williams, 2014) with the 12 Apostles through the lens of Paul's 1 Corinthians 12:12–31. Directions for the essay and essay rubric are at the end of the lesson.

Differentiation

Think about your students' skill levels, intelligences, and learning styles. How are you going to make this lesson meet the needs of all of your students?

Scaffolds: Introduce foundational concept first, through short story/reading, then expanding into the concept of layers of perspective through the film. Have the students engage in comparing and contrasting the film while analyzing the primary source.
Connection to Real-Life: Have the students recognize the importance of diverse abilities to help the community as a whole through tangible experiences of teamwork and athletics.

Summarizing Strategies/Synthesizing Activity

What strategies are you going to use to allow students to summarize what they learned in the lesson?

- Discussion with reference to film clips/documents/evidence

References

Are there any additional resources that might be relevant to your lesson? Are there sources that you need to reference? Please add any citations using APA.

DaBoss. (Ed.). (2013, December14). *The four oxen and the lion.* Fables of Aesop. https://fablesofaesop.com/the-four-oxen-and-the-lion.html
Hall, D., & Williams, C. (Directors). (2014). *Big Hero 6* [Film]. Walt Disney Studios.
U.S. Conference of Catholic Bishops. (2000a). *Catechism of the Catholic Church* (2nd ed.) Libreria Editrice Vaticana.
U.S. Conference of Catholic Bishops. (2000b). *Doctrinal elements of a curriculum framework for the development of catechetical materials for young people of high school age.*

Additional Resources

Aranjuez, A. (2015). Power from a different perspective: Race, gender, and grief in *Big Hero 6*. Screen Education 79, 8–15. https://go.gale.com/ps/i.do?id=GALE%7CA440821101&sid=googleScholar&v=2.1&it=r&linkaccess=abs&issn=1449857X&p=AONE&sw=w&userGroupName=anon%7Ef8b521b4
List of Disney's *Big Hero 6* Characters. (2021, December 24). In Wikipedia. https://en.wikipedia.org/w/index.php?title=List_of_Disney%27s_Big_Hero_6_characters&oldid=1061795895
Malewitz, T. (2020). Community: Establishing a foundation for authentic relationship. In *Authenticity, passion, and advocacy: Approaching adolescent spirituality from the life and wisdom of Thomas Merton* (pp. 152–163). Wipf & Stock.
Tulloch, B., & Meyers, E. M. (2018). Children's film as design fiction: Ethics, data, and technology in *Big Hero 6* and *Zootopia*. *iConference 2018 Proceedings*. https://www.ideals.illinois.edu/handle/2142/100221
Who Were the 12 Disciples? (n.d.). Bibleinfo. https://www.bibleinfo.com/en/questions/who-were-twelve-disciples

Chapter 1: Faith in Action ■ 9

Hollywood or History?
Big Hero 6 (2014)

Big Hero 6 (2014) depicts the story of a group of friends working together, for the common good. Read the account of Paul of Tarsus's analogy of the parts of the body and their purpose in the Body of Christ (1 Corinthians 12:12–31), as well as Aesop's Fable "The Four Oxen and the Lion," and offer concrete examples from all the three sources to compare how working together can support a goal, while focusing on an individual choices could hurt a team goal. Offer a concrete example to support your decision.

Do you think that the Hollywood film *Big Hero 6* (2014) offered a good example of Paul of Tarsus's concept well? Explain your decision in the Hollywood or History? box at the bottom of the page.

Big Hero 6 (2014)	1 Corinthians 12:12–31	Secondary Source (Aesop)

What do you think? Hollywood or History?

Hollywood or History?
Big Hero 6 (2014) Character Notes

Unity and teamwork are important aspects for a community to come together. Diversity can play an important role in a community as each individual's talents or abilities can help the whole community. In this lesson we will compare Paul of Tarsus's call for community in the early Christian church (1 Corinthians 12:12–31) with the plot of *Big Hero 6* (2014).

While watching the film take note below of the role, abilities, actions, and contributions of the family or members of the Big Hero 6 (2014) community. Use your notes to help write an essay that compares and contrasts the film and Jesus' community of the 12 Apostles.

Characters in the Film
- Hiro Hamada
- Tadashi Hamada (Hiro's brother)
- Aunt Cass
- Fred
- Go Go Tomago
- Honey Lemon
- Wasabi

Jesus and the 12 Apostles
- Jesus
- Simon (Peter)
- Andrew
- James
- John
- Matthew
- Judas

Character Resources

- "List of Disney's *Big Hero 6* characters" (Wikipedia: https://en.wikipedia.org/w/index.php?title=List_of_Disney%27s_Big_Hero_6_characters&oldid=1061795895)
- "Who Were the 12 Disciples?" (Bibleinfo: https://www.bibleinfo.com/en/questions/who-were-twelve-disciples)

Hollywood or History?
Big Hero 6 (2014) Essay Directions

Purpose: Using *Big Hero 6* (2014) as a parable, "What can we learn about the nature of the community of the 12 Apostles?"; "How did each of their abilities bring something important to the wholeness of their community?"

In at least a 2-page essay, compare and contrast the characters of Big Hero 6 (2014) and the 12 Apostles to illustrate the importance of coming together in a community. Explain the role of each of the characters mentioned below and how the character could serve as a parallel to the calling and mission of Jesus and the 12 Apostles.

Use correct citations, 12 pt font.

Due:

Compare and contrast the following characters of *Big Hero 6* (2014) to Jesus and the early Church.

Use your notes from the film to recall specific scenes while writing your essay. Here are a few examples:

1. Baymax
   a. What role does Baymax play throughout the film?
   b. What was its original purpose?
   c. How did it grow beyond its purpose?

2. Who would these characters relate to in Jesus' time period? Why?
   a. Hiro
   b. Tadashi (Hiro's brother)
   c. Aunt Cass
   d. Fred
   e. Go Go
   f. Honey Lemon
   g. Wasabi

3. What could these relationships be symbolic of?
   a. Hiro and Tadashi
   b. Baymax and Hiro
   c. Tadashi's Friends and Hiro
   d. Tadashi and Professor Callaghan

Essay Rubric

Name: _____

Content (40 points)
- Descriptions and explanations show thoughtful reflection on each character's comparison to Jesus and his followers.
- Offer good knowledge about the reaction of the early Church in a correct culture and cultural expectations of the time
- Correct page length

    40 _____ 30 _____ 20 _____ 10 _____ 5 _____

Mechanics (20 points)
- Grammar
- Spelling
- Punctuation
- Appropriate vocabulary, no slang

    20 _____ 15 _____ 10 _____ 5 _____ 0 _____

Format (10 points)
- Correct Citations
- 1-inch margin
- 12-point font
- Neatness

    10 _____ 8 _____ 6 _____ 4 _____ 2 _____

Total points possible: 70 points   Total points earned: _____

(*Note:* A lower point value may be assigned in any area if a student is missing a section or has not completed the assignment sufficiently.

The Death and Resurrection of the Dark Knight

Adam P. Zoeller

FILM: *The Dark Knight Rises* (2012)

Grade	Subject	Topic
10–12	Christianity; Judaism	The Paschal Mystery

Chapter Theme	Estimated Time Needed for Lesson
Faith in Action: Paschal Mystery, Salvation History, Stages of Grief, Afterlife	Part 1: 30 minutes Part 2: 2 hours 45 minutes

National Association for Media Literacy Education

Standard Number	Detailed Description of Each Standard You Are Discussing

Core Principles of Media Literacy Education in the United States	3. MLE builds and reinforces skills for learners of all ages. Like print literacy, those skills necessitate integrated, interactive, and repeated practice.
	
	Implications for Practice
	  3.3 MLE engages students with varied learning styles.
	  3.4 MLE is most effective when used with co-learning pedagogies, in which teachers learn from students and students learn from teachers and from classmates.

State Standard Description

State	Detailed Description of Each Standard You Are Discussing
Florida Psychology strand SS.912.P	**SS.912.P.9.2.** Describe the relationship between attitudes (implicit and explicit) and behavior. **SS.912.P.9.7.** Discuss how an individual influences group behavior.

Massachusetts English Language Arts and Literacy (Grades 9–10 Writing Standards)	1. Write arguments (e.g., essays, letters to the editor, advocacy speeches) to support claims in an analysis of substantive topics or texts, using valid reasoning and relevant and sufficient evidence.
	  a. Introduce precise claim(s), distinguish the claim(s) from alternate or opposing claims, and create an organization that establishes clear relationships among claim(s), counterclaims, reasons, and evidence.
	  b. Develop claim(s) and counterclaims fairly, supplying evidence for each while pointing out the strengths and limitations of both in a manner that anticipates the audience's knowledge level and concerns.
	  c. Use words, phrases, and clauses to link the major sections of the text, create cohesion, and clarify the relationships between claim(s) and reasons, between reasons and evidence, and between claim(s) and counterclaims.
	  d. Establish and maintain a style appropriate to audience and purpose (e.g., formal for academic writing) while attending to the norms and conventions of the discipline in which they are writing.
	  e. Provide a concluding statement or section that follows from and supports the argument presented.

North Carolina Standards for World History Inquiry 9–12	Apply the inquiry models to analyze and evaluate social studies topics and issues in order to communicate conclusions and take informed actions. I.1.3 Summarize the central ideas and meaning of primary and secondary sources through the use of literacy strategies. I.1.4 Analyze causes, effects, and correlations. I.1.4 Determine the relevance of a source in relation to the compelling and supporting questions.

USCCB Curriculum Framework

Standard Number	Detailed Description of Each Standard You Are Discussing

Course III: The Mission of Jesus Christ	VII. Challenges
	  C. Isn't making sacrifices and putting up with suffering a sign of weakness (CCC, nos. 1808, 1831)?
	    1. No. Making sacrifices and putting up with suffering requires a great deal of courage and strength. Jesus teaches us, by example, about the value of unselfish living and the courage and strength that requires. It takes grace and personal holiness to live as Jesus Christ has taught us.

	2. Jesus shows us through the whole Paschal mystery (suffering, death, resurrection, and ascension) that giving of ourselves is the path to eternal life and happiness (CCC, nos. 571–655). 3. He gives us the example of accepting the Father's will even when it involves suffering.

NCSS C3 Framework

Dimension	Detailed Description of Each NCSS Dimension You Are Incorporating (should have all four).
D1.2.9-12	Explain points of agreement and disagreement experts have about interpretations and applications of disciplinary concepts and ideas associated with a compelling question.
D2.His.5.9-12.	Analyze how historical contexts shaped and continue to shape people's perspectives.
D3.3.9-12	Identify evidence that draws information directly and substantively from multiple sources to detect inconsistencies in evidence in order to revise or strengthen claims.
D4.1.9-12	Construct arguments using precise and knowledgeable claims, with evidence from multiple sources, while acknowledging counterclaims and evidentiary weaknesses.

NCSS Core Themes and Description

Theme Number	Detailed Description of Each Aligned NCSS Theme
IV Individual Development and Identity	The study of individual development and identity will help students to describe factors important to the development of personal identity. They will explore the influence of peoples, places, and environments on personal development. Students will hone personal skills such as demonstrating self-direction when working towards and accomplishing personal goals, and making an effort to understand others and their beliefs, feelings, and convictions.

Handouts/Materials/Web Links

Handout/Materials:
- "Hollywood or History?" graphic organizer
- Appendix A: "New Man in Christianity"
- Appendix B: "The Dark Knight Rises Venn Diagram"

Web Links:
- *The Dark Knight Rises: Sacred Art* [Blog] (Johnson, 2012)
  https://catholicveritas.com/blog/dark-night-rises-sacred-art
- *The Dark Knight Rises* [Film] (Nolan, 2012)
  https://www.warnerbros.com/movies/dark-knight-rises

Primary Source(s):
- *On Death and Dying* (Kübler-Ross, 1969)
- *Batman: Knightfall* (Moench, 1993)
- *The New American Bible* (Catholic Book, 1991)

Secondary Source(s):
- *Hero With a Thousand Faces* (Campbell, 2012)
- *New Man* (Merton, 1961)

Guiding Questions

What should students know or understand at the completion of the unit or lesson?

Primary Questions:
1. Provide evidence of foreshadowing in the film.
2. Apply Hebrew numerology to the intentional numbers mentioned in the film.
3. Provide examples of scripture and/or theological concepts presented in the dialogue by and between main characters.
4. Describe symbols associated with scripture stories and Christian theology in the film.
5. Evaluate evidence to support the film as a modern-day Christian allegory.

Important Vocabulary

List all of the important indicators of achievement (important people, places, and events) and vocabulary that students will need to know at the conclusion of the lesson.

Allegory: a story with a hidden meaning.
Christian Symbols: images and symbols from sacred stories that are visual reminders of the lessons and morals of said stories.
Foreshadowing: a literary technique that provides clues to future events.
Gematria: the study of symbolic numbers in the Bible.
Original Sin: the fallen state of human nature into which all generations of people are born.
Protoevangelium: A Latin term meaning "first gospel" and is the initial sign of the very good news that God did not abandon humanity's first parents or their descendants

after they committed sin. Eve's offspring (Jesus) would someday destroy the snake (sin and death).
Paschal Mystery: the passion, death, resurrection, and ascension of Jesus Christ.
Passion Narratives: the Gospel accounts of the Paschal mystery.
Scriptural Exegesis: analyzing a story in sacred scripture from different perspectives.
Sheol: a place where all souls reside upon death.
Stages of Grief: emotional responses to grief and loss as outlined and credited by Kubler-Ross.

Assessment Strategies

Describe the assessments that will be used during the unit.

Formative Assessment: Guided questions for the film, classroom discussion, and Venn diagram comparing Bruce Wayne/Batman to Jesus of Nazareth/Son of God.
Summative Assessment: Essay Topic—Defend the film, *The Dark Knight Rises* (Nolan, 2012) as a modern-day Christian allegory with evidence from scripture and Christian theology to support characters, themes, and the plot.

Teaching Strategies Day 1

10 min	Sparking Strategy	10 min	Independent Study: Students complete guided questions from *Thomas Merton: Essential Writings* (Bochen, 2000).	5 min	Preview questions for film.
10 min	Read Gospel passage from John 3:1–8. Explain the concept of being "born again."	10 min	Student sharing of responses to questions	**Time Remaining/ HMWK**	

Times are highly flexible and should be adjusted according to the number of sources used, length of introduction, period/ block schedule, etc.

Teaching Strategies Days 2 through 5

10 min	Provide guided questions to the film based on the specific day.	35 min	Watch film *The Dark Knight Rises* (Nolan, 2012) and allow students to complete guided questions.	10 min	Questions and answers

Times are highly flexible and should be adjusted according to the number of sources used, length of introduction, period/ block schedule, etc.

Sparking Strategy/Warm-Up

Sparking Strategy (Lesson introduction)

Invite students to define Paschal mystery. Write the four parts (passion, death, resurrection, and ascension) on the board in class so that it is visible to all students. Ask students how we see certain aspects of the Paschal mystery in nature. Provide the answers: "winter as death and spring as resurrection" in the life cycle of trees, plants, and so on. Ask the rhetorical question to the class without soliciting a response, "What good can come from death?"

Lesson Procedures

In a numerical list, provide a step by step outline of what you plan to do in the lesson. Include questions you will ask the students and materials you will use.

Outline

Day 1

Read the Gospel of John 3:1–8 to introduce the main theme of this unit of study. Explain to class the theological concept of being "born again" in light of the conversation between Jesus Christ and Nicodemus. Assign reflection from *Thomas Merton: Essential Writings* (Bochen, 2000, pp. 62–67). Assign guided questions which focus on contemplation, discernment, identity, and conversion [Appendix A]. This assignment is to be completed independently.

Day 2

Introduce the concepts of allegory and describe the target learning objective which involves understanding the film as a modern-day Christian allegory. View film Part 1: *The Dark Knight Rises* (Nolan, 2012, 00:00–36:37). For homework, assign students to complete the guided questions for Part 1 of the film.

1. Define Paschal mystery
2. Define allegory.
3. Define foreshadowing. Predict a possible example of foreshadowing present in the film.
4. Describe how Alfred has a prophetic voice.
5. Explain what the numbers 7 and 8 represent symbolically according to Hebrew numerology.
6. Define bane. Which definitions connect most appropriately to the antagonist?
7. What is the main theme of John's Gospel? How does this relate to John Blake's knowledge of Bruce Wayne's true identity?
8. The stages of grief are identified as the following: denial, bargaining, anger, depression, and acceptance. Apply one or more of these stages to Bruce Wayne's mental state at the beginning of the film.
9. Provide examples of the passion/suffering of Bruce Wayne/Batman in the film.
10. The three main police officers are named James Gordon, Peter Foley, and John Blake. Consider that these three men's names are similar to three main apostles. What do you expect from these characters in the film? (*Hint:* James became the first bishop of Jerusalem, Peter denied Christ in the passion narratives, and John was present at the foot of the cross during Jesus' crucifixion).

Day 3

Review scriptural exegesis and Hebrew numerology with the class in order to prepare them for answering assigned guided questions for Parts 2–4 of the film. View film Part 2: *The Dark Knight Rises* (Nolan, 2012, 36:37–1:18:33). For homework, assign students to complete the guided questions for Part 2 of the film.

11. Define terrorism. How were the Zealots understood in ancient Judaism?
12. Read Isaiah 53:4–6. Explain how the treatment of the Batman by the police connects to this passage from the prophet Isaiah.
13. Bane says, "Speak of the devil and he shall appear." What is significant about this statement as it relates to his symbolic identity in the film?
14. Read Isaiah 53:8–11 and explain how this is present in the film.
15. Bane claims to have been "born in the dark." What is significant about this statement in relation to his symbolic identity?
16. What does the pit in the ancient part of the world represent in light of your knowledge of the Paschal mystery?
17. Read Revelation 21:1–4. What does Gotham City represent a symbolic kingdom?

Day 4

Invite students to share important themes present in the film. Possible answers may include, but are not limited to: allegory, foreshadowing, or scriptural exegesis. Students may access their guided questions for review. Review the conversation between Jesus Christ and Nicodemus from the Gospel of John. Focus on the theme of being born again. View film Part 3: *The Dark Knight Rises* (Nolan, 2012, 1:18:33–2:01). For homework, assign students to complete the guided questions for Part 3 of the film.

18. How is order and disorder present in the film?
19. Sheol is the realm of the dead in the Jewish religion. Jesus Christ enters Sheol on Holy Saturday to free those souls that are trapped. Explain how this is present in the film.
20. In the film, Bruce is going through depression at the beginning (figurative pit) and then is thrown in a pit in the ancient part of the world (literal pit). Explain what would be more challenging for you…a literal pit or a figurative pit.
21. How many times does it take Bruce to climb out of the pit? What does this symbolize?
22. How are the death and Resurrection aspects of the Paschal mystery present in the film today?
23. According to Thomas Merton's (1961) *A New Birth*, "What has to happen to Bruce before he can rise out of the pit?"
24. Why is the film called "The Dark Knight Rises"?
25. Selina Kyle/Catwoman is searching for the "clean slate" for the entire film. She wants to start over and move beyond her past mistakes. Many people in the film say that the clean slate does not exist. Who eventually gives the clean slate to her? What is interesting about the timing of when Selina gets the clean slate? How does the clean slate reflect themes of Protoevangelium?
26. "It was the best of times, it was the worst of times, it was the age of wisdom, it was the age of foolishness, it was the epoch of belief, it was the epoch of incredulity, it was the season of Light, it was the season of Darkness, it was the spring of hope, it was the winter of despair, we had everything before us, we had noth-

ing before us..."—*A Tale of Two Cities* by Charles Dickens (1859/2004, p. 7). Apply this line to the hope and despair of Gotham City.

Day 5

Explore the theological concept of the Paschal mystery. Read 1 Corinthians 15:1–28. Discuss how the Paschal mystery is present in the film. View film Part 4: *The Dark Knight Rises* (Nolan, 2012, 2:01–2:45). For homework, assign students to complete the guided questions for Part 4 of the film.

27. Read Matthew 16:13–23. Connect this scripture passage to the conversation between Catwoman and Batman: "You don't owe these people any more...you've given them everything."—Catwoman (Nolan, 2012, 2:09:19–2:10:46)
28. Read John 21:18. Apply this scripture to the film.
29. Read Luke 24:50–53. Apply this scripture to the film.
30. Explain the inclusion of the character Robin (represented at the end of the movie) in light of the beginning of the Church.
31. Compare Selina Kyle to the Church (bride of Jesus) as it relates to the destruction of evil (the anti-Christ).
32. Read Revelation 17:1–6. Apply this scripture to the film.
33. How is the Ascension represented at the end of the film? An epic hero represents the virtues and values of a culture; defends those virtues and values against an existential threat. Because of the epic hero's greatness, the virtues and values of the culture survive, though the hero may or may not. Apply this concept to the film.

Day 6

Instruct students to submit their answers to the guided questions for grading. Assign students to work with a partner to complete the Venn diagram comparing Bruce Wayne/Batman to that of Jesus of Nazareth/second person in the Holy Trinity (Appendix B). Invite students to share the results of their Venn diagram prior to the end of the class period. For homework, assign the essay topic to the class, "Defend the Film *The Dark Knight Rises* (Nolan, 2012) as a Modern-Day Christian Allegory."

Differentiation

Think about your students' skill levels, intelligences, and learning styles. How are you going to make this lesson meet the needs of all of your students?

Collaborative Learning: Complete Venn diagram in groups.
Introverts: Independently answering guided questions to the film.
Extraverts: Participation in class discussion on themes in film.
Visual Learners: The opportunity to engage in and appreciate the value of media literacy by watching the film.

Summarizing Strategies/Synthesizing Activity

What strategies are you going to use to allow students to summarize what they learned in the lesson?

- Guided questions analyzing the film and completing an essay on the topic of modern Christian allegories.
- Comparing and contrasting the main character of Bruce Wayne/Batman to that of Jesus Christ.
- Analyzing scripture passages to evaluate application of the main message present in film.

References

Are there any additional resources that might be relevant to your lesson? Are there sources that you need to reference? Please add any citations using APA.

Bochen, C. (Ed.). (2000). *Thomas Merton: Essential writings*. Orbis Books.
Campbell, J. (2012). *Hero with a thousand faces*. New World Library.
Catholic Book. (1991). *The New American Bible—Saint Joseph Edition*.
Dickens, C. (2004). *A tale of two cities*. Barnes and Noble Classics. (Original work published in 1859)
Johnson, J. (2012, August 8). *The dark knight rises: Sacred art* [Blog]. Veritas. https://catholicveritas.com/blog/dark-night-rises-sacred-art
Kübler-Ross, E. (1969). *On death and dying*. Scribner.
Merton, T. (1961). *New man*. Farrar, Straus, and Giroux.
Moench, D. (1993). *Batman: Knightfall*. DC Comics.
Nolan, C. (Director). (2012). *The dark knight rises* [Film]. Warner Bros., Legendary Pictures, Syncopy, DC Entertainment.
U.S. Conference of Catholic Bishops. (2000). *Catechism of the Catholic Church* (2nd ed.) Libreria Editrice Vaticana.

Additional Resources

Center for Media Literacy. (2001). *National Association for Media Literacy Education*. http://www.medialit.org/reading-room/what-media-literacy-namles-short-answer-and-longer-thought

Hollywood or History?
The Dark Knight Rises (2012)

Directed by Christopher Nolan, *The Dark Knight Rises* (2012) is the end of his Batman trilogy. This film focused on the journey of Bruce Wayne within his physical pain and emotional distress. Mr. Wayne must learn to discover that recognizing his fear may indeed be the source of his strength.

Evaluate each source provided and summarize your observations and analysis in corresponding spaces provided. In the section located at the bottom of the page, explain whether you think the scenes from *The Dark Knight Rises* (2012) should be evaluated as an accurate account of what it means to be "born again" in Christianity using the Gospel of John (3:1–21) or *Thomas Merton: Essential Writings* (Bochen, 2000, pp. 62–67). Use examples from your sources/documents to explain your answer.

Primary Source	*The Dark Knight Rises* (2012)	Secondary Source

What do you think? Hollywood or History?

Appendix A
New Man in Christianity

Film Description: Directed by Christopher Nolan (2012), *The Dark Knight Rises* is the end of his Batman trilogy. This film focused on the journey of Bruce Wayne within his physical pain and emotional distress. In order to understand the theological concepts present in the film, it is recommended that the film in its entirety is shown to the class. This culminating lesson for Christianity will allow the opportunity to analyze the primary teachings of the largest world religions.

Directions: For this supplemental assignment, please complete the following reflection questions based on the writing of *Thomas Merton: Essential Writings* (Bochen, 2000).

1. What is meant by a new creation in relation to an inner revolution?

2. According to Merton, "Why does one look to be born again?"

3. Provide a possible explanation or application to the following line from Merton: "He feels himself a prisoner in himself, depressed and weighed down by the falsity and illusions of his own life."

4. Complete the following sentence: "To be born again is not to become somebody else, but . . ."

5. In order to become a new self, "What must happen to the old self?"

6. Explain Merton's explanation of being born again in regards to the ego and being born of the spirit.

7. Identify the qualities of the "New Man" according to Thomas Merton.

Appendix B
The Dark Knight Rises Venn Diagram

Film Description: Directed by Christopher Nolan (2012), *The Dark Knight Rises* is the end of his Batman trilogy. This film focused on the spiritual journey of Bruce Wayne within his physical pain and emotional distress. In order to understand the theological concepts present in the film, it is recommended that the film in its entirety is shown to the class. This culminating lesson for Christianity will allow the opportunity to analyze the primary teachings of the largest world religions.

Directions: Compare and contrast Bruce Wayne/Batman and Jesus of Nazareth/second person of the Trinity using the Venn diagram. Identify at least five similarities and three differences using the Gospel of John as your primary reference. Write down keywords or ideas for each category.

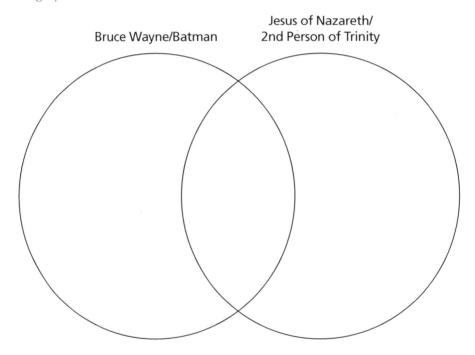

Evaluate: Defend the Batman in *The Dark Knight Rises* (2012) as a modern Christ figure.

The Hero's Journey of Frodo Baggins

Adam P. Zoeller

FILM: *The Lord of the Rings: The Fellowship of the Ring* (2001)

Grade	Subject	Topic
9	Christianity	Biblical Criticism and Inspiration

Chapter Theme	Estimated Time Needed for Lesson
Faith in Action: Christology, Hero's Journey, Mythology, Struggles of War	Part 1: Historical, Form, and Source Criticism (45 minutes) Part 2: Hero's Journey (30 minutes)

National Association for Media Literacy Education

Standard Number	Detailed Description of Each Standard You Are Discussing

Core Principles of Media Literacy Education in the United States	3. MLE builds and reinforces skills for learners of all ages. Like print literacy, those skills necessitate integrated, interactive, and repeated practice.
	
	Implications for Practice
	  3.3 MLE engages students with varied learning styles.
	  3.4 MLE is most effective when used with co-learning pedagogies, in which teachers learn from students and students learn from teachers and from classmates.

State Standard Description

State	Detailed Description of Each Standard You Are Discussing
Maryland 9th grade Reading Standards for Literature	**CCSS.ELA-LITERACY.RL.9-10.6** Analyze a particular point of view or cultural experience reflected in a work of literature from outside the United States, drawing on a wide reading of world literature.

Ohio English Language Arts Key Ideas and Details (9th grade)	RL.9-10.2 Analyze literary text development. a. Determine a theme of a text and analyze in detail its development over the course of the text, including how it emerges and is shaped and refined by specific details. b. Provide an objective summary of the text that includes the theme and relevant story elements.
Washington K–12 Learning Standards for Social Studies (Grade 9)	H1: Understands Historical Chronology H1.9-10.2 Assess how historical events and developments were shaped by unique circumstances of time and place as well as broader historical contexts.

USCCB Curriculum Framework

Standard Number	Detailed Description of Each Standard You Are Discussing

Course I. The revelation of Jesus Christ in scripture (Grade 9)	III. Understanding Scripture
	
	Criteria for interpreting the Sacred Scripture (CCC, nos. 109–114, 137).
	1. Read and interpret sacred Scripture within the tradition and teaching of the Church.
	2. Give attention both to what the human authors intended to say and to what God reveals to us by their words.
	3. Take into account the conditions of the time when it was written and the culture where it was written.
	
	Senses of Scripture (CCC, nos. 115, 118–119).
	1. The literal sense: the meaning conveyed by the words of Scripture and discovered by exegesis (CCC, nos. 109–110, 116).
	2. The spiritual sense (CCC, no. 117).
	   a. Allegorical sense: recognizing the significance of events in the Bible as they relate to Christ.
	   b. Moral sense: Scripture teaches us and encourages us how to live and act.

Course II. Who is Jesus Christ (Grade 9)	IV. Jesus Christ teaches us about ourselves 2. He reveals the way to repentance and conversion, teaching us to leave sin behind and to live a new life in him; he gives us the spiritual power and grace to overcome evil; he also teaches us about God's forgiveness (CCC, nos. 1847–1848). 3. He teaches us how to be single-hearted in our desire for God, to offset the disordered affections and divided hearts with which we live (CCC, nos. 1716–1717).

NCSS C3 Framework

Dimension	Detailed Description of Each NCSS Dimension You Are Incorporating (should have all four).
D1.2.9-12	Explain points of agreement and disagreement experts have about interpretations and applications of disciplinary concepts and ideas associated with a compelling question.
D2.His.5.9-12.	Analyze how historical contexts shaped and continue to shape people's perspectives.
D3.3.9-12	Identify evidence that draws information directly and substantively from multiple sources to detect inconsistencies in evidence in order to revise or strengthen claims.
D4.1.9-12	Construct arguments using precise and knowledgeable claims, with evidence from multiple sources, while acknowledging counterclaims and evidentiary weaknesses.

NCSS Core Themes and Description

Theme Number	Detailed Description of Each Aligned NCSS Theme
I Culture	The study of culture examines the socially transmitted beliefs, values, institutions, behaviors, traditions and way of life of a group of people; it also encompasses other cultural attributes and products, such as language, literature, music, arts and artifacts, and foods. Students come to understand that human cultures exhibit both similarities and differences, and they learn to see themselves both as individuals and as members of a particular culture that shares similarities with other cultural groups, but is also distinctive. In a multicultural, democratic society and globally connected world, students need to understand the multiple perspectives that derive from different cultural vantage points.
IV Individual Development and Identity	The study of individual development and identity will help students to describe factors important to the development of personal identity. They will explore the influence of peoples, places, and environments on personal development. Students will hone personal skills such as demonstrating self-direction when working towards and accomplishing personal goals, and making an effort to understand others and their beliefs, feelings, and convictions.

Handouts/Materials/Web Links

Handout/Materials:
- "Hollywood or History?" graphic organizer

Web Links:
- *The Lord of the Rings: The Fellowship of the Ring* (Jackson, 2001)
  https://www.imdb.com/title/tt0120737/

  Clip to video
  1. Mythology   (00:00–7:21)
  2. Ordinary World   (7:21–20:00)
  3. Call to Adventure   (27:20–31:23)
  4. Refusal of the Call (31:23–34:30)
  5. Crossing the Threshold (36:28–38:22)
  6. Meeting the Mentor   (54:15–57:41)
  7. Allies, Tests, Enemies (1:01:54–1:03:27 & 1:26:33–1:36:18)

Primary Source(s):
- *Hero With a Thousand Faces* (Campbell, 2012)
- *The Lord of the Rings: The Fellowship of the Ring* (Tolkien, 1954/1987)

Secondary Source(s):
- *The Lord of the Rings: The Fellowship of the Ring* (Jackson, 2001)
- "How J. R. R. Tolkien Found Mordor on the Western Front" (Locante, 2016)
  https://www.nytimes.com/2016/07/03/opinion/sunday/how-jrr-tolkien-found-mordor-on-the-western-front.html

Guiding Questions

What should students know or understand at the completion of the unit or lesson?

Primary Questions:
- Describe how Tolkien's Catholic faith and experience of fighting in World War I influenced his writing of *The Lord of the Rings* trilogy.
- Apply Joseph Campbell's hero's journey stages to the main protagonist in *The Lord of the Rings* trilogy.

Important Vocabulary

List all of the important indicators of achievement (important people, places, and events) and vocabulary that students will need to know at the conclusion of the lesson.

Part 1

Allegory: a story that has an implicit or hidden meaning.
Battle of Somme: one of the deadliest battles in World War I in northern France.

Fellowship: friendly association especially with someone who shares one's interest.
Form Criticism: determining the literary genre of a specific text.
Historical Criticism: studying the text to determine the culture, audience, and theme.
Mordor: mythical location in Tolkien's Middle Earth characterized by a dark and desolate landscape.
Source Criticism: determining where authors got their material and/or inspiration.
Tolkien, J. R. R. (1892–1973): 20th century Catholic author who wrote *The Hobbit* (1932) and *The Lord of the Rings* (1954).

Part 2

Antagonist: a person who is actively opposed or is hostile to someone or something.
Campbell, Joseph (1904–1987): 20th century American professor of literature.
Christian Discipleship: responding to the spiritual call of God to live a life based in the teachings of Jesus Christ.
Jackson, Peter (1961–): film director of *The Lord of the Rings: Fellowship of the Ring* (2001).
Mythology: the study of sacred stories that teach truthful lessons but may or may not be entirely based in fact.
Protagonists: the leading character or one of the major characters in a drama, movie, novel, or other fictional text.

Assessment Strategies

Describe the assessments that will be used during the unit.

Formative Assessment:

- Collaborative learning as students make relevant connections between the Battle of Somme and the landscape of Mordor after reading the *New York Times* opinion article "How J. R. R. Tolkien Found Mordor on the Western Front" (Locante, 2016).
- Classroom discussion about technological obstacles to discipleship after students read the blog "My iPhone, My Precious" (Sri, 2016)

Summative Assessment:

- Essay Options
    1. Defend the valuable 21st century skill of media literacy.
    2. Defend the importance of source, form, and historical criticism when studying literary texts.
    3. Relate the primary protagonist to the hero's journey (Stages 1–6).

Teaching Strategies Part 1

10 min	Sparking Strategy: Value of myths	10 min	Assign articles to the class to read in order to discover Tolkien's inspiration.	5 min	Invite students to share how Tolkien's work is an allegory (a story with a hidden meaning).
10 min	Explain inspiration as it relates to source, historical, and form criticism.	10 min	Share the results with a classmate	Time Remaining/ HMWK	

Times are highly flexible and should be adjusted according to the number of sources used, length of introduction, period/block schedule, etc.

Teaching Strategies Part 2

10 min	What makes someone heroic? Introduce the stages of the hero's Journey	10 min	Continue watching and apply the hero's journey motif to the main character of Frodo Baggins.	5 min	Questions and answers
10 min	List the first 6 stages on the board and begin watching the selected scenes from the film.	10 min		Time Remaining/ HMWK	

Times are highly flexible and should be adjusted according to the number of sources used, length of introduction, period/block schedule, etc.

Sparking Strategy/Warm-Up

Sparking Strategy (Lesson introduction)

Define myth and explain the value of myths to examine religious truths of primeval stories. Watch the film theatrical trailer for *The Lord of the Rings: The Fellowship of the Ring* (https://www.youtube.com/watch?v=V75dMMIW2B4). Invite students to share their impression and understanding of the plot of the story. Request students who may have seen the film or read the book to elaborate on the plot and themes of the story as a means to guarantee accurate information. Watch the first scene of the film (Jackson, 2001, 00:00–7:21) in order to fully understand Tolkien's story as a myth.

Lesson Procedures

In a numerical list, provide a step by step outline of what you plan to do in the lesson. Include questions you will ask the students and materials you will use.

Outline

Part 1

1. Explore the importance of studying scripture contextually through the lens of the Catholic church by defining the following: historical criticism, source criticism, and form criticism.
2. Divide the class into two large groups.
   - Assign one half to take notes on the Catholic themes in Tolkien's work from (Barron, 2007)
     https://youtu.be/Pio5pf-Eoi8
   - Assign the other half to read the following article analyzing how Tolkien's experience of fighting in World War I inspired his writing. *How J. R. R. Tolkien Found Mordor on the Western Front* (Locante, 2016): https://www.nytimes.com/2016/07/03/opinion/sunday/how-jrr-tolkien-found-mordor-on-the-western-front.html
3. After ample time to read articles, inform students that they need to find a partner from the opposite article and provide a brief report explaining either the Inspiron Catholicism or war respectively.
4. Invite students to share how Tolkien's work can be classified as a Christian allegory.

Part 2

1. Ask the rhetorical question, "What makes someone heroic?" Solicit answers from the class. Write the responses on the board.
2. Introduce the 20th century author Joseph Campbell and his exploration of the hero's Journey.
3. List the parts of the hero's journey on the board while focusing on the first six stages that the main protagonist, Frodo Baggins, will experience:
   - ordinary world
   - call to adventure
   - refusal of the call
   - crossing the threshold
   - meeting the mentor
   - allies, tests, enemies
4. List the stages on the board and have students view the following film clips that support Campbell's work.
   1. Ordinary World (7:21–20:00)
   2. Call to Adventure (27:20–31:23)
   3. Refusal of the Call (31:23–34:30)
   4. Crossing the Threshold (36:28–38:22)
   5. Meeting the Mentor (54:15–57:41)
   6. Allies, Tests, Enemies (1:01:54–1:03:27 and 1:26:33–1:36:18)

   Transition into temptation (of the ring) as the primary obstacle to a hero's journey towards Christian discipleship. Provide examples of what the ring could represent in today's society. Distribute blog "My iPhone, My Precious" (Sri, 2013). Have students read how technology can be addictive and distract from our call to become a Christian hero. Invite students to share their understanding of the article as well as how the main message can be applied to the students' lives.

Differentiation

Think about your students' skill levels, intelligences, and learning styles. How are you going to make this lesson meet the needs of all of your students?

Visual learners: benefit from viewing film clips in light of the themes of faith and history.
Student choice: in assessments to evaluate comprehension of the material. These student-centered assessments allow the student to reach higher level critical thinking skills such as analysis and evaluation by promoting student choice that challenge and/or meet their cognitive abilities.
Introverted Learners: benefit from creating a Word Cloud associating themes from the film into a medium that promotes 21st century skills of technology implementation.
Extroverted Learners: benefit from discussing the limitations of interpersonal skills and the challenges associated with using/abusing technology.
Independent Learners: Guided questions will help students break major themes and plot development into smaller parts.

Summarizing Strategies/Synthesizing Activity

What strategies are you going to use to allow students to summarize what they learned in the lesson?

- Create a word cloud demonstrating at least 15 themes from the study of *The Lord of the Rings: the Fellowship of the Ring* (Jackson, 2001).
- Completion of guided questions to the film that draw upon the themes, plot, and character developments.

References

Are there any additional resources that might be relevant to your lesson? Are there sources that you need to reference? Please add any citations using APA.

Barron, R. (2007, May 11). *Bishop Barron on "The Lord of the Rings" (Part 1 of 2)* [YouTube]. https://www.youtube.com/watch?v=Pio5pf-Eoi8
Campbell, J. (2012). *Hero with a thousand faces.* New World Library.
Jackson, P. (Director). (2001). *The Lord of the Rings: The Fellowship of the Ring.* New Line Productions.
Kreeft, P. (2005). *The philosophy of Tolkien: The worldview behind the Lord of the Rings.* Ignatius Press.
Locante, J. (2016, July 3). How J. R. R. Tolkien found Mordor on the western front. *New York Times* Opinion. https://www.nytimes.com/2016/07/03/opinion/sunday/how-jrr-tolkien-found-mordor-on-the-western-front.html
Sri, E. P. (2016, January 28). *My iPhone, my precious.* edwardsri.com. https://edwardsri.com/2016/01/28/01-my-iphone-my-precious
Tolkien, J. R. R. (1987). *The lord of the rings: The fellowship of the ring.* Houghton Mifflin Company. (Original work published in 1954)
U.S. Conference of Catholic Bishops. (2000). *Catechism of the Catholic Church* (2nd ed.) Libreria Editrice Vaticana.

U.S. Conference of Catholic Bishops. (2008). *Doctrinal elements of a curriculum framework for the development of catechetical materials for young people of high school age.* United States Conference of Catholic Bishops. https://www.usccb.org/beliefs-and-teachings/how-we-teach/catechesis/upload/high-school-curriculum-framework.pdf

Additional Resources

Catford, L., & Ray, M. (1991). *The path of the everyday hero.* Creative Quest Publishing.

Malewitz, T. E. (2020). True/false self: Refining the search for authenticity. *Authenticity, passion, and advocacy: Approaching adolescent spirituality from the life and wisdom of Thomas Merton* (pp. 62–72). Wipf & Stock.

Raglan, F. S. (2011). *The hero: A study in tradition, myth and drama.* Dover Books.

Zoeller, A. P., & Malewitz, T. E. (2019). Tolkien's allegory: Using Peter Jackson's vision of fellowship to illuminate male adolescent Catholic education. *Journal of Catholic Education, 22*(1). http://dx.doi.org/10.15365/joce.2201042019

Hollywood or History?

The Lord of the Rings: Fellowship of the Ring (2001)

The hero's journey motif is present in many Hollywood films that focus on storytelling techniques associated with journey, mission, and quests. In this inquiry lesson, students will analyze the work of J. R. R. Tolkien through the lens of director Peter Jackson, *The Lord of the Rings: The Fellowship of the Ring* (2001) in order to determine how and where themes of Joseph Campbell's Hero's Journey are evident. In addition, an examination of the religious themes from Catholicism will be explored by using the work of Peter Kreeft.

Evaluate each source provided and summarize your observations and analysis in corresponding spaces provided. In the section located at the bottom of the page, explain whether you think the scenes from *The Lord of the Rings: The Fellowship of the Ring* should be evaluated as an accurate account of the hero's journey (Campbell, 2012), Catholic theology (Barron, 2007), or both. Use examples from your sources/documents to explain your answer.

Primary Source	*The Lord of the Rings: The Fellowship of the Ring* (2001)	**Secondary Source**

What do you think? Hollywood or History?

The Nature of the 10 Plagues Against Egypt and the Egyptian Gods

Thomas E. Malewitz

FILMS: *The Prince of Egypt* (1998) and *Exodus: Gods and Kings* (2014)

Grade	Subject	Topic
6–12	Judaism; Egyptian Mythology	Analyzing the 10 plagues of Egypt

Chapter Theme	Estimated Time Needed for Lesson
Faith in Action: Addressing violence in scripture; Egyptian gods and plagues	55 minutes

National Association for Media Literacy Education

Standard Number	Detailed Description of Each Standard You Are Discussing

Core Principles of Media Literacy Education in the United States	1. Media Literacy Education (MLE) requires active inquiry and critical thinking about the messages we receive and create.
	
	Implications for Practice
	   1.4 MLE trains students to use document-based evidence and well-reasoned arguments to support their conclusions.
	   1.7 For MLE teachers, fostering critical thinking is routine. MLE calls for institutional structures to support their efforts by actively encouraging critical thinking in all classrooms.

	3. MLE builds and reinforces skills for learners of all ages. Like print literacy, those skills necessitate integrated, interactive, and repeated practice.
	
	Implications for Practice
	   3.3 MLE engages students with varied learning styles.
	   3.4 MLE is most effective when used with co-learning pedagogies, in which teachers learn from students and students learn from teachers and from classmates.

State USCCB Standard Description

State	Detailed Description of Each Standard You Are Discussing
Illinois High School Social Studies	**SS.H.1.9-12; SS.H.2.9-12; SS.H.3.9-12** Evaluate how historical developments were shaped by time and place as well as broader historical contexts; analyze change and continuity within and across historical eras; evaluate the methods utilized by people and institutions to promote change.
Kentucky (Grade 6) Development of Civilizations	**6.I.CC.3** Evaluate how individuals and groups addressed local, regional, and global problems throughout the development of civilizations. **6.C.PR.1** Analyze the purposes and effects of laws in River Valley Civilizations and Classical Empires between 3500 BCE–600 CE.
Michigan (Grade 7) Civics Growth and Development of World Religions	**W3.2.1** Identify and describe the core beliefs of major world religions and belief systems, including Hinduism, Judaism, Buddhism, Christianity, Confucianism, Sikhism, and Islam. *Examples may include, but are not limited to:* comparing major figures, sacred texts, and basic beliefs (ethnic vs. universalizing; monotheistic vs. polytheistic) among religions; case studies of continuity of local indigenous belief systems or animistic religions; comparisons with religious traditions that developed after 1500 CE such as Protestantism.
United States Conference of Catholic Bishops (USCCB) Curriculum Framework	**Doctrinal Elements of a Curriculum Framework for the Development of Catechetical Materials for Young People of High School Age** (USCCB, 2008)
USCCB.I Revelation of God—VI.C.2	The Bible has a definite historic basis for events recounted in both the Old and the New Testaments
USCCB.Option A Sacred Scripture— II.C.1-3	Analyze the Book of Exodus: Prominence and the call of Moses; Divine liberation from slavery to freedom
USCCB.Option A Sacred Scripture— VI.A.1-3	Recognize the Purpose of a Prophet: To interpret signs of the times in light of covenant; Afflict the comfortable and comfort the afflicted; Understand that prophesies (and works) were medicinal, meant to convert listeners to God.

NCSS C3 Framework

Dimension	Detailed Description of Each NCSS Dimension You Are Incorporating (should have all four).
D1.2.9-12	Explain points of agreement and disagreement experts have about interpretations and applications of disciplinary concepts and ideas associated with a compelling question.
D2.His.5.9-12.	Analyze how historical contexts shaped and continue to shape people's perspectives.
D3.3.9-12	Identify evidence that draws information directly and substantively from multiple sources to detect inconsistencies in evidence in order to revise or strengthen claims.
D4.1.9-12	Construct arguments using precise and knowledgeable claims, with evidence from multiple sources, while acknowledging counterclaims and evidentiary weaknesses.

NCSS Core Themes and Description

Theme Number	Detailed Description of Each Aligned NCSS Theme
II Time, Continuity, and Change	Studying the past makes it possible for us to understand the human story across time. Historical analysis enables us to identify continuities over time in core institutions, values, ideals, and traditions, as well as processes that lead to change within societies and institutions, and that result in innovation and the development of new ideas, values, and ways of life.
V Individuals, Groups, and Institutions	Social studies programs should include experiences that provide for the study of interactions among individuals, groups, and institutions.
VI Power, Authority, and Governance	Social studies programs should include experiences that provide for the study of how people create, interact with, and change structures of power, authority, and governance.

Handouts/Materials/Web Links

Handout/Materials:
- "Hollywood or History?" graphic organizer

Web Links:
- *Exodus: God and Kings* (Scott, 2014) [~18 mins total]
  – 1:21:18–1:34:50 (Plagues 1–9)
  – 1:42:46–1:47:50 (Plague 10)

- "The Ten Plagues Scene (6/10)" from *The Prince of Egypt* (Chapman et al., 1998) [3 mins] https://www.youtube.com/watch?v=GJleW4TCQM0

Primary Source:
- Exodus 7:14–11:10

Secondary Source:
- "Three ways to look at the ten plagues: Were they natural disasters, a demonstration of the impotence of the Egyptian gods, or an undoing of Creation?" (Zevit, 1990) https://www.biblicalarchaeology.org/daily/biblical-topics/exodus/exodus-in-the-bible-and-the-egyptian-plagues

Guiding Questions

What should students know or understand at the completion of the unit or lesson?

Primary Questions:
- What was the purpose of the 10 Plagues?
- Examine ways the action of the 10 Plagues be interpreted.
- Is the Hollywood depiction of the 10 Plagues the only perspective to understand the 10 Plagues?

Important Vocabulary

List all of the important indicators of achievement (important people, places, and events) and vocabulary that students will need to know at the conclusion of the lesson.

> **Israelites:** The descendants of Jacob (Israel) and followers of the LORD, YHWH. A nation enslaved to Egypt and then led out of slavery by Moses.
> **Monotheism:** A faith or religion that worships one deity.
> **Moses:** The leader/liberator of the Israelites from their slavery in Egypt; a prophet and messenger of the LORD, YHWH.
> **Pestilence:** an epidemic or disease.
> **Pharaoh:** The leader of the Egyptian people. The pharaohs were revered as gods while they lived.
> **Plague:** A disease or disaster that affects the economic, social, or lives of a community or nation.
> **Polytheism:** A faith or religion that worships more than one deity.

Assessment Strategies

Describe the assessments that will be used during the unit.

> **Formative Assessment:** lecture, compare/contrasting, analysis/discussion
> **Summative Assessment:** class discussion/participation, "Hollywood or History?" graphic organizer

Teaching Strategies

5 min	Warm-up activity	15 min	View clips from: *Exodus: Gods and Kings* (Scott, 2014)	10 min	Analysis/discussion of depiction of the plagues from the clips to the sources
5 min	View clips from: *Prince of Egypt* (Chapman et al., 1998)	10 min	Compare to the primary and secondary sources	**Time Remaining/ HMWK**	"Hollywood or History?" graphic organizer

Times are highly flexible and should be adjusted according to the number of sources used, length of introduction, period/block schedule, etc.

Sparking Strategy/Warm-Up

Sparking Strategy (Lesson introduction)

Connect the upcoming lesson plan to the challenges of the pandemic of 2020–2021. Ask the students how their lives were disrupted, changed, or affected; namely, "What did the pandemic mean to them?" Explain that the story of the 10 plagues, that affected Egypt from the book of Exodus, has several layers of meaning. Scholars state that it could have been: (a) a series of natural disasters; (b) a spiritual sign of the Israelite God's power over the Egyptian gods; and/or (c) an example of the Bible theme of order, disorder, and reorder.

Lesson Procedures

In a numerical list, provide a step by step outline of what you plan to do in the lesson. Include questions you will ask the students and materials you will use.

1. Introduce the vocabulary to the students as they prepare to view the video clips.
2. Invite the students to take notes (bullet points) while they watch the video clips, so that the students can find examples of the layers of meaning in the video clips.
3. Show *Prince of Egypt* (Chapman et al., 1998; 5 mins)
4. Take a few minutes to explore some of the visuals of the plagues as well as the lyrics, feeling, emotion, and/or music from the clip to help the students clarify their notes.
5. Show *Exodus: Gods and Kings* (Scott, 2014; 15 mins)
6. Take a few minutes to compare and contrast the visual representations between *Prince of Egypt* (Chapman et al., 1998) and *Exodus: Gods and Kings* (Scott, 2014). Invite the students to offer the differences they noticed.
7. Have the students read/or read to the students from Exodus 7:14–11:10
8. Lead a discussion with the students and analyze the differences between the video clips and the focus of the passage from Exodus.
9. Have the students complete the "Hollywood or History?" graphic organizer in-class, or as a homework assignment.

Differentiation

Think about your students' skill levels, intelligences, and learning styles. How are you going to make this lesson meet the needs of all of your students?

> **Scaffolds:** Introduce vocabulary first, then expanding into the concept of layers of perspective of a story. Have the students engage in comparing and contrasting each film before analyzing the primary source.
>
> **Connection to Real-Life:** Introduce the topic through the lens of the 2020–2021 pandemic. Connecting the material directly to the memory, lives, and experience of the students for a relatable context.

Summarizing Strategies/Synthesizing Activity

What strategies are you going to use to allow students to summarize what they learned in the lesson?

- Discussion with reference to film clips/documents/evidence of Hollywood or History?

References

Are there any additional resources that might be relevant to your lesson? Are there sources that you need to reference? Please add any citations using APA.

Chapman, B., Hickner, S., & Wells, S. (Directors). (1998). *The prince of Egypt.* DreamWorks.

Scott, R. (Director). (2014). *Exodus: God and kings.* 20th Century Fox.

Zevit, Z. (1990). Three ways to look at the ten plagues: Were they natural disasters, a demonstration of the impotence of the Egyptian gods or an undoing of Creation? *The Bible Review, 6*(3), 16–23, 42. https://www.biblicalarchaeology.org/daily/biblical-topics/exodus/exodus-in-the-bible-and-the-egyptian-plagues/

Additional Resources

Barron, R. (2015, January 1). Bishop Barron on "Exodus: Gods and Kings" [YouTube]. 5:15–6:46. https://www.youtube.com/watch?v=h5syURgIL94

Berlin, A., & Brettler, M. (Eds.). (2004). Exodus 7:14–13:16. In *The Jewish study bible: TANAKH translation* (pp. 117–133). Oxford University.

Brueggemann, W. (2009). *An unsettling God: The heart of the Hebrew bible.* Fortress.

Monreal, T., & Varga, B. A. (2021). Representing ancient Egypt(ians)/visual mediums and public perception. In S. Roberts & C. Elfer (Eds.), *Hollywood or history? An inquiry-based strategy for using film to teach world history* (pp. 67–79). Information Age Publishing.

Seibert, E. (2009). *Disturbing divine behavior: Troubling old testament images of God.* Fortress.

Hollywood or History?

Prince of Egypt (1998) and *Exodus: Gods and Kings* (2014)

Prince of Egypt (1998) and *Exodus: Gods and Kings* (2014) are two films that depict the 10 Plagues of Egypt. Read the account of the 10 plagues from the Book of Exodus (7:14–11:10) and compare which account best matches the following perspective. Offer a concrete example to support your decision.

Do you think that Hollywood films *Prince of Egypt* (1998) and *Exodus: Gods and Kings* (2014) offered the three perspectives of understanding the 10 plagues well? Explain your decision in the Hollywood or History? box at the bottom of the page.

Natural Disasters	YHWH's power over the Egyptian gods	Order, Disorder, Reorder
Prince of Egypt?	*Prince of Egypt?*	*Prince of Egypt?*
Exodus: Gods and Kings?	*Exodus: Gods and Kings?*	*Exodus: Gods and Kings?*
Exodus (7:14–11:10)	Exodus (7:14–11:10)	Exodus (7:14–11:10)

What do you think? Hollywood or History?

CHAPTER 2

Historical Contexts

Understanding the surrounding context of historical events and culture is key to an authentic approach of analyzing events and significant individuals from the past. I (Thomas) remember a graduate professor who compared approaching the subject of Church history to a detective novel, where a scholar needs to seek out the clues that give meaning to the actions and motivations that define the context of the life and culture of an examined historical subject. In Scripture study, the term *exegesis* refers to breaking open or bringing out the truth of an ancient passage for a critical eye of explanation. It is equally important to do the same with media representations of contexts surrounding historical individuals and the legacy of their lived experiences. This chapter of *Hollywood or History? An Inquiry-Based Strategy for Teaching World Religions* offers four films that are based on historical events. These biopics or documentaries engage a contextual understanding of how world religions have influenced the historical record, in the positive or in the negative. Through these lesson plans secondary students will be challenged to research the surrounding context to reach a better understanding of the historical context of an event or religious figures in light of a religious significance.

The first lesson plan in this section examines a call to ethical action and human dignity using the example of the life of Eunice Kennedy Shriver (1921–2009). Through Mitchell's (2015) *ESPN 30-for-30 Shorts: Brave in the Attempt* documentary, secondary students will explore the development of the Special Olympics, the recognition of the dignity of individuals with disabilities through the advocacy of Shriver, and its connection with Catholic social teaching. This example of a woman of faith and force illustrates a clear message that global change can start from the humblest grassroot beginnings, like inspiration from within a family or a neighborhood backyard.

The second lesson explores the role of art through the visual eye and photojournalism of holocaust survivor, Henri Dauman (1933–). Through Jones' (2020) award-winning documentary—*Henri Dauman: Looking Up*—students will engage the history of 20th century America through the photos of Dauman's collection of celebrities and socialites from the perspective of a refugee and immigrant photographer. The dissonance between Dauman's war life and photography of American affluence strikes a profound contention for historical analysis for the students.

The third lesson again challenges historical realities through the power of truth telling and the search for reconciliation. Villeneuve's (2017) short film *Holy Angels* offers a poignant testimony through the remembrances of Lena Wandering Spirit's experience at Holy Angels Residential School in Alberta. Through the film students are challenged to engage a history that is still being unearthed, the effects of nationalism of the North American 20th century. Ethical implications are challenged and discussed to understand the deep wounds and challenges of seeking Truth and Reconciliation for wrongs of the past, especially wrongs perpetrated in the name of religion.

The final film in this section also presents a topic that challenges the limits of one's faith. Through Scorsese's (2016) *Silence*, students will research the effects of the Japanese nationalism of the 16th century. The topic presented in this lesson plumbs the spiritual depths of one's identity and faith to engage the concept of the Greek term, *martyr*, witness.

REFERENCES

Jones, P. K. (Director). (2020). *Henri Dauman: Looking up* [Film]. Nocturnal Media.
Mitchell, F. (Director). (2015). *ESPN 30-for-30 shorts: Brave in the Attempt* [Film]. ESPN.
Scorsese, M. (Director). (2016). *Silence* [Film]. Paramount Pictures.
Villeneuve, J. C. (Director). (2017). *Holy Angels* [Film]. National Film Board of Canada. https://www.nfb.ca/film/holy-angels

Catholic Social Teachings and Eunice Kennedy Shriver's Catholic Faith

Daniel E. Martin

FILM: *Brave in the Attempt* (2015)

Lesson Name
Part 1: Introducing Catholic Social Teaching and Eunice Kennedy Shriver's Catholic Faith
Part 2: Analyze and Discuss *Brave in the Attempt* in Preparation for an Essay used as an Assessment

Grade	Subject	Topic
7–12	Christianity; Social Justice; Female Leadership	Catholic Social Teaching: An Embodied Example of Catholic Social Thought

Chapter Theme	Estimated Time Needed for Lesson
Historical Context: Social Justice, Equal Rights, Discipleship, Special Olympics	45 minutes (Part 1)
45 minutes (Part 2)

National Association for Media Literacy Education

Standard Number	Detailed Description of Each Standard You Are Discussing

Core Principles of Media Literacy Education in the United States	4. Media Literacy Education (MLE) develops informed, reflective and engaged participants essential for a democratic society.
	
	Implications for Practice
	    4.1 MLE promotes student interest in news and current events as a dimension of citizenship, and can enhance student understanding of First Amendment rights and responsibilities.
	6. MLE affirms that people use their individual skills, beliefs, and experiences to construct their own meanings from media messages.
	
	Implications for Practice
	    6.1 MLE is not about teaching students what to think; it is about teaching them how they can arrive at informed choices that are most consistent with their own values.

State and USCCB Standard Description

State	Detailed Description of Each Standard You Are Discussing
Kentucky High School Social Studies K.H.CO.1 (Parts 1 and 2)	H: Conflict and Compromise K.H.CO.1 Describe interactions that occur between individuals/groups in families, classrooms, and communities. Whether working independently or cooperatively, people learn in the context of families, peers, schools, and communities. Groups found in a student's community may, at times, conflict with one another; however, members of a community must cooperate through work, play, or learning to complete tasks.
The College, Career, and Civic Life (C3) Framework for Social Studies State Standards (Part 2)	D1.5.6-8. Determine the kinds of sources that will be helpful in answering compelling and supporting questions, taking into consideration multiple points of views represented in the sources.
United States Conference of Catholic Bishops (USCCB) Curriculum Framework	**Doctrinal Elements of a Curriculum Framework for the Development of Catechetical Materials for Young People of High School Age** (USCCB, 2008)

High School Curriculum Framework: Elective Option C—Living as a Disciple of Jesus Christ in Society (Parts 1 and 2)	B. Call to family, community, and participation.
	   1. What is a family (CCC, nos. 2202–2203)?
	   2. The family—foundation of society—needs support.
	   3. Society should protect the dignity and growth of the family.
	   4. *All people should participate in society* (emphasis added)—work for common good

High School Curriculum Framework: Elective Option C—Living as a Disciple of Jesus Christ in Society (Parts 1 and 2)	Major Themes of Catholic Social Teaching (CCC, nos. 1877–1948, 2196–2257)
	A. The dignity of human life.
	   1. All human life created and redeemed by God is sacred.
	   2. Dignity due to being an image and likeness of God.

Common Core	
Reading CCR 3 (Part 1)	Analyze how and why individuals, events, and ideas develop and interact over the course of a text.

Grade 8: RL.8.3. (Parts 1 and 2)	Analyze how particular lines of dialogue or incidents in a story or drama propel the action, reveal aspects of a character, or provoke a decision.
Grades 11–12: RL.11-12.3. (Parts 1 and 2)	Analyze the impact of the author's choices regarding how to develop and relate elements of a story or drama (e.g., where a story is set, how the action is ordered, how the characters are introduced and developed).
California Arts Standards for Media Arts	
5.MA:Re7 (Parts 1 and 2)	a. Identify, describe, and differentiate how messages and meaning are created by components in media artworks.
8.MA:Re7 (Part 2)	b. Compare, contrast, and analyze how various forms, methods, and styles in media artworks manage audience experience and create intention.
Colorado 21st Century Skills and Readiness Competencies in Reading, Writing, and Communicating (Part 2 and Essay)	Critical Thinking and Reasoning (9th Grade) Critical thinking and reasoning are vital to advance in the technologically sophisticated world we live in. In order for students to be successful and powerful readers, writers, and communicators, they must incorporate critical thinking and reasoning skills. Students need to be able to successfully argue a point, justify reasoning, evaluate for a purpose, infer to predict and draw conclusions, problem-solve, and understand and use logic to inform critical thinking.

NCSS C3 Framework

Dimension	Detailed Description of Each NCSS Dimension You Are Incorporating (should have all four).
D1.2.9-12	Explain points of agreement and disagreement experts have about interpretations and applications of disciplinary concepts and ideas associated with a compelling question.
D2.His.5.9-12.	Analyze how historical contexts shaped and continue to shape people's perspectives.
D3.3.9-12	Identify evidence that draws information directly and substantively from multiple sources to detect inconsistencies in evidence in order to revise or strengthen claims.
D4.1.9-12	Construct arguments using precise and knowledgeable claims, with evidence from multiple sources, while acknowledging counterclaims and evidentiary weaknesses.

NCSS Core Themes and Description

Theme Number	Detailed Description of Each Aligned NCSS Theme
III People, Places, Environments	The study of people, places, and environments enables us to understand the relationship between human populations and the physical world. Students learn where people and places are located and why they are there. They examine the influence of physical systems, such as climate, weather and seasons, and natural resources, such as land and water, on human populations. They study the causes, patterns and effects of human settlement and migration, learn of the roles of different kinds of population centers in a society, and investigate the impact of human activities on the environment. This enables them to acquire a useful basis of knowledge for informed decision-making on issues arising from human-environmental relationships.
V Individuals, Groups and Institutions	Institutions are the formal and informal political, economic, and social organizations that help us carry out, organize, and manage our daily affairs. Schools, religious institutions, families, government agencies, and the courts all play an integral role in our lives. They are organizational embodiments of the core social values of those who comprise them, and play a variety of important roles in socializing individuals and meeting their needs, as well as in the promotion of societal continuity, the mediation of conflict, and the consideration of public issues.
X Civics Ideals and Practices	An understanding of civic ideals and practices is critical to full participation in society and is an essential component of education for citizenship, which is the central purpose of social studies. All people have a stake in examining civic ideals and practices across time and in different societies. Through an understanding of both ideals and practices, it becomes possible to identify gaps between them, and study efforts to close the gaps in our democratic republic and worldwide.

Handouts/Materials/Web Links

Handout/Materials:
- "Hollywood or History?" graphic organizer

Web Links:
- A. Primary Source(s):
    - *Brave in the Attempt* (Mitchell, 2015)
      https://www.espn.com/watch/player?id=80dc5e9f-49b0-496b-b224-a9917b09f0e9
    - "Education + Advocacy" (n.d.)
      https://www.cctwincities.org/education-advocacy/

- "Populorum Progressio (On the Development of Peoples)" (Pope Paul VI, 1967) https://www.cctwincities.org/wp-content/uploads/2015/10/Populorum-Progressio.pdf (uploaded in 2015)
B. Secondary Source(s):
- *The Kennedy Women: The Saga of an American Family* (Leamer, 1994)
- *Catholic Social Teaching and Movements* (Krier Mich, 1998)
- *Living Justice: Catholic Social Teaching in Action* (Massaro, 2012)
- *Sarge: The Life and Times of Sargent Shriver* (Stossel, 2004)

Guiding Questions

What should students know or understand at the completion of the unit or lesson?

Primary Questions:

- What idea is the basis for the Roman Catholic church's commitment to human dignity?
- What 19th century global phenomenon spurred the development of modern Catholic social teaching? Why?
- What was the condition of many disabled people prior to the development of the Special Olympics? Why would the commitment to human dignity found in Catholic social teaching respond to this set of conditions?
- How did Eunice Kennedy Shriver embody the beliefs that she held?

Additional Questions:

- What evidence do we have that Eunice Kennedy Shriver was a dedicated Roman Catholic?
- What biographical data do we have about Eunice Kennedy Shriver that suggests she would apply her Catholic faith to people in the disabled community?

Important Vocabulary

List all of the important indicators of achievement (important people, places, and events) and vocabulary that students will need to know at the conclusion of the lesson.

Catholic Social Teaching: A sustained body of reflection on social and economic questions in light of Catholic moral commitments initiated by Pope Leo XIII that continues to this day.
- **Full Participation in Society as relates to Catholic Social Teaching:** "Every person has at once a right and a duty to participate in the full range of activities and institutions of all aspects of social life" (Massaro, 2012, p. 86).
- **Industrialization as Relates to Catholic Social Teaching:** Unsafe working conditions and deplorable poverty prompted Catholic figures in the 19th century to analyze, critique, and engage social systems from a standpoint of Catholic moral principles.

Eunice Kennedy Shriver (1921–2009): Sister of President John F. Kennedy who created the Special Olympics.

Human Dignity: From the Roman Catholic perspective, all humans have dignity/value due to reflecting God's image and likeness. Catholics believe this human dignity cannot be lost therefore all humans from conception to natural death are valuable.

Rosemary Kennedy (1918–2005): Sister of President John F. Kennedy and Eunice Kennedy Shriver who had a mental disability and helped to inspire the Special Olympics

Assessment Strategies

Describe the assessments that will be used during the unit.

Formative Assessment: Round table discussion, Complete "Hollywood or History?" graphic organizer, and discuss with peers.

Summative Assessment: Essays that analyze Eunice Kennedy Shriver's work with the Special Olympics in light of Catholic social teaching principles of human dignity and full participation in society.

Teaching Strategies (Part 1)

8 min	Roundtable Group Discussion/ Lecture	10 min	Primary Sources and Secondary Source Individual Analysis	10 min	Begin "Hollywood or History?" graphic organizer
12 min	View clips from *Brave in the Attempt.* 0:00–12:03 (Mitchell, 2015)	5 min	Confer with students to clear up misconceptions	**Time Remaining/ HMWK**	Continue with graphic organizer with any extra time

Times are highly flexible and should be adjusted according to the number of sources used, length of introduction, period/ block schedule, etc.

Teaching Strategies (Part 2)

3 min	Recap Part 1	10 min	How does the documentary represent embodied notions of human dignity?	10 min	Completion of "Hollywood or History?" graphic organizer
12 min	View clips from *Brave in the Attempt.* 12:03–23:39 (Mitchell, 2015)	10 min	Use whiteboard to post plural, particular examples of answers to the above question.	**Time Remaining/ HMWK**	Work on essay

Times are highly flexible and should be adjusted according to the number of sources used, length of introduction, period/ block schedule, etc.

Sparking Strategy/Warm-Up

Sparking Strategy (Lesson introduction)

Have students discuss the treatment of people with disabilities in present time. Have them extrapolate what that treatment might have looked like 100 years ago and 50 years ago.

Lesson Procedures

In a numerical list, provide a step by step outline of what you plan to do in the lesson. Include questions you will ask the students and materials you will use.

Outline

Preliminary: Students Should have read: Thomas Massaro, SJ's (2012) work *Living Justice: Catholic Social Teaching in Action* (pp. 84–87), Laurence Leamer's (1994) *The Kennedy Women: The Sage of an American Family* (pp. 225–227), as well as Section 47 of Pope Paul VI's (1967) *Populorum Progressio*.

Part 1:

1. Start with a roundtable group discussion: spark ideas about how people in the disability community have been and are treated. Ask for examples of both discrimination and movements toward inclusivity. Anecdotes are acceptable starting points for broadening this discussion.
2. Deliver a mini-lecture on industrialization in the 19th-century and its disproportionate economic impacts on areas with large Roman Catholic populations such as southern and central Europe, Latin America, Ireland, as well as immigrant populations that migrated to the United States. Explore how and why in 1891 that Pope Leo XIII launched a sustained analysis of social conditions in light of Roman Catholic thought known as Catholic social teaching that continues to this day.
3. Explain to students the religious reasoning behind the Roman Catholic church's commitment to human dignity. Demonstrate how this commitment to human dignity connected to the economic concerns of Pope Leo XIII but also broadened to concerns about nuclear warfare, societal participation, and other topics.
4. Have students read a short excerpt from *Sarge: The Life and Times of Sargent Shriver* (Stossel, 2004, pp. 112, 113) in which Eunice Kennedy became engaged to Sargent Shriver after attending Mass together. Sargent Shriver noted Eunice's deep devotion to Mary.
5. Have students explore the idea of full participation in society from Thomas Massaro, SJ's (2012) work *Living Justice: Catholic Social Teaching in Action* (pp. 84–87) as well as Section 47 of Pope Paul VI's (1967) *Populorum Progressio*. In a guided discussion, have students lay out concrete examples of public actions and policies that have attempted to broaden social participation for groups other than the disabled to help students see how Eunice Kennedy Shriver's work fits into broader societal movements ahead of Lesson 2.

Part 2:

1. Remind students of Pope Paul VI's (1967) words on social participation "The struggle against destitution, though urgent and necessary, is not enough. It is a question, rather, of building a world where every man, no matter what his race, religion or nationality, can live a fully human life…" (*Populorum Progressio*, Section 47).

2. Show more clips from *Brave in the Attempt* (Mitchell, 2015).
   - Pause at the footage of disabled people in institutional settings in the United States prior to Eunice Kennedy Shriver's work (07:35). Ask students to reflect on how this relates to the Roman Catholic commitment to human dignity.
   - Pause at the image of "Our Lady of Guadalupe" in Eunice Kennedy Shriver's office to briefly discuss her Catholic faith. Ask if the documentary sufficiently addresses her faith with this image?
3. Have students post a number of particular instances in which the Special Olympics highlighted human dignity.
4. Have students work together to finalize their graphic organizer ahead of responding to the essay prompt.

Differentiation

Think about your students' skill levels, intelligences, and learning styles. How are you going to make this lesson meet the needs of all of your students?

Scaffolds: Work with students individually if needed to answer questions and further explain any material. Make sure that the student table groups have mixed students so that higher achieving students are working with/helping their classmates.

ESL Interventions: Provide vocabulary terms pertaining to Catholic social teaching and the development of the Special Olympics. Consider selecting among the sources with images, or finding additional documents, from the source collections provided.

Extensions: Have students write a letter or make a video telling a younger student about the complexities of choosing what to focus upon and what to leave out when producing a compact (23 minutes in this case) documentary.

Summarizing Strategies/Synthesizing Activity

What strategies are you going to use to allow students to summarize what they learned in the lesson?

- Hollywood or History? Was Eunice Kennedy Shriver's religious conviction underplayed in the documentary?
- Student-generated position statements with reference to documents/evidence
- Roundtable discussion

References

Are there any additional resources that might be relevant to your lesson? Are there sources that you need to reference? Please add any citations using APA.

Education + Advocacy. (n.d.). Catholic Charities of Saint Paul and Minneapolis. https://www.cctwincities.org/education-advocacy/

Krier Mich, M. L. (1998). *Catholic social teaching and movements*. Twenty-Third Publications.

Leamur, L. (1994). *The Kennedy women: The saga of an American family*. Villard Books.

Massaro, T. (2012). *Living justice: Catholic social teaching in action*. Rowman and Littlefield.

Mitchell, F. (Director). (2015). *ESPN 30-for-30 shorts: Brave in the attempt* [Film]. ESPN.

Pope Paul VI. (1967, March 26). *Populorum progressio* (On the Development of Peoples). Libreria Editrice Vaticana. https://www.cctwincities.org/wp-content/uploads/2015/10/Populorum-Progressio.pdf

Stossel, S. (2004). *Sarge: The life and times of Sargent Shriver*. Smithsonian Books.

Chapter 2: Historical Contexts ▪ 53

Hollywood or History?
Brave in the Attempt (2015)

Inspirational stories are a part of the landscape for Hollywood films, short films, and documentaries. *Brave in the Attempt* (2015) highlights the inspiring work of Eunice Kennedy Shriver and the development of the Special Olympics.

Evaluate each source provided and summarize your observations and analysis in the corresponding spaces provided. In the section located at the bottom of the page, explain whether you think the main themes from *Brave in the Attempt* (2015) should be evaluated as accurate accounts of *Populorum Progressio* (On the Development of Peoples) by Pope Paul VI (1967) and *Living Justice: Catholic Social Teaching in Action* (2010), pure Hollywood creations, or a mixture of both. Use examples from your sources/documents to explain your answer.

Primary Source	*Brave in the Attempt* (2015)	Secondary Source
What do you think? Hollywood or History?		

Henri Dauman and Telling the Untold Stories

Stephanie Garrone-Shufran and Rory Tannebaum

FILM: *Henri Dauman: Looking Up* (2020)

Grade	Subject	Topic
7–12	Judaism; U.S. History	The American Experience and Jewish Refugees

Chapter Theme	Estimated Time Needed for Lesson
Historical Context: Judaism, Rituals, Symbols	Two days of class.

National Association for Media Literacy Education

Standard Number	Detailed Description of Each Standard You Are Discussing

Core Principles of Media Literacy Education in the United States	1. Media Literacy Education (MLE) requires active inquiry and critical thinking about the messages we receive and create.
	
	Implications for Practice
	  1.3 MLE emphasizes strong sense critical thinking, i.e., asking questions about all media messages, not just those with which we may disagree.
	  1.4 MLE trains students to use document-based evidence and well-reasoned arguments to support their conclusions.
	
	6. MLE affirms that people use their individual skills, beliefs, and experiences to construct their own meanings from media messages.
	
	Implications for Practice
	  6.1 MLE is not about teaching students what to think; it is about teaching them how they can arrive at informed choices that are most consistent with their own values.

State and Common Core Standard Description

State	Detailed Description of Each Standard You Are Discussing
Massachusetts 8th Grade U.S. History	Topic 4. The Great Wars, 1914–1945 [WHII.T4] Supporting Question: What were the causes and consequences of the 20th century's two world wars? 13. Describe the Holocaust, including its roots in Christian anti-Semitism, 19th century ideas about race and nation, and the Nazi dehumanization and planned extermination of the Jews and persecution of LGBT and Gypsy/Roma people.
Massachusetts High School U.S. History	Topic 3. Defending democracy: responses to fascism and communism [USII.T3] Supporting Question: What kind of a role should the U.S. play in world affairs? 2. Explain the rise of fascism and the forms it took in Germany and Italy, including ideas and policies that led to the Holocaust. Topic 5. The Cold War Era, 1945–1991 [WHII.T5] Supporting Question: How did the Cold War manifest itself in conflicts and shifting alliances in the second half of the 20th century? 7. Explain the background for the establishment of the modern state of Israel in 1948, and subsequent military and political conflicts b. anti-Semitism and the Holocaust
Michigan High School World History	7.2.6 Case Studies of Genocide Analyze the development, enactment, and consequences of, as well as the international community's responses to, the Holocaust (or Shoah), Armenian Genocide, and at least one other genocide.
New York Grade 10: Global History and Geography	10.10 Human Rights Violations Since the Holocaust, human rights violations have generated worldwide attention and concern. The United Nations *Universal Declaration of Human Rights* has provided a set of principles to guide efforts to protect threatened groups and has served as a lens through which historical occurrences of oppression can be evaluated.
Common Core	
CCSS.ELA LITERACY. RH.9-10.2	Determine the central ideas or information of a primary or secondary source; provide an accurate summary of how key events or ideas develop over the course of the text.

CCSS.ELA LITERACY. RH.9-10.9	Compare and contrast treatments of the same topic in several primary and secondary sources.

NCSS C3 Framework

Dimension	Detailed Description of Each NCSS Dimension You Are Incorporating (should have all four).
D2.His.1.9-12	Evaluate how historical events and developments were shaped by unique circumstances of time and place as well as broader historical contexts.
D2.His.2.9-12	Analyze change and continuity in historical eras.
D2.His.3.9-12	Use questions generated about individuals and groups to assess how significance of their actions changes over time and is shaped by the historical context.
D2.His.6.9-12	Analyze the ways in which the perspectives of those writing history shaped the history that they produced.

NCSS Core Themes and Description

Theme Number	Detailed Description of Each Aligned NCSS Theme
II Time, Continuity, and Change	Studying the past makes it possible for us to understand the human story across time. Historical analysis enables us to identify continuities over time in core institutions, values, ideals, and traditions, as well as processes that lead to change within societies and institutions, and that result in innovation and the development of new ideas, values, and ways of life.
V Individuals, Groups and Institutions	Social studies programs should include experiences that provide for the study of interactions among individuals, groups, and institutions.
VI Power, Authority and Governance	Social studies programs should include experiences that provide for the study of how people create, interact with, and change structures of power, authority, and governance.

Handouts/Materials/Web Links

Handout/Materials:
- "Hollywood or History?" graphic organizer

Web Links:

A. *Henri Dauman: Looking Up* (Jones, 2020)
   https://www.amazon.com/Henri-Dauman-Looking-Up/dp/B084Z8KNBK/ref=sr_1_1?dchild=1&keywords=henri+dauman&qid=1631456669&s=instant-video&sr=1-1
   (available on Amazon Prime Video for free regardless of membership)
B. Primary Source(s):
   – Henri Dauman's Digital Portfolio
     https://daumanpictures.com/magazine-covers
     [Iconic photos taken by Henri Dauman: Marilyn Monroe, Andy Warhol, John and Jackie Kennedy, Elvis Presley, Brigitte Bardot, Groucho Marx, and hundreds of other well-known celebrities]
C. Secondary Source(s):
   – "Henri Dauman: Looking Up—Official Trailer" (2021)
     https://www.youtube.com/watch?v=ohJmWYtvOCg [2 mins].
   – "Guidelines for Teaching About the Holocaust" (United States Holocaust Memorial Museum, n.d.)
     https://www.ushmm.org/teach/fundamentals/guidelines-for-teaching-the-Holocaust

Guiding Questions

What should students know or understand at the completion of the unit or lesson?

Primary Questions:
- How does Henri Dauman's photography tell a story in images?
- To what extent can photographs impact someone's perception of an event or era?
- How did the United States view Jewish immigrants/refugees during World War II?

Additional Questions:
- Why are stories important in history?
- Whose stories get told? Whose stories do not? Why does that matter?

Important Vocabulary

List all of the important indicators of achievement (important people, places, and events) and vocabulary that students will need to know at the conclusion of the lesson.

Emigration: Leaving a country to search for a better life—be it social conditions, professional opportunities, or to escape turmoil.
Henri Dauman (1933–): An iconic photographer throughout the 20th century who documented politicians, celebrities, and artists.
Immigration: The process in which individuals seek residency in another country.
Refugee: "A refugee is someone who has been forced to flee his or her country because of persecution, war or violence. A refugee has a well-founded fear of persecution for reasons of race, religion, nationality, political opinion or membership in a particular social group. Most likely, they cannot return home or are afraid to do so. War and ethnic, tribal and religious violence are leading causes of refugees fleeing their countries" ("What is a Refugee?," n.d., para. 1).

58 ▪ Hollywood or History?

Assessment Strategies

Describe the assessments that will be used during the unit.

Formative Assessment: Throughout the lesson, the teacher will have many opportunities to both assess students and correct any misconceptions that students may have. This can occur during the first day—in which students are analyzing Dauman's iconic photographs—as well as on the second day during either the think–pair–share or the Jigsaw portion of the lesson.

Summative Assessment: Students will write a brief essay on the impact of photography and its connection to storytelling. This will then be connected to a discussion on how immigrants chose to document their experiences (and how this practice has both remained the same and evolved since Dauman's photography was popularized).

Teaching Strategies (Part 1 and 2)

5 min	Sparking Strategy	30 min	View clips from: "Henri Dauman: Looking Up—Official Trailer" (2021)	20 min	Group discussion on emigration, World War II, and photography as a means of storytelling
15 min	Students find photographs for sharing				
5 min	Students share photos and provide explanation			Time Remaining/ HMWK	"Hollywood or History?" graphic organizer
10 min	Teacher provides an overview of emigration during WWII (both Jewish individuals others)				

Times are highly flexible and should be adjusted according to the number of sources used, length of introduction, period/block schedule, etc.

Sparking Strategy/Warm-Up

Sparking Strategy (Lesson introduction)

Teacher shows a photo (some examples are listed above).

Writing prompt: Look closely at this photo. Tell a story based on what you see.

Lesson Procedures

In a numerical list, provide a step by step outline of what you plan to do in the lesson. Include questions you will ask the students and materials you will use.

Outline

Part 1:

1. Hook: Use a photograph to tell a story.
2. Introduce Henri Dauman—short biography. This will be followed by showing a single photo of his (https://daumanpictures.com/wp-content/uploads/2012/12/HENRI-263-62399.jpg) in order to model for students how to analyze his work.
3. Carousel Brainstorm: posters for Kennedys, Elvis Presley, Muhammad Ali, Malcolm X, Marilyn Monroe (can add other of Dauman's subjects if there are many students). Small group of students visit each station and brainstorm what they know about the person/people.
4. Teachers visit each poster. Corrects any misconceptions and adds any pertinent information that has not been written by students.
5. Show a film clip from Henri Dauman: Looking Up (Jones, 2020, at 1 hour in, exactly) about how photos tell a story.
6. Short discussion of what it means to tell a story in photographs.
7. Teacher models completing a writing assignment: Show one photo from the Kennedys. Write a description of exactly what is in the photo. Construct a story of what the photo means/shows/symbolizes. Explain how that story is connected to the history of the time.
8. Summative Assessment: Teacher shows students a variety of Dauman's photos. They each choose one to write about—description, constriction of story, explanation.

Part 2:

9. Quick Write: What do you know of your family's immigration history? How did you learn this information?
10. The teacher will remind students that yesterday they learned about the stories Dauman told of public figures through his photography. Today we will be talking about the private story of his own life and the Jewish refugees who entered the United States during World War II.
11. Think–Write–Pair–Share: Students will be shown a photograph of refugee children on the SS Saint Louis ("Passengers Aboard the St. Louis," 1939; https://encyclopedia.ushmm.org/content/en/photo/passengers-aboard-the-st-louis). As a review from the previous day, they will describe the photo and construct a story. They will turn and talk with a partner about their description and their story. A few teacher-chosen volunteers will share.
12. The teacher will then briefly present on the real-life story behind the photo and the United States' actions regarding Jewish refugees and immigrants in that timeframe. Use information from "What Americans Thought of Jewish Refugees on the Eve of World War II" (Tharoor, 2015).
13. Clips in which Dauman tells his story of survival in France during and immediately after World War II will be played.
14. Students will then read "The Secret History of America's Only WWII Refugee Camp" (Blankfeld, 2020).

15. Jigsaw: Before they begin reading, students will be assigned to expert and home groups. In their expert groups, they will be assigned one of the following questions to answer:
    - What parallels do you see between this article and Dauman's story?
    - What parallels do you see between this story and the story of American immigration today?
    - Why do you think this story is a "secret history" in the United States? How does this compare to the stories of those people in Dauman's photos?
    - What was Dauman's reason for not sharing his story until the film? How might others feel about sharing their personal immigration stories?
16. In their home groups, students will share their answers to their assigned questions and lead brief discussions among their classmates.
17. Summative Assessment: Find a photo of immigration today. Create a caption that tells the immigration story of those involved.

Differentiation

Think about your students' skill levels, intelligences, and learning styles. How are you going to make this lesson meet the needs of all of your students?

Scaffolds:
- Provide a worksheet for students to complete in Jigsaw activity.
- Allow for student choice of photos for their writing.
- Create intentional groupings in which students of various levels would be supported.

ESL Interventions:
- For writing:
  - Allow students to label the pictures instead of using sentences (WIDA Level 1).
  - Encourage use of the L1 to write (WIDA Levels 1 & 2).
  - Pre-choose photos for their summative assessments and provide necessary vocabulary (WIDA Levels 1 & 2).
  - Provide unfamiliar vocabulary in word banks for them to use in their writing (WIDA Levels 1–3).
  - Provide sentence frames for the summative writing assessments (WIDA Levels 1–3).
- For reading:
  - Pair ELs with other speakers of their L1 for support in discussion (WIDA Levels 1–3).
  - Replace the article with video: "The Only World War II Refugee Camp in America" (The Saturday Evening Post, n.d.; WIDA Levels 1 & 2).
  - Place ELs in an expert group for this question: "What was Dauman's reason for not sharing his story until the film and how might others feel about sharing their personal immigration stories?"
  - In discussions:
    - Provide sentence frames (WIDA Levels 1 & 2).
    - Provide comprehensible input through visuals (WIDA Levels 1 & 2).
    - Provide a note-taking guide to help them organize information (WIDA Levels 1–4).

Extensions: Have students take their own photos within their communities to create stories of their place and time, as Dauman did. Write a short explanation.

Summarizing Strategies/Synthesizing Activity

What strategies are you going to use to allow students to summarize what they learned in the lesson?

Ideally, teachers will be discussing issues of immigration throughout the course of the academic year—not solely when discussing World War II. In order to help students understand that immigration is always occurring, teachers can connect much of this lesson (and the telling of stories) with other moments in history where immigration was occurring throughout the world. This could be showing students stories from Syrian refugee Crisis ("Syria Refugee Crisis Explained," 2022), the Rohingya Refugee Crisis ("Rohingya Refugee Crisis Explained," 2022), or the immigration occurring just south of the U.S. border ("Central America Refugee Crisis," n.d.). Such conversations will help students to understand that immigration is still incredibly prevalent today and that we have to understand that such events happen and are told by differing voices and with varying perspectives.

References

Are there any additional resources that might be relevant to your lesson? Are there sources that you need to reference? Please add any citations using APA.

Blankfeld, K. (2020, September 11). The secret history of America's only WWII refugee camp. *The New York Times.* https://www.nytimes.com/2020/09/11/nyregion/oswego-jewish-refugees-world-war-two.html

Central America Refugee Crisis. (n.d.). United Nations High Commissioner for Refugees. https://www.unrefugees.org/emergencies/central-america/

Henri Dauman: Looking Up—Official Trailer. (2021, February 13). [YouTube video]. https://www.youtube.com/watch?v=ohJmWYtvOCg

Jones, P. K. (Director). (2020). *Henri Dauman: Looking up* [Film]. Nocturnal Media.

Passengers Aboard the St. Louis. (1939). [Photo]. Holocaust Encyclopedia. https://encyclopedia.ushmm.org/content/en/photo/passengers-aboard-the-st-louis

Rohingya Refugee Crisis Explained. (2022, July 13). United Nations High Commissioner for Refugees. https://www.unrefugees.org/news/rohingya-refugee-crisis-explained/

Syria Refugee Crisis Explained. (2022, July 8). United Nations High Commissioner for Refugees. https://www.unrefugees.org/news/syria-refugee-crisis-explained/

Tharoor, I. (2015, November 17). What Americans thought of Jewish refugees on the eve of World War II. *The Washington Post.* https://www.washingtonpost.com/news/worldviews/wp/2015/11/17/what-americans-thought-of-jewish-refugees-on-the-eve-of-world-war-ii/

The Saturday Evening Post. (n.d.). *The only World War II refugee camp in America* [YouTube video]. https://www.youtube.com/watch?v=WyAN1O3Dv7M

What Is a Refugee? (n.d.). United Nations High Commissioner for Refugees. https://www.unrefugees.org/refugee-facts/what-is-a-refugee/

United States Holocaust Memorial Museum. (n.d.). *Guidelines for teaching about the holocaust.* https://www.ushmm.org/teach/fundamentals/guidelines-for-teaching-the-Holocaust

Additional Resource

Engle, M. (2009). *Tropical secrets. Holocaust refugees in Cuba.* Henry Holt and Company.

Lieb, S. R. (2020, April 22). Photographer Henri Dauman shot Hollywood greats after being shot at by Nazis. *The Times of Israel.* https://www.timesofisrael.com/photographer-henri-dauman-shot-hollywood-greats-after-being-shot-at-by-nazis/

United States Holocaust Memorial Museum. (n.d). Holocaust awareness. https://www.ushmm.org

Hollywood or History?
Henri Dauman: Looking Up (2020)

Inspirational stories are a part of the landscape for Hollywood, short films, and documentaries. The documentary *Henri Dauman: Looking Up* (2020) explores inspiration art and culture through the lens of holocaust survivor and photographer, Henri Dauman.

Evaluate and summarize your observations and analysis in the corresponding spaces provided. In the section located at the bottom of the page, explain whether you think the main themes from *Henri Dauman: Looking Up* (2020) should be evaluated as an accurate portrayal, pure Hollywood creations, or a mixture of both, based on evidence from the primary and secondary sources. Use examples from your sources/documents to explain your answer.

Primary Source(s)	*Henri Dauman: Looking Up* (2020)	**Secondary Source**

What do you think? Hollywood or History?

Understanding the Effects of Residential Schools and Initial Steps of Reconciliation

Thomas E. Malewitz

FILM: *Holy Angels* (2017)

Grade	Subject	Topic
11–12	Christianity; First Nations	First Nations, Christianity, and Truth and Reconciliation

Chapter Theme	Estimated Time Needed for Lesson
Historical Context: First Nations, Christianity, Ethics, Genocide, Reconciliation	45 minutes

National Association for Media Literacy Education

Standard Number	Detailed Description of Each Standard You Are Discussing

Core Principles of Media Literacy Education in the United States	3. Media Literacy Education (MLE) builds and reinforces skills for learners of all ages. Like print literacy, those skills necessitate integrated, interactive, and repeated practice.
	
	Implications for Practice
	   3.3 MLE engages students with varied learning styles.
	   3.4 MLE is most effective when used with co-learning pedagogies, in which teachers learn from students and students learn from teachers and from classmates.
	
	4. MLE develops informed, reflective, and engaged participants essential for a democratic society.
	
	Implications for Practice
	   4.1 MLE promotes student interest in news and current events as a dimension of citizenship, and can enhance student understanding of First Amendment rights and responsibilities.
	   4.4 MLE invites and respects diverse points of view.
	   4.5 MLE explores representations, misrepresentations, and lack of representation of cultures and countries in the global community.

State and USCCB Standard Description

State	Detailed Description of Each Standard You Are Discussing
Illinois (Part 1 & 2) High School Social Studies	**SS.H.1.9-12.** Evaluate how historical developments were shaped by time and place as well as broader historical contexts. **SS.H.2.9-12.** Analyze change and continuity within and across historical eras. **SS.H.3.9-12.** Evaluate the method utilized by people and institutions to promote change.
Kentucky (Part 1 & 2) High School History: Cause and Effect	**UH.CE.5** Evaluate the ways in which groups facing discrimination worked to achieve expansion of rights and liberties from 1877–present.
Michigan (Part 1 & 2) High School Social Studies: Civics	**C – 6.4.2** Identify, discuss, and analyze methods individuals and/or groups have chosen to attempt social and legal change. Assess the effects of civil disobedience, social movements, demonstrations, protests on society and law.
New York (Part 1) High School Social Studies	**11.4c.2** Federal policies regarding westward expansion had positive effects on the national economy but negative consequences for Native Americans: the effect of federal policies on Native Americans on the Great Plains, including reservation policies, the Dawes Act (1887), and forced acculturation efforts (Carlisle Indian School).
United States Conference of Catholic Bishops (USCCB) Curriculum Framework	**Doctrinal Elements of a Curriculum Framework for the Development of Catechetical Materials for Young People of High School Age (USCCB, 2008)**
USCCB.Option C Social Justice— II.B.1-4	Evaluate several types and concepts of justice in society: distributive, legal, commutative, and social justice.
USCCB.Option C Social Justice— III.A.1-3	Analyze the foundational social justice teaching of dignity of the human person.
USCCB.Option C Social Justice— III.F	Integrate and evaluate multiple sources of information presented to define and explore the concept of solidarity and working for the common good.

NCSS C3 Framework

Dimension	Detailed Description of Each NCSS Dimension You Are Incorporating (should have all four).
D1.2.9-12	Explain points of agreement and disagreement experts have about interpretations and applications of disciplinary concepts and ideas associated with a compelling question.
D2.His.5.9-12	Analyze how historical contexts shaped and continue to shape people's perspectives.
D3.3.9-12	Identify evidence that draws information directly and substantively from multiple sources to detect inconsistencies in evidence in order to revise or strengthen claims.
D4.1.9-12	Construct arguments using precise and knowledgeable claims, with evidence from multiple sources, while acknowledging counterclaims and evidentiary weaknesses.

NCSS Core Themes and Description

Theme Number	Detailed Description of Each Aligned NCSS Theme
II Time, Continuity, and Change	Studying the past makes it possible for us to understand the human story across time. Historical analysis enables us to identify continuities over time in core institutions, values, ideals, and traditions, as well as processes that lead to change within societies and institutions, and that result in innovation and the development of new ideas, values, and ways of life.
V Individuals, Groups and Institutions	Social studies programs should include experiences that provide for the study of interactions among individuals, groups, and institutions.
VI Power, Authority and Governance	Social studies programs should include experiences that provide for the study of how people create, interact with, and change structures of power, authority, and governance.

Handouts/Materials/Web Links

Handout/Materials:
- "Hollywood or History?" graphic organizer

Web Links:
A. Link to Film Clips:
   - *Holy Angels* (Villeneuve, 2017) [14 mins]
     https://www.nfb.ca/film/holy-angels/
   - "Residential School Survivor Explains the Impact on Her Family" (CBC News, 2018) [4 mins]
     https://www.youtube.com/watch?v=nJ64DItsIi0
   - "The Stranger" Official Video—Secret Path" (GordDownieVideos, 2016) [Animated music video, 6 mins]
     https://www.youtube.com/watch?v=za2VzjkwtFc
B. Primary Source(s):
   - "The Lonely Death of Chanie Wenjack" (Adams, 1967)
     https://www.macleans.ca/society/the-lonely-death-of-chanie-wenjack/
   - United Nations Declaration on the Rights of Indigenous Peoples (United Nations, n.d.-b)
     https://www.un.org/development/desa/indigenouspeoples/declaration-on-the-rights-of-indigenous-peoples.html
C. Secondary Source(s):
   - *Secret Path* (Downie & Lamire, 2016)

Guiding Questions

What should students know or understand at the completion of the unit or lesson?

Primary Questions:
- Explain the impact that the residential/industrial indian school system had on the identity and culture of the First Nations during the 20th century in the United States and Canada.
- Explore how the association of Christian leadership of the residential schools affected the faith of generations of First Nations individuals.
- What do you think are the most striking similarities between the personal reflection of *Holy Angels* (Villeneuve, 2017), "The Stranger" (GordDownieVideos, 2016), and the testimony of the residential school survivor's stories?
- After hearing the testimony offered in the video clips, do you think that the Canada's Truth and Reconciliation was accurate in labeling the residential school system a "cultural genocide" or, as some First Nations scholars argue, a genocide? Why or why not?

Important Vocabulary

List all of the important indicators of achievement (important people, places, and events) and vocabulary that students will need to know at the conclusion of the lesson.

Atone/Atonement: to make amends or reparation for an action.
Cultural genocide: acts and measures undertaken to destroy nations' or ethnic groups' culture through spiritual, national, and cultural destruction ("Cultural Genocide," n.d., para. 1).

Genocide: a deliberate/criminal act of any of the following committed with intent to destroy, in whole or in part, a national, ethnical, racial, or religious group, such as:
  (a) killing members of the group,
  (b) causing serious bodily or mental harm to members of the group,
  (c) deliberately inflicting on the group conditions of life calculated to bring about its physical destruction in whole or in part,
  (d) imposing measures intended to prevent births within the group, and
  (e) forcibly transferring children of the group to another group (United Nations, n.d.-a, "Convention on the Prevention and Punishment of the Crime of Genocide, Article II").

Residential/Industrial school (circa 1875–late 1990s): A government/religious sponsored boarding school for First Nations/Native Americans.

Testimony: A formal written or oral statement, especially when given as personal evidence in a court of law.

Tribunal: A court of justice.

Truth and Reconciliation Commission: "A commission (1) focused on the past, rather than in ongoing events; (2) investigates a pattern of events that took place over a period of time; (3) engages directly and broadly with the affected population, gathering information on their experiences; (4) is a temporary body, with the aim of concluding with a final report; and (5) is officially authorized or empowered by the state under review" (Hayner, 2011, pp. 11–12).

Assessment Strategies

Describe the assessments that will be used during the unit.

Formative Assessment: Class Discussion, Reflection

Summative Assessment: Reflection Essay

Teaching Strategies (Part 1 and 2)

10 min	Warm Up	15 min	View *Holy Angels* (Villeneuve, 2017).	**Time Remaining/ HMWK**	Introduce and allow students to work on the reflection essay.
15 min	Explore the power of music; View *The Stranger* (GordDownie Videos, 2016); class discussion.	20 min	Reflection and analyze *Holy Angels* (Villeneuve, 2017).		

Times are highly flexible and should be adjusted according to the number of sources used, length of introduction, period/block schedule, etc.

Sparking Strategy/Warm-Up

Sparking Strategy (Lesson introduction)

Create a dialogue on the historical concept and need for countries and communities to work together toward better future collaboration. Frame the concept within the ethical challenge of how to re-establish trust within a community when violence has led to loss of life between countries and communities, such as in abuse, religious war, and violence introducing terms such as: genocide, tribunal, and Truth/Reconciliation Commission. All students have time to reflect and process the severity of affect violence on communities—using a contemporary example in the news (if available) could be helpful as a tangible example for the conversation.

Lesson Procedures

In a numerical list, provide a step by step outline of what you plan to do in the lesson. Include questions you will ask the students and materials you will use.

Please note: *This lesson only offers a brief introduction into the topic of residential/industrial schools and the Canadian Truth and Reconciliation Commission.*

Understanding the effect of Residential Schools on Faith:

1. Invite students to reflect on the power of storytelling to understand and convey experiences. Have them think of a favorite song, music video, and ask: "What is the musician trying to say through the lyrics or video of the song (e.g., What story is the musician telling the audience? What did you learn from the musician?)?"
2. Explain to the student that historical experiences can also be understood from storytelling. Use GordDownieVideos (2016) "The Stranger" (4 mins) as an example.
3. Have the students write down five themes from the GordDownieVideos (2016) music video for reflection on the story of the music video.
4. Invite some of the students to share one of their themes, and explore what the students experienced from the music video.
5. Explain to the students that storytelling is also used in formal matters, such as in court of law and justice proceedings. Define "testimony" and briefly explain how a testimony is used when a witness explains their experience to a court.
6. Play *Holy Angels* (Villeneuve, 2017) [14 mins].
7. Have the students examine the testimony within *Holy Angels* (Villeneuve, 2017) using guiding questions (e.g., "What did the narrator explain happened at the school?"; "What was the narrator afraid of?"; "Why?"). If a second testimony clip is needed for further reflection use "Residential School Survivor Explains the Impact on Her Family" (CBC News, 2018) [4 mins].
8. Relate the topic back to ethics and religion—most of the residential schools were led by government and Christian religious sponsored leadership. Invite the students to reflect on the ethical issues of such leadership (e.g., "How do you think the First Nations would view Christianity and/or the government because of the treatment in such schools?"; "Would trust be lost between First Nations and the leadership of such schools?")
9. Define and explain the term atone or atonement in context for the students.

10. Have the students write a reflection essay (250 words or so) addressing how they think the Christian and government leaderships should try to atone for the actions affecting the First Nations.

Differentiation

Think about your students' skill levels, intelligences, and learning styles. How are you going to make this lesson meet the needs of all of your students?

Scaffolds: Offer concrete context for new vocabulary terms for the students. Be sure to illustrate the meaning and offer an application to a tangible example, such as storytelling and lyrics in contemporary music.

Multi-modal assessments: Allow students to create a project, letter, or commercial to demonstrate their abilities and creative problem solving instead of an essay reflection in Lesson Procedure 10.

Summarizing Strategies/Synthesizing Activity

What strategies are you going to use to allow students to summarize what they learned in the lesson?

- Hollywood or History?
- student-generated reflection essay with reference to documents/evidence
- class discussion

References

Are there any additional resources that might be relevant to your lesson? Are there sources that you need to reference? Please add any citations using APA.

Adams, I. (1967, February 1). The lonely death of Chanie Wenjack. *Maclean's* https://www.macleans.ca/society/the-lonely-death-of-chanie-wenjack/

CBC News. (2018, March 19). *Residential school survivor explains the impact on her family* [YouTube video]. https://www.youtube.com/watch?v=nJ64DItsIi0

Cultural Genocide. (n.d.). The Armenian Genocide Museum-Institute Foundation. http://www.genocide-museum.am./eng/cultural_genocide.php

Downie, G., & Lamire, J. (2016). *Secret path.* Simon & Schuster.

GordDownieVideos. (2016, October 13). *"The stranger" official video—Secret path* [YouTube video]. https://www.youtube.com/watch?v=za2VzjkwtFc

Hayner, P. B. (2011). *Unspeakable truths: Transitional justice and the challenge of Truth Commissions* (2nd ed.). Routledge.

United Nations. (n.d.-a). *Genocide.* https://www.un.org/en/genocideprevention/genocide.shtml

United Nations. (n.d.-b). *United Nations declaration on the rights of Indigenous peoples.* https://www.un.org/development/desa/indigenouspeoples/declaration-on-the-rights-of-indigenous-peoples.html

United States Conference of Catholic Bishops. (2008). *Doctrinal elements of a curriculum framework for the development of catechetical materials for young people of high school age.*

Villeneuve, J. C. (2017). *Holy angels* [Film]. National Film Board of Canada. https://www.nfb.ca/film/holy-angels/

Additional Resource

Canadian Conference of Catholic Bishops. (2021, September 24). *Statement of apology by the Catholic bishops of Canada to the indigenous peoples of this land.* https://www.cccb.ca/letter/statement-of-apology-by-the-catholic-bishops-of-canada-to-the-indigenous-peoples-of-this-land/

GCIndigenous. (2020, December 15). S*tatement by Minister Bennett on the 5th anniversary of the truth and reconciliation final report* [YouTube video]. https://www.youtube.com/watch?v=c0iuGsGGe2I&t=5s

Hanson, E., Gamez, D. P., & Manuel, A. (2020). T*he residential school system.* Indigenous Foundations .arts.ubc.ca. (Original work published 2009) https://indigenousfoundations.arts.ubc.ca/the_residential_school_system/

LeBlanc, T. (2016, May 25). Walking in reconciled relationships. *Consensus, 37*(1), Article 4. https://scholars.wlu.ca/consensus/vol37/iss1/4

Malewitz, T. E. (2020). The arts, Part II—Painting/photography: The appreciation of beauty. In *Authenticity, passion, and advocacy: Approaching adolescent spirituality from the life and wisdom of Thomas Merton* (pp. 105–116). Wipf & Stock.

National Congress of American Indians. (2020). *The tribal nations of the United States: An introduction.* http://www.ncai.org/tribalnations/introduction/Indian_Country_101_Updated_February_2019.pdf

Regan, P. (2010). *Unsettling the settler within: Indian residential schools, truth telling, and reconciliation in Canada.* University of British Columbia.

Robinson, D., & Martin, K. (Eds.). (2016). *Arts of engagement: Taking aesthetic action in and beyond the truth and reconciliation commission of Canada.* Wilfrid Laurier University.

Toulouse, P. R. (2018). *Truth and reconciliation in Canadian schools.* Portage & Main.

Truth and Reconciliation Commission. (2016). *A knock on the door: The essential history of residential schools from the Truth and Reconciliation Commission of Canada.* University of Manitoba.

Twiss, R. (2015). *Rescuing the gospel from the cowboys: A Native American expression of the Jesus way.* IVP Books.

Hollywood or History?
Holy Angels (2017)

Inspirational stories are a part of the landscape for Hollywood, short films, and documentaries. The documentary *Holy Angels* (2017) offers the witness of Lena Wandering Spirit's experience of the Canadian residential school at Holy Angels in Fort Chipewyan, Alberta which operated from 1874–1974.

Evaluate and summarize your observations and analysis in the corresponding spaces provided. In the section located at the bottom of the page, explain whether you think the main themes from *Holy Angels* (2017) should be evaluated as an accurate portrayal, pure Hollywood creations, or a mixture of both, based on evidence from the primary and secondary sources. Use examples from your sources/documents to explain your answer.

Primary Source(s)	***Holy Angels* (2017)**	**Secondary Source**

What do you think? Hollywood or History?

In the Face of Martyrdom: Testing the Bedrock of Faith

Thomas E. Malewitz

FILM: *Silence* (2016)

Grade	Subject	Topic
9–12	Christianity; Japanese Nationalism	Declaring Faith in the Face of Martyrdom

Chapter Theme	Estimated Time Needed for Lesson
Historical Context: Missionary, Martyrdom, Courage, Jesuit	45 minutes

National Association for Media Literacy Education

Standard Number	Detailed Description of Each Standard You Are Discussing

Core Principles of Media Literacy Education in the United States	4. Media Literacy Education (MLE) develops informed, reflective, and engaged participants essential for a democratic society.
	
	Implications for Practice
	  4.1 MLE promotes student interest in news and current events as a dimension of citizenship, and can enhance student understanding of First Amendment rights and responsibilities.
	
	6. MLE affirms that people use their individual skills, beliefs, and experiences to construct their own meanings from media messages.
	
	Implications for Practice
	  6.1 MLE is not about teaching students what to think; it is about teaching them how they can arrive at informed choices that are most consistent with their own values.

State and USCCB Standard Description

State	Detailed Description of Each Standard You Are Discussing
Michigan World History and Geography	**F.6.2.2** Growth of Nationalism and Nation-States—compare and contrast the rise of nation-states in a Western and non-Western context. Examples may include but are not limited to: case studies of Germany, Italy, Japan.
New York Global History and Geography II	**10.1a** Powerful Eurasian states and empires faced and responded to challenges ca. 1750. Students will compare and contrast the Mughal Empire and the Ottoman Empire in 1750 in terms of religious and ethnic tolerance, political organization, and commercial activity. Students will examine efforts to unify, stabilize, and centralize Japan under the rule of the Tokugawa Shogunate. Students will compare and contrast the Tokugawa Shogunate in Japan with France under the rule of the Bourbon Dynasty, looking at the role of Edo and Paris/Versailles, attempts to control the daimyo and nobles, and the development of bureaucracies. **10.1b** Perceptions of outsiders and interactions with them varied across Eurasia. Students will compare and contrast the Tokugawa and Mughal responses to outsiders, with attention to the impacts of those decisions. Students will create a world map showing the extent of European maritime empires, the Russian Empire, the Ottoman Empire, Mughal Empire, China under the Qing Dynasty, Japan under the Tokugawa Shogunate, Ashanti, Benin, and Dahomey ca. 1750.
United States Conference of Catholic Bishops (USCCB) Curriculum Framework	**Doctrinal Elements of a Curriculum Framework for the Development of Catechetical Materials for Young People of High School Age (USCCB, 2008)**
USCCB.II Who is Jesus? (Christology)— V.A.3b	The testimony and witness of others who have gone before us: people whose stories appear in the Bible; Apostles, saints, and martyrs (CCC, nos. 823, 828, 857, 946, 1258, 2473).
USCCB.Option 2 History of the Catholic Church—II.8.A-D	The Age of Exploration: Church's Missionaries Confront New Cultures (Japan)

USCCB.Option 3 Social Justice—V.C	Isn't not fighting back or getting even with someone who hurts or offends you a sign of weakness? We have the example of the martyrs, which shows the strength and power that faith and God's grace give.

NCSS C3 Framework

Dimension	Detailed Description of Each NCSS Dimension You Are Incorporating (should have all four).
D1.2.9-12	Explain points of agreement and disagreement experts have about interpretations and applications of disciplinary concepts and ideas associated with a compelling question.
D2.His.5.9-12	Analyze how historical contexts shaped and continue to shape people's perspectives.
D3.3.9-12	Identify evidence that draws information directly and substantively from multiple sources to detect inconsistencies in evidence in order to revise or strengthen claims.
D4.1.9-12	Construct arguments using precise and knowledgeable claims, with evidence from multiple sources, while acknowledging counterclaims and evidentiary weaknesses.

NCSS Core Themes and Description

Theme Number	Detailed Description of Each Aligned NCSS Theme
II Time, Continuity, and Change	Studying the past makes it possible for us to understand the human story across time. Historical analysis enables us to identify continuities over time in core institutions, values, ideals, and traditions, as well as processes that lead to change within societies and institutions, and that result in innovation and the development of new ideas, values, and ways of life.
V Individuals, Groups and Institutions	Social studies programs should include experiences that provide for the study of interactions among individuals, groups, and institutions.
VI Power, Authority and Governance	Social studies programs should include experiences that provide for the study of how people create, interact with, and change structures of power, authority, and governance.

Handouts/Materials/Web Links

Handout/Materials:
- "Hollywood or History?" graphic organizer

Web Links:
A. Link to Film Clips:
   – *Silence* (Scorsese, 2016)
     51:13–1:01:24 [10 mins]
B. Primary Source(s):
   – Matthew 26:31–35; 69–75 (version)
   – *Silence: A novel* (Endo, 2016)
C. Secondary Source(s):
   – *Journey to the East: The Jesuit Mission to China, 1579–1724* (Brockey, 2007)
   – "Bishop Barron on 'Silence [Spoilers]'" (Barron, 2017)
     https://www.youtube.com/watch?v=5Th7Tiz1cEk [11:21]

Guiding Questions

What should students know or understand at the completion of the unit or lesson?

Primary Questions:
- What does it mean to stand up for what you believe in, in the midst of persecution?
- What does a lived faith look like?
- How is Peter's denial/betrayal of Jesus an archetype for the temptation of denial?
- How can we find courage in the midst of pressure to do something against what we believe?

Important Vocabulary

List all of the important indicators of achievement (important people, places, and events) and vocabulary that students will need to know at the conclusion of the lesson.

Japanese Nationalism: a government vision that desired to cleanse Japan from foreign teachings, focusing on a single culture and identity.
Jesuit: A Catholic religious community of missionaries focused on education, research, cultural dialogue, and sharing faith. Founded in 1540. Known for missionaries to India, Japan, China, North America.
Martyrdom: A witness of faith to the point of death.
Missionary: An individual who travels to another country to preach, share, and convert followers to their belief.
Tokugawa Shogunate (1603–1868): a forceful military-led governmental structure that strictly banned/removed foreign influence to promote political unity and stability.

Assessment Strategies

Describe the assessments that will be used during the unit.

Formative Assessment: Small group discussion, Line of Contention
Summative Assessment: "Hollywood or History?" graphic organizer

Teaching Strategies (Part 1 and 2)

10 min	Warm-Up/ Lecture	15 min	Read Matthew 26:31–35; 69–75 comparison/contrast small group discussion	10 min	Line of Contention
10 min	View clip from: *Silence* (Scorsese, 2016)	12 min	View clip from *Bishop Barron on "Silence"* [*Spoilers*] (Barron, 2017)	**Time Remaining/ HMWK**	"Hollywood or History?" graphic organizer

Times are highly flexible and should be adjusted according to the number of sources used, length of introduction, period/block schedule, etc.

Sparking Strategy/Warm-Up

Sparking Strategy (Lesson introduction)

Introduce the concept of authoritarian nationalism. Have students discuss some movies, documentaries or books that focus on structural policies in the plot of the story that isolate or segregate groups based on their identities/ideologies (examples such as *Star Wars* [Lucas, 1977]; *X-Men* [Singer, 2000], *Captain America: Civil War* [Russo & Russo, 2016]). What happens if people stand up to the authoritarian structure? What does it mean to become a witness for one's belief in the face of isolation or segregation? Are they seen as a hero, someone who is crazy, or should the individual give up and merely follow what they are told to do? Transition the conversation to historical events in Part 1.

Lesson Procedures

In a numerical list, provide a step by step outline of what you plan to do in the lesson. Include questions you will ask the students and materials you will use.

Please note: *This lesson only offers a brief introduction into the topic of residential/industrial schools and the Canadian Truth and Reconciliation Commission.*

Outline:

1. Start with a brief lesson on tangible examples of individuals who stood up against authoritarian laws of their time, such as Rosa Parks, 1955; "Tank Man" in Tiananmen Square, 1989. What consequences occurred historically to individuals that stood against authoritarian policies in history? Explore briefly some of the experiences of such individuals.

2. Transition the conversation to the historical context of 17th century Japan, under the Tokugawa Shogunate. Additional information on the policies of the Tokugawa Shogunate can be found at: https://www.britannica.com/event/Tokugawa-period (The Editors of Encyclopaedia Britannica, n.d.).

3. Explain to students that there have been several films depicting the martyrdom of foreign missionaries during the Tokugawa Shogunate. However, the films may or may not attempt to offer an accurate account of the events of martyrdom and Tokugawa Shogunate policies. Introduce the "Hollywood or History?" graphic organizer hand-

out and work with students to detail how they can use the outline to record information during the film clip and document analysis that they will take part in.
4. Display the clip of the *Silence* (Scorsese, 2016; section of the film included above) [10 mins]. If teachers want to show the entire film, we recommend finding time to show the film in full but breaking it up into sections and have students use multiple sources to analyze each segment of the film.
5. Have students compare and contrast the film clip with the position of Peter as described in Matthew 26:31–35; 69–75. For more advanced students, teachers may elect to use selected passages from Endo's novel or Brockey's text.
6. Have students discuss the similarities and differences of Peter and the Japanese martyrs in small groups, having them take bullet point notes in a T-chart.
7. After 10 minutes, recollect the students' attention and show the film critique by Robert Barron (2017): *Bishop Barron on "Silence"* [*Spoilers*] [12 mins].
8. Use a "line of contention," or similar whole group debriefing approach, to allow students to share their thoughts. Draw a line on the board to demonstrate the continuum of thoughts. On one side of the line, write 100% history. Students who stand there are making the claim that the movie clip is 100% accurate and factual. On the other side of the line, write 100% Hollywood. If students stand next to this part of the line they are making the claim that there is nothing factual about the scene they watched. Allow studies to stand at any point of the line they wish (i.e., 25% history, 75% Hollywood, etc.). Most important are student explanations and efforts should be made to reference the document collections.

Differentiation

Think about your students' skill levels, intelligences, and learning styles. How are you going to make this lesson meet the needs of all of your students?

Scaffolds: Work with students individually if needed to answer questions and further explain any material. Make sure that the student table groups have mixed students so that higher achieving students are working with/helping their classmates.

ESL Interventions: Provide vocabulary terms pertaining to the era of prohibition with useful synonyms and definitions/description in order to give students background knowledge and vocabulary help as they move through the lesson itself. Consider selecting among the sources with images, or finding additional documents, from the source collections provided.

Extensions: Have students write a letter or make a video telling a younger student about the complexities, the potential biases and inaccuracies found in Hollywood films and what they should do to be better informed about historical figures and events that are portrayed in movies.

Summarizing Strategies/Synthesizing Activity

What strategies are you going to use to allow students to summarize what they learned in the lesson?

- Hollywood or History?
- student-generated position statements with reference to documents/evidence

- line of contention
- Small group discussion

References

Are there any additional resources that might be relevant to your lesson? Are there sources that you need to reference? Please add any citations using APA.

Barron, R. (2017, January 17). *Bishop Barron on "Silence"* [*spoilers*] [YouTube video]. https://www.youtube.com/watch?v=5Th7Tiz1cEk

Brockey, L. M. (2007). *Journey to the East: The Jesuit mission to China, 1579–1724.* Belknap.

Endo, S. (2016). *Silence: A novel.* Picador.

Lucas, G. (Director). (1977). *Star Wars* [Film]. Lucasfilm.

Russo, A., & Russo, J. (Directors). (2016). *Captain America: Civil war* [Film]. Marvel Studios.

Scorsese, M. (2016). *Silence* [Film]. Paramount Pictures.

Singer, B. (2000). *X-Men* [Film]. Marvel Enterprises, The Donners' Company, Bad Hat Harry Productions.

The Editors of Encyclopaedia Britannica. (n.d.). *Tokugawa period: Japanese history.* https://www.britannica.com/event/Tokugawa-period

Additional Resource

Malewitz, T. (2020). *Authenticity, passion, and advocacy: Approaching adolescent spirituality from the life and wisdom of Thomas Merton* (pp. 62–72). Wipf & Stock.

Marcus, A. S., Metzger, S. A., Paxton, R. J., & Stoddard, J. D. (2018). *Teaching history with film: Strategies for secondary social studies.* Routledge.

Matz, K., & Pingatore, L. (2005) Reel to real: Teaching the twentieth century with classic Hollywood films. *Social Education, 69*(4), 189–192.

Mayward, J. (2021). The cinematic summoned self: The call of Christ in Martin Scorsese's *Silence*. *Pro Ecclesia: A Journal of Catholic and Evangelical Theology, 30*(4). https://doi.org/10.1177/10638512211025007

McEntire, J. L. (2020). Confessions of 'the Weak': The ecclesiastical hindrance of determinism in silence. *Exchange, 49*(2), 164–178. https://doi.org/10.1163/1572543X-12341560

Montevecchio, C. A. (2017). Silence. *Journal of Religion & Film, 21*(1). https://digitalcommons.unomaha.edu/jrf/vol21/iss1/26

Ng, T. (2019). Of faith and faithlessness: Adaptive fidelity in Shusaku Endo's and Martin Scorsese's *Silence*. *Literature and Theology, 33*(4), 434–450. https://doi.org/10.1093/litthe/frz024

Russell, W. B. (2012). The reel history of the world: Teaching world history with major motion pictures. *Social Education, 76*(1), 22–28. https://eric.ed.gov/?id=EJ1002090

Russell, W. B. & Waters, S. (2017). *Cinematic social studies: A resource for teaching and learning social studies through film.* Information Age Publishing.

United States Conference of Catholic Bishops. (2000). *Catechism of the Catholic Church* (2nd ed.) Libreria Editrice Vaticana.

Hollywood or History?
Silence (2016)

Silence (2016) is a film that depicts a challenge of faith and the choice of martyrdom. Read the account of Peter in Matthew 26:31–35; 69–75 and compare which account is the most logical to you. Offer a concrete example to support your decision.

How do you think the Hollywood film *Silence* (2016) and Bishop Barron's critique (2017) on *Silence* illustrate the difference between fact and fiction? Explain your decision in the Hollywood or History? box at the bottom of the page.

Silence (2016)	Peter (Matthew 26:31–35; 69–75)	"Bishop Barron on *Silence*" (2017)
What do you think? Hollywood or History?		

CHAPTER 3

Religious Figures

Havelock (1995) argues,

>There is a beginning to every "change," and it usually starts when something is wrong and the system is not functioning properly. Initially there is care and concern. It is this care and concern that brings about the desire for change." (p. 58)

In addition, Havelock (1995) claims that a "change agent" is someone who deliberately tries to bring about change or innovation in a social organization (p. 8). The "guide" in the change agents is characterized by the following elements: care, relate, examine, acquire, try, extend, and renew (p. 2). Although the concept of a change agent is typically applied to a secular industry, there is merit in relating the main ideas of a change agent to an organized religion or primary religious figures in the 20th century whose goals were to work towards implementing systemic change. The systemic change in which religious figures in this chapter are passionate about range from poverty and oppression to racism and inequality. Through this lens we can see the influence of a religious figure and/or a movement of social reform in light of the numerous social injustices that have existed throughout the history of the world.

What is social justice? Oxford Reference (n.d.) describes social justice as "the objective of creating a fair and equal society in which each individual matters, their rights are recognized and protected, and decisions are made in ways that are fair and honest" (para. 1). This includes maintaining empathy towards all people regardless of nationality, race, gender, and so on. "Awareness that questions of justice involve issues of how decisions are made, as well as what those decisions are, underlies several important theoretical statements about social justice" (Tyler & Smith, 2015, p. 10). Understanding injustices within a neighborhood, community, city, state, or nation requires vigilance, introspection and active participation. The balance of Ignatian spirituality rests on contemplation and action. Professor at Boston College, Marina Berzins McCoy (n.d.), describes this balance as learning how to be, learning how to see, and learning how to love. Her reflection centers on being cognizant of the world and your place in it, seeing the injustices in the world and through love, work towards ending injustice. "Contemplation moves into action when we *learn how to love*. We are asked to love those who are poor, hungry, sick, in prison, lonely, or marginalized in any way" (McCoy, n.d., para. 4, emphasis in original). The compassion of Dorothy Day and the Catholic Worker Houses of Hospitality in the Journey Film documentary, *Revolution of the Heart: The Dorothy Day Story* (Doblmeier, 2020), epitomizes the idea of contemplation and action. The recognition of the economic conditions of the Great Depression inspired Dorothy Day to work towards meeting the basic needs of the impoverished. Likewise, the recognition of racial injustices in the 1960s prompted the perseverance of Dr. Martin Luther King Jr. and the African-American community in the film *Selma* (DuVernay, 2014) to stand united for their dignity as equal members of the human race.

In the films, *Malcolm X* (Lee, 1992) and *Gandhi* (Attenborough, 1982), the exploration of two religious figures of Islam and Hinduism, respectively, are central in seeking that "their rights are recognized and protected and decisions are made that are fair and honest" (Oxford Reference, n.d., para. 1). Within different countries, different issues, and different time periods, these two men sought an end to oppression of their people through passionate pleas and nonviolent resistance. The devotion of these religious figures as well as the Trappist monks from the film *Of Gods and Men* (Beauvois, 2010) is a reminder of the courage needed to activate change in the lives of our neighbor.

REFERENCES

Attenborough, R. (Director). (1982). *Gandhi* [Film]. Goldcrest Films; International Film Investors; National Film Development Corporation of India; Indo-British Films.
Beauvois, X. (Director). (2010). *Of gods and men* [Film]. Why Not Productions, Armada Films.
Doblmeier, M. (Director). (2020). *Revolution of the heart: The Dorothy Day story* [Film]. Journey Films.
DuVernay, A. (Director). (2014). *Selma* [Film]. Paramount Pictures. Pathé; Harpo Films; Plan B Entertainment; Cloud Eight Films; Ingenious Media; Redgill Selma Productions.
Havelock, R. G. (with Zlotolow, S.). (1995). *The change agents guide* (2nd ed.). Educational Technology Publications.
Lee, S. (Director). (1992). *Malcolm X* [Film]. Warner Bros.
McCoy, M. B. (n.d.). *Contemplation in action*. Ignatian Spirituality. https://www.ignatianspirituality.com/contemplation-in-action/
Oxford Reference. (n.d.). *Social Justice*. https://www.oxfordreference.com/view/10.1093/oi/authority.20110803100515279
Tyler, T. R., & Smith, H. J. (1995). *Social justice and social movements* [Working paper]. University of California Berkeley. https://escholarship.org/content/qt54d3j035/qt54d3j035.pdf

Guidance on Non-Violence: *Gandhi*, Living for Change Through Faith

Thomas E. Malewitz

FILM: *Gandhi* (1982)

Grade	Subject	Topic
9–12	Hinduism: Gandhi	Gandhi and nonviolence as a viable option

Chapter Theme	Estimated Time Needed for Lesson
Religious Figures: Gandhi, Nonviolence, Systemic Change	45 minutes

National Association for Media Literacy Education

Standard Number	Detailed Description of Each Standard You Are Discussing

Core Principles of Media Literacy Education in the United States	3. Media Literacy Education (MLE) builds and reinforces skills for learners of all ages. Like print literacy, those skills necessitate integrated, interactive, and repeated practice.
	
	Implications for Practice
	    3.3 MLE engages students with varied learning styles.
	    3.4 MLE is most effective when used with co-learning pedagogies, in which teachers learn from students and students learn from teachers and from classmates.
	
	4. MLE develops informed, reflective, and engaged participants essential for a democratic society.
	
	Implications for Practice
	    4.1 MLE promotes student interest in news and current events as a dimension of citizenship, and can enhance student understanding of First Amendment rights and responsibilities.
	    4.4 MLE invites and respects diverse points of view.
	    4.5 MLE explores representations, misrepresentations, and lack of representation of cultures and countries in the global community.

State and USCCB Standard Description

State	Detailed Description of Each Standard You Are Discussing
Michigan High School World History and Geography	**7.2.5** Revolution, decolonization, and democratization—evaluate the causes and consequences of revolutionary and independence movements in different world regions. *Examples may include but are not limited to:* case studies of the Russian Revolution, Mexican Revolution, and/or Iranian Revolution; legacy of imperialism in Africa, Southeast Asia, and Latin America; importance of the massive resistance and nonviolent philosophy of Mahatma Gandhi; independence movements and formation of new nations in the Indian subcontinent.
New York High School Global History and Geography II	**10.7a** Independence movements in India and Indochina developed in response to European control. • Students will explore Gandhi's nonviolent nationalist movement and nationalist efforts led by the Muslim League aimed at the masses that resulted in a British-partitioned subcontinent.
United States Conference of Catholic Bishops (USCCB) Curriculum Framework	**Doctrinal Elements of a Curriculum Framework for the Development of Catechetical Materials for Young People of High School Age** (USCCB, 2008)
USCCB.Option 5 Ecumenical and Interreligious Dialogue—IV.B.1	Find dialogue between Christian and non-Christian religious beliefs held in common, including major world religions such as Hinduism and Buddhism, and others such as Sikhs, Mormons, and Bahai. Such as sharing a common origin and end, compassionate action, moral restraint, spiritual discipline, and respect for human dignity.

NCSS C3 Framework

Dimension	Detailed Description of Each NCSS Dimension You Are Incorporating (should have all four).
D1.2.9-12	Explain points of agreement and disagreement experts have about interpretations and applications of disciplinary concepts and ideas associated with a compelling question.
D2.His.5.9-12.	Analyze how historical contexts shaped and continue to shape people's perspectives.

D3.3.9-12	Identify evidence that draws information directly and substantively from multiple sources to detect inconsistencies in evidence in order to revise or strengthen claims.
D4.1.9-12	Construct arguments using precise and knowledgeable claims, with evidence from multiple sources, while acknowledging counterclaims and evidentiary weaknesses.

NCSS Core Themes and Description

Theme Number	Detailed Description of Each Aligned NCSS Theme
III People, Places, Environments	The study of people, places, and environments enables us to understand the relationship between human populations and the physical world. Students learn where people and places are located and why they are there. They examine the influence of physical systems, such as climate, weather and seasons, and natural resources, such as land and water, on human populations. They study the causes, patterns and effects of human settlement and migration, learn of the roles of different kinds of population centers in a society, and investigate the impact of human activities on the environment. This enables them to acquire a useful basis of knowledge for informed decision-making on issues arising from human-environmental relationships.
V Individuals, Groups and Institutions	Social studies programs should include experiences that provide for the study of interactions among individuals, groups, and institutions.
VI Power, Authority and Governance	Social studies programs should include experiences that provide for the study of how people create, interact with, and change structures of power, authority, and governance.

Handouts/Materials/Web Links

Handout/Materials:
- "Hollywood or History?" graphic organizer
- "Hollywood or History?" group project directions and rubric

Web Links:
- A. Link to Film Clip(s):
  - "Gandhi Clip on the Salt March" (Rudy, 2012)
    https://www.youtube.com/watch?v=WW3uk95VGes [5 mins]
  - "The Father of the Nation: *Gandhi* (7/8) CLIP" (Movieclips, 2012)
    https://www.youtube.com/watch?v=pAs8uvKNkcU [3 mins]

B. Primary Source(s):
- "Mahatma Gandhi Arrives in the U.K. (1931)" (British Pathé, 2014) https://www.youtube.com/watch?v=P6njRwz_dMw [3 mins]
- "Mahatma Gandhi First Television Interview (30 April 1931)" (DeputyDoug829, 2011) https://www.youtube.com/watch?v=Zt_MmVBUv84 [4 mins]

C. Secondary Source(s):
- "Martin Luther King on Gandhi" (India Political Center, 2016) https://www.youtube.com/watch?v=B3Ife3CTBnQ [6 mins]
- "Sir Richard Attenborough on Mahatma Gandhi | EMMA Awards" (EmmaAwards, 2010) https://www.youtube.com/watch?v=FuYbLkFT2mM [2 mins]

Guiding Questions

What should students know or understand at the completion of the unit or lesson?

Primary Questions:
- What does nonviolent resistance look like?
- What are strengths of nonviolent resistance to discrimination?
- How did Gandhi's actions influence other nonviolent civil rights leaders?

Additional Questions:
- What is a primary/secondary source?
- What are ways to gain a better understanding of an historical event?
- Which type of source is the most accurate primary/secondary? Why?

Important Vocabulary

List all of the important indicators of achievement (important people, places, and events) and vocabulary that students will need to know at the conclusion of the lesson.

Mahātmā: an honorific title given to Gandhi since 1914, meaning "great-souled."
Mohandas Karamchand Gandhi (1869–1948): Indian lawyer, civil rights advocate, nonviolent resistance leader that led India's independence from British colonial rule.
Nonviolent resistance: the nonviolent practice or opposition to a governmental structure through civil disobedience, protest, or noncooperation.

Assessment Strategies

Describe the assessments that will be used during the unit.

Formative Assessment: Round table discussion, "Hollywood or History?" graphic organizer
Summative Assessment: Group research project

Teaching Strategies (Part 1 and 2)

10 min	Roundtable group discussion/ View clip "Mahatma Gandhi Arrives in the U.K." (British Pathé, 2014)	15 min	Primary Sources and Secondary Source analysis	10 min	Group project
8 min	View clips from: *Gandhi* (Attenborough, 1982)	10 min	Research/graphic organizer	**Time Remaining/ HMWK**	

Times are highly flexible and should be adjusted according to the number of sources used, length of introduction, period/ block schedule, etc.

Sparking Strategy/Warm-Up

Sparking Strategy (Lesson introduction)

Define nonviolent resistance for students. Have students discuss some movies, video games, documentaries, or books that focus on nonviolence resistance. Offer historical examples of nonviolent resistance including pictures or stories to assist students to understand the concept.

Lesson Procedures

In a numerical list, provide a step by step outline of what you plan to do in the lesson. Include questions you will ask the students and materials you will use.

Outline

1. Start with a roundtable group discussion: Spark ideas about how social elements like movies, video games, documentaries, or books that focus on history shape our understanding of people and events.
2. Show clip "Mahatma Gandhi Arrives in the U.K. (1931)" (British Pathé, 2014) [3 min]. Explain how short newsreels were used in the film to convey news at that time. Ask the students how the news reel described Gandhi. What words/phrases were used? List these on the board. Summarize and reflect upon the descriptions of Gandhi listed on the board for the students.
3. Show the film clips from *Gandhi* (Attenborough, 1982) [8 mins total]. Compare and contrast the presentation on Gandhi in the film versus the newsreel clip with the terms on the board. Do they match? What are the differences? Ask the students why there is a difference.
4. Explain to the students that Gandhi's belief was revered and became an example for future nonviolent leaders, such as Martin Luther King Jr. Show clip "Martin Luther King on Gandhi" (India Political Center, 2016) [6 mins]. Ask the students, "How did MLK describe Gandhi and his teachings?"

5. Analyze how King and Attenborough ("Sir Richard Attenborough on Mahatma Gandhi" (EmmaAwards, 2010) [2 mins]) explain the importance and inspiration of Gandhi's nonviolent advocacy. What similarities exist between the video clips?
6. Have the students choose another nonviolent resistor to research (a list could include individuals such as: Martin Luther King Jr., Dorothy Day, Thomas Merton, Nelson Mandela, Desmond Tutu, Cesar Chavez, Rosa Parks, 1913 Suffrage Parade, etc.)
7. Use the "Hollywood or History?" graphic organizer to compare and contrast the life events and actions of Gandhi to the chosen nonviolent resistor.
8. After the graphic organizer activity, place students in groups to create a project on the life of Gandhi and how his life and advocacy influenced future nonviolent resistors.
9. Have the student-groups present their findings for the class.

Differentiation

Think about your students' skill levels, intelligences, and learning styles. How are you going to make this lesson meet the needs of all of your students?

Scaffolds: Work with students individually if needed to answer questions and further explain any material. Make sure that the student table groups have mixed students so that higher achieving students are working with/helping their classmates.

ESL Interventions: Find reading level appropriate research readings on web sources such as Newsela.

Summarizing Strategies/Synthesizing Activity

What strategies are you going to use to allow students to summarize what they learned in the lesson?

- Hollywood or History? graphic organizer
- Student-generated position statements with reference to documents/evidence
- Roundtable discussion
- Group research project and class presentation

References

Are there any additional resources that might be relevant to your lesson? Are there sources that you need to reference? Please add any citations using APA.

Attenborough, R. (Director). (1982). *Gandhi* [Film]. Goldcrest Films; International Film Investors; National Film Development Corporation of India; Indo-British Films.

British Pathé. (2014, April 13). *Mahatma Gandhi arrives in the U.K. (1931)* [YouTube video]. https://www.youtube.com/watch?v=P6njRwz_dMw

DeputyDoug829. (2011, October 29). *Mahatma Gandhi first television interview* [YouTube video]. https://www.youtube.com/watch?v=Zt_MmVBUv84

EmmaAwards. (2010, April 16). *Sir Richard Attenborough on Mahatma Gandhi | EMMA awards* [YouTube video]. https://www.youtube.com/watch?v=FuYbLkFT2mM

Kay, K., & Greenhill, V. (2012). *Leader's guide to 21st century education: 7 steps for schools and districts.* Pearson.

India Political Center. (2016, November 4). *Martin Luther King on Gandhi* [YouTube video]. https://www.youtube.com/watch?v=B3Ife3CTBnQ

Movieclips. (2012, October 7). *Gandhi (7/8) movie CLIP—The father of the nation (1982)* [YouTube video]. https://www.youtube.com/watch?v=pAs8uvKNkcU

Rudy, M. (2012, February 22). *Gandhi clip on the salt march* [YouTube video]. https://www.youtube.com/watch?v=WW3uk95VGcs

Additional Resources

Dalton, D. (2021). *Mahatma Gandhi: Nonviolent power in action*. Columbia University.

Marcus, A., & Stoddard, J. (2007). Tinsel Town as teacher: Hollywood film in the high school classroom. *The History Teacher, 40*(3), 303–330.

O'Brien, A. S., & O'Brien, P. E. (2018). *After Gandhi: One hundred years of nonviolent resistance*. Charlesbridge.

Roberts, S. L. (2014). Effectively using social studies textbooks in historical inquiry. *Social Studies Research and Practice, 9*(1), 119–128. https://doi.org/10.1108/SSRP-01-2014-B0006

Russell, W. B. (2007). *Using film in social studies*. University Press of America.

Russell, W. B. (2012). The reel history of the world: Teaching world history with major motion pictures. *Social Education, 76*(1), 22–28. https://www.socialstudies.org/system/files/publications/articles/se_760122.pdf

Russell, W. B., & Waters, S. (2017). *Cinematic social studies: A resource for teaching and learning social studies through film*. Information Age Publishing.

Hollywood or History?

Gandhi (1982)

Gandhi exemplified nonviolent resistance advocacy to assist his country's freedom from the British colonial rule. In the following chart identify TWO other famous nonviolent resistors (individuals such as: Martin Luther King Jr., Dorothy Day, Thomas Merton, Nelson Mandela, Desmond Tutu, Cesar Chavez, Rosa Parks, 1913 Suffrage Parade, etc.). Compare and contrast their life and advocacy experience to Gandhi's.

Ganghi	Name:	Name:
Birth	Birth	Birth
Death	Death	Death
Country	Country	Country
Challenge	Challenge	Challenge
Nonviolent examples:	Nonviolent examples:	Nonviolent examples:
1	1	1
2	2	2
3	3	3
4	4	4
5	5	5
Research Resources Used		
1		
2		
3		
4		
5		
6		

Hollywood or History?
Gandhi (1982) Group Project

Name(s): _____
　　　　　_____
　　　　　_____
　　　　　_____

Due: 80 points (slides/information)

Your quest is:

Create a **10 slide Powerpoint/Keynote/Google Slides** project to explore the life, beliefs, and nonviolent resistance and inspiration of Gandhi.

Use your notes, powerpoints and/or book, and Internet to research and offer information about Gandhi. Include information about his birth, death, struggles, direct quotations, direct influences, and resources

Expectations:

Context: List, define, and explain Gandhi's life and beliefs surrounding non-violent resistance to the British colonial rule of India.

References: 5 credible references in MLA style

Evidence: (at least) 5 direct quotations about Gandhi's life and beliefs

Creativity: (at least) 6 to 8 pictures in context and description
(*Hint:* Be sure to include a title and works cited slide with Scripture citations and all references.)

Project Rubric

Grade: _____ / 80   Name(s)

1. Context				
Biographical information: clear information; direct connect to previous course material	A—20 points	B—15 points	C—10 points	D—5 points

2. Scriptural connections				
Synthesize and make connections between Gandhi and those he influenced.	A—20 points	B—15 points	C—10 points	D—5 points

3. Evidence				
Clear supporting evidence about Gandhi's life and nonviolent advocacy	A—20 points	B—15 points	C—10 points	D—5 points

4. Organization for presentation				
Mechanics—spelling, proper designations, clear	A—10 points	B—7 points	C—5 points	D—2 points

5. References				
Proper references, not just copy/pasting ULRs	A—5 points	B—4 points	C—3 points	D—2 points

Adapted from essay rubric template resources Kay, K. and Greenhill, V. Pearson Education, Inc. 2012

The Legacy of Authentic Discipleship

Adam P. Zoeller

FILM: *Revolution of the Heart: The Dorothy Day Story* (2020)

Grade	Subject	Topic
11–12	Christianity	Social Justice, Faith in Action

Chapter Theme	Estimated Time Needed for Lesson
Religious Figures: Community, Human Dignity, Human Rights, Social Justice	Day 1: Video clips and vocabulary worksheet Day 2: Collaboration: Project based learning

National Association for Media Literacy Education

Standard Number	Detailed Description of Each Standard You Are Discussing
Core Principles of Media Literacy Education in the United States	3. Media Literacy Education (MLE) builds and reinforces skills for learners of all ages. Like print literacy, those skills necessitate integrated, interactive, and repeated practice. *Implications for Practice* 3.3 MLE engages students with varied learning styles. 3.4 MLE is most effective when used with co-learning pedagogies, in which teachers learn from students and students learn from teachers and from classmates.

State and USCCB Standard Description

State	Detailed Description of Each Standard You Are Discussing
California State Board of Education Grade 12 History-Social Science Content Standards.	12.3 Students evaluate and take and defend positions on what the fundamental values and principles of civil society are (i.e., the autonomous sphere of voluntary personal, social, and economic relations that are not part of government), their interdependence, and the meaning and importance of those values and principles for a free society.

Florida Psychology strand SS.912.P	**SS.912.P.9.7** Discuss how an individual influences group behavior.
North Carolina Standards for World History 9–12 Inquiry	Apply the inquiry models to analyze and evaluate social studies topics and issues in order to communicate conclusions and take informed actions. I.1.3 Summarize the central ideas and meaning of primary and secondary sources through the use of literacy strategies. I.1.4. Analyze causes, effects, and correlations.
USCCB Curriculum Framework	

Elective Option C:
Living as a Disciple
of Jesus Christ in
Society
	II. Social Teaching of the Church
	   D. Principles of Catholic social teaching from the Universal Magisterium
	      3. The perfection of the person by the common good: man is perfected not only by private goods such as food and shelter but by "common goods" such as peace and truth that come about through his life with others in community (CCC, nos. 1905–1912, 1925–1927).
	         a. Respect for and promotion of the fundamental rights of the person.
	         b. Prosperity, or the development of the spiritual and temporal goods of society.

	III. Major Themes of Catholic Social Teaching
	   D. Preferential option for the poor
	      1. Moral principle: universal destination of the goods of the earth (CCC, nos. 2402–2406).
	      2. Goods of the earth for every human being.
	      3. Why all need these goods (CCC, no. 2402).
	      4. See Christ in homeless, outcast, unpopular.
	      5. Appropriate use of wealth and other resources.
	         a. Be a voice for the voiceless.
	         b. Assess social acts and their impacts on the poor.
	      6. Concern for the spiritually poor.
	   E. Dignity of work and the rights of workers.
	      1. God's creation plan includes work.
	      2. Right to work in just conditions.
	   F. Solidarity: individuals should work for the common good (CCC, nos. 2437–2442).

NCSS C3 Framework

Dimension	Detailed Description of Each NCSS Dimension You Are Incorporating (should have all four).
D1.2.9-12	Explain points of agreement and disagreement experts have about interpretations and applications of disciplinary concepts and ideas associated with a compelling question.
D2.His.5.9-12.	Analyze how historical contexts shaped and continue to shape people's perspectives.
D3.3.9-12	Identify evidence that draws information directly and substantively from multiple sources to detect inconsistencies in evidence in order to revise or strengthen claims.
D4.1.9-12	Construct arguments using precise and knowledgeable claims, with evidence from multiple sources, while acknowledging counterclaims and evidentiary weaknesses.

NCSS Core Themes and Description

Theme Number	Detailed Description of Each Aligned NCSS Theme
I Culture	The study of culture examines the socially transmitted beliefs, values, institutions, behaviors, traditions, and way of life of a group of people; it also encompasses other cultural attributes and products, such as language, literature, music, arts and artifacts, and foods. Students come to understand that human cultures exhibit both similarities and differences, and they learn to see themselves both as individuals and as members of a particular culture that shares similarities with other cultural groups, but is also distinctive. In a multicultural, democratic society and globally connected world, students need to understand the multiple perspectives that derive from different cultural vantage points.
IV Individual Development and Identity	The study of individual development and identity will help students to describe factors important to the development of personal identity. They will explore the influence of peoples, places, and environments on personal development. Students will hone personal skills such as demonstrating self-direction when working towards and accomplishing personal goals, and making an effort to understand others and their beliefs, feelings, and convictions.

Handouts/Materials/Web Links

Handout/Materials:

- "Hollywood or History?" graphic organizer

Web Links:

A. Link to Film Clip(s):
   - *Revolution of the Heart: The Dorothy Day Story: A Film by Martin Doblmeier* (Journey Films, n.d.)
   https://www.journeyfilms.com/store/p/milk-dip-cup-8ry6x

B. Primary Source(s):
   - *The Long Loneliness* (Day, 1952)
   - "Rerum Novarum" (Encyclical of Pope Leo XIII on Capital and Labor, 1891)
   https://www.vatican.va/content/leo-xiii/en/encyclicals/documents/hf_l-xiii_enc_15051891_rerum-novarum.html
   - Matthew 25:31–46 (New American Bible, 1987).
   - "Universal Declaration of Human Rights" [web booklet] (United Nations, 2015).
   https://www.un.org/en/udhrbook/pdf/udhr_booklet_en_web.pdf

Guiding Questions

What should students know or understand at the completion of the unit or lesson?

Primary Questions:

- Describe Dorothy Day's impact on the 20th century American Catholic church.
- Explain how the Catholic Worker Movement reinforces the primary themes of *Rerum Novarum* (Encyclical of Pope Leo XIII on Capital and Labor, 1891).
- Match articles in the *Universal Declaration of Human Rights* (United Nations, 2015) to the mission of Dorothy Day and Peter Maurin.

Important Vocabulary

List all of the important indicators of achievement (important people, places, and events) and vocabulary that students will need to know at the conclusion of the lesson.

Anarchist: a person who rebels against any authority, established order, or ruling power.
Catholic Worker Houses of Hospitality: communities led by Dorothy Day and Peter Maurin to live and serve the marginalized in solidarity.
Catholic Worker Newspaper: social justice focused New York newspaper debuting May 1, 1933 which highlighted the dignity of humans and the rights of workers.
Empathy: the capacity for seeing things from another person's perspective.
Pacifism: opposition to war or violence as a means of settling disputes.
Peter Maurin (1877–1949): contemporary and mentor of Dorothy Day who helped her understand Catholic Social Teaching.
Pope Leo XIII (1810–1903): Holy Father of the Catholic church who authored *Rerum Novarum*.
Saint: title bestowed on Catholic credited with living a virtuous life.
Social Justice: the Church's commitment, and mandate to its members, to engage in conscious efforts to fight against social sin.

Social Teachings: Catholic justice teachings primarily focused on the dignity of the human person, but specifically evident in seven themes ranging from the rights of workers to caring for the poor as the most vulnerable members of society.

***Rerum Novarum*:** A response to the industrial revolution; Papal encyclical in 1891 that focuses on the dignity of work and the rights of workers.

Assessment Strategies

Describe the assessments that will be used during the unit.

Formative Assessment: completing a vocabulary worksheet including essential terms such as those listed in the "Important Vocabulary" section of the lesson plan. This to be completed while watching the video clips.

Summative Assessment: Students are invited to choose which project-based assignment to complete for their summative assessment.

A. Explore the legacy of Dorothy Day in light of Catholic social justice themes including but not limited to: Rights of Workers, Just-War theory, UN Declaration of Human Rights, and so on.
B. Create a skit arguing for and against World War II with the main characters being Dorothy Day, FDR, and Winston Churchill.
C. Research presentation on the four most important figures in U.S. history according to Pope Francis: Thomas Merton, Dorothy Day, Martin Luther King Jr., and Abraham Lincoln.
D. Compare and contrast the moral figures of Eleanor Roosevelt and Dorothy Day (see English, 2020; https://www.imdb.com/title/tt13345084/?ref_=ttep_ep4).
E. Create 3–5 prayers that focus on community and communal identity in light of Dorothy Day legacy with the Catholic Worker Movement and isolation associated with the pandemic and social distancing.
F. Create a WANTED poster inviting more people to become an advocate for the rights of workers and the dignity of work in light of Rerum Novarum.
G. Create an advertisement illustrating how Dorothy Day's legacy encompasses the Sermon on the Mount (Matthew 5:1–12, NAB).

Teaching Strategies (Day 1)

10 min	Sparking Strategy	10 min	Watch selected scenes from the documentary on Dorothy Day and her mission (Doblmeier, 2020)	5 min	Explore the idea of personalism in light of Dorothy Day's actions.
10 min	Introduce the person Dorothy Day, the time period and economic conditions of her time, and other pertinent vocabulary.	10 min		**Time Remaining/ HMWK**	

Times are highly flexible and should be adjusted according to the number of sources used, length of introduction, period/ block schedule, etc.

Teaching Strategies (Day 2)

10 min	Review legacy of Dorothy Day.	10 min	Provide class time to begin and/or complete assessment options on Dorothy Day.	5 min	Questions and answers
10 min	Introduce assessment options for completion.	10 min		Time Remaining/HMWK	Complete assessment option for homework.

Times are highly flexible and should be adjusted according to the number of sources used, length of introduction, period/block schedule, etc.

Sparking Strategy/Warm-Up

Sparking Strategy (Lesson introduction)

Allow students to read the Gospel of Matthew (25:31–46, NAB). Invite students to the board to list examples of marginalized groups in the story of the Judgment of Nations. Based upon the results listed, solicit volunteers to answer the question, "Who is my neighbor?"

Lesson Procedures

In a numerical list, provide a step by step outline of what you plan to do in the lesson. Include questions you will ask the students and materials you will use.

Outline

Day 1

1. Discussing the call to the marginalized from the Judgment of Nations, read the parable of the Good Samaritan (Luke 10:25–37, NAB) to reinforce the theme of "Who is my neighbor?" Introduce how the generalizations and stereotypes within a culture limits people from living Gospel values.
2. Introduce the person and legacy of Dorothy Day.
3. Distribute a handout on essential vocabulary that include the following terms and people without the description: social justice, social teachings, empathy, anarchist, saint, *Catholic Worker* newspaper, Catholic Worker Houses of Hospitality, Peter Maurin, pacifism, *Rerum Novarum*, and Pope Leo XIII.
4. Invite students to read the list aloud. Inform students that during the video, the task for students is to complete the vocabulary handout.
5. Watch the following scenes from *Revolution of the Heart: The Dorothy Day Story* (Doblmeier, 2020). Select the following scenes to view: *Open, Catholic Worker, Peter Maurin*, and *Pacifism*.
6. At the conclusion of the film clips, invite students to share answers to the vocabulary worksheet.
7. Teachers should define the term "personalism" in light of Gospel values. Invite students to complete a journal reflection question on how he/she can work for the marginalized in the community.

Day 2

1. Review the material from Day 1 by writing the following two questions on the board and solicit volunteers to answer aloud: "What can the school community do 'to be a voice for the voiceless' and specifically assist the poor and marginalized in the community?" and "Describe how an individual such as Dorothy Day influences group behavior."
2. Distribute the choices for students to assess knowledge of Dorothy Day in relation to social justice. Allow students to choose their own group of three. Provide time in class to work on projects.

Differentiation

Think about your students' skill levels, intelligences, and learning styles. How are you going to make this lesson meet the needs of all of your students?

Visual learners will benefit from viewing a documentary in class. The multiple commentaries on Dorothy Day will reinforce the preferential learning of auditory learners by hearing various voices and opinions.

Student choice in assessments to evaluate comprehension of the material. These student centered assessments allow the student to reach higher level critical thinking skills such as analysis and evaluation by promoting student choice that challenge and/or meet their cognitive abilities.

Introverted Learners will benefit from reflection through journaling about the concept of personalism in light of how he/she can work for the marginalized of the community.

Extroverted Learners will benefit from opportunities in class to dialogue in question and answer sessions.

Summarizing Strategies/Synthesizing Activity

What strategies are you going to use to allow students to summarize what they learned in the lesson?

After students complete vocabulary quiz on essential terms and the project-based assignment, students will be assigned to complete the following questions:

1. What can the school community do "to be a voice for the voiceless" and specifically assist the poor and marginalized in the community?
2. Describe how an individual such as Dorothy Day influences group behavior.

References

Are there any additional resources that might be relevant to your lesson? Are there sources that you need to reference? Please add any citations using APA.

Day, D. (1952). *The long loneliness.* HarperOne.
Doblmeier, M. (Director). (2020) *Revolution of the heart: The Dorothy Day story* [Film]. Journey Films.
Encyclical of Pope Leo XIII on Capital and Labor. (1891, May 15). *Rerum novarum.* Vatican. https://www.vatican.va/content/leo-xiii/en/encyclicals/documents/hf_l-xiii_enc_15051891_rerum-novarum.html
English, K. (2020, October 25). Eleanor Roosevelt (Season 1, Episode 4) [TV series episode]. In J. Gaspin, B. Kaplan, A. Cooley, P. Hatoupis, A. Feltes, V. Davis, J. Tennon, Andrew Wang, C.

Schulman, & S. Bier (Executive Producers), *First ladies*. Welle Entertainment; Pathless Woods Productions; Lionsgate Television. https://www.imdb.com/title/tt13345084/?ref_=ttep_ep4

Francis. (2015, September 24). Transcript: Pope Francis speech to Congress. *Washington Post.* https://www.washingtonpost.com/local/social-issues/transcript-pope-franciss-speech-to-congress/2015/09/24/6d7d7ac8-62bf-11e5-8e9e-dce8a2a2a679_story.html

Journey Films. (n.d.). Revolution of the heart: The Dorothy Day story: A film by Martin Doblmeier [Video trailer]. https://www.journeyfilms.com/store/p/milk-dip-cup-8ry6x

New American Bible. (1987). World Bible Publishing.

United Nations. (2015). Universal declaration of human rights. https://www.un.org/en/udhrbook/pdf/udhr_booklet_en_web.pdf

Additional Resources

Dorothy Day, Servant of God. (2022, February 11). Catholicworker.org. https://www.catholicworker.org/dorothyday/canonization.html

Journey Films. (2019, October 24). *Revolution of the heart: The Dorothy Day story* [YouTube]. https://youtu.be/DRQLnJJZnCo

Journey Films. (2021, February 16). *Personalism—Revolution of the heart* [YouTube video]. https://youtu.be/AEQnad4MFI4

Loughery, J., & Randolph, B. (2020). *Dorothy Day: Dissenting voice of the American century*. Simon & Schuster.

Pycior, J. L. (2020). *Dorothy Day, Thomas Merton and the greatest commandment: Radical love in times of crisis*. Paulist Press.

Singer-Towns, B. (2004). *The Catholic faith handbook for youth*. Saint Mary's Press.

United States Conference of Catholic Bishops. (n.d.). *Seven themes of Catholic social teachings* https://www.usccb.org/beliefs-and-teachings/what-we-believe/catholic-social-teaching/seven-themes-of-catholic-social-teaching

Hollywood or History?

Revolution of the Heart: The Dorothy Day Story (2020)

Dorothy Day was a 20th century American Catholic whose passion for the marginalized led to the development of the Catholic Worker Houses of Hospitality during the Great Depression. Her life and dedication to this ministry is currently under review by the Vatican's Congregation for the Causes of Saints.

Evaluate each source provided and summarize your observations and analysis in corresponding spaces provided. In the section located at the bottom of the page, explain whether you think the scenes from *Revolution of the Heart: The Dorothy Day Story* (2020) should be evaluated as accurate accounts of the Gospel of Matthew (25:31–46), or *Rerum Novarum* (1891) or a mixture of both. Use examples from your sources/documents to explain your answer.

Primary Source	***Revolution of the Heart*** **(2020)**	**Secondary Source**

What do you think? Hollywood or History?

Through the Eyes of Dr. King and Malcolm X: The Intersection of Civil Rights and Religion

Colleen Fitzpatrick and Ariel Cornett

FILM: *Selma* (2014) and *Malcolm X* (1992)

Grade	Subject	Topic
7–12	Christianity, Islam, U.S. History	Civil Rights Religion • Christianity • Islam

Chapter Theme	Estimated Time Needed for Lesson
Religious Figures: Religion, Faith, Politics, Civil Rights Movement	55 minutes (Part 1) 55 minutes (Part 2)

National Association for Media Literacy Education

Standard Number	Detailed Description of Each Standard You Are Discussing

Core Principles of Media Literacy Education in the United States	3. Media Literacy Education (MLE) builds and reinforces skills for learners of all ages. Like print literacy, those skills necessitate integrated, interactive, and repeated practice.
	
	Implications for Practice
	    3.3 MLE engages students with varied learning styles.
	    3.4 MLE is most effective when used with co-learning pedagogies, in which teachers learn from students and students learn from teachers and from classmates.
	
	4. MLE develops informed, reflective, and engaged participants essential for a democratic society.
	
	Implications for Practice
	    4.1 MLE promotes student interest in news and current events as a dimension of citizenship, and can enhance student understanding of First Amendment rights and responsibilities.
	    4.4 MLE invites and respects diverse points of view.
	    4.5 MLE explores representations, misrepresentations, and lack of representation of cultures and countries in the global community.

State and Common Core Standard Description

State	Detailed Description of Each Standard You Are Discussing
New York 11th grade	**11.10** Racial, gender, and socioeconomic inequalities were addressed by individuals, groups, and organizations. Varying political philosophies prompted debates over the role of the federal government in regulating the economy and providing a social safety net. 　a) After World War II, long-term demands for equality by African Americans led to the civil right movement. The efforts of individuals, groups, and institutions helped to redefine African American civil rights, though numerous issues remain unresolved. 　b) Individuals, diverse groups, and organizations have sought to bring about change in American society through a variety of methods.
North Carolina 11th grade	**AH2.H.4.3** Analyze the social and religious conflicts, movements, and reforms that impacted the United States since Reconstruction in terms of participants, strategies, opposition, and results. • How the African American civil rights movement of the 20th century was led by a variety of individuals and organizations with different strategies. • How and to what extent various civil rights events and movements successfully tested segregation and gained greater equality for different groups of Americans.
Virginia 11th grade	**VUS.13c** The student will apply social science skills to understand the social, political, and cultural movements and changes in the United States during the second half of the 20th century by explaining how the National Association for the Advancement of Colored People (NAACP), the 1963 March on Washington, the Civil Rights Act of 1964, the Voting Rights Act of 1965, and the Americans with Disabilities Act (ADA) had an impact on all Americans.
National and State English Language Arts Standards	
North Carolina 11th grade	Reading: Integration of Ideas and Analysis **RI.11-12.7** Integrate and evaluate multiple sources of information presented in different media or formats, including visually and quantitatively, as well as in words in order to address a question or solve a problem. Writing: Text Types, Purposes, and Publishing **W.11-12.1** Write arguments to support claims in an analysis of substantive topics or texts, using valid reasoning and relevant and sufficient evidence. B. Introduce precise, knowledgeable claim(s), establish the significance of the claim(s), distinguish the claim(s)

	from alternate or opposing claims, and create an organization that logically sequences claim(s), counterclaims, reasons, and evidence. Speaking and Listening: Collaboration and Communication **SL.11-12.1** Initiate and participate effectively in a range of collaborative discussions (one-on-one, in groups, and teacher-led) with diverse partners on Grades 11–12 topics, texts, and issues, building on others' ideas and expressing their own clearly and persuasively. A. Come to discussions prepared, having read and researched material under study; explicitly draw on that preparation by referring to evidence from texts and other research on the topic or issue to stimulate a thoughtful, well-reasoned exchange of ideas.

Virginia
11th grade
	Reading
	
	11.4 The student will read, comprehend, and analyze relationships among American literature, history, and culture.
	   j) Generate and respond logically to literal, inferential, evaluative, synthesizing, and critical thinking questions about the text(s).
	   k) Compare/contrast literary and informational nonfiction texts.
	
	Writing
	
	11.6 The student will write in a variety of forms, to include persuasive/argumentative, reflective, interpretive, and analytic with an emphasis on persuasion/argumentation.
	   b) Produce arguments in writing/developing a thesis that demonstrates knowledgeable judgments, addresses counterclaims, and provides effective conclusions.
	   d) Adapt evidence, vocabulary, voice, and tone to audience, purpose, and situation.

NCSS C3 Framework

Dimension	**Detailed Description of Each NCSS Dimension You Are Incorporating (should have all four).**
D1.2.9-12	Explain points of agreement and disagreement experts have about interpretations and applications of disciplinary concepts and ideas associated with a compelling question.
D2.His.5-9-12.	Analyze how historical contexts shaped and continue to shape people's perspectives.
D3.3.9-12	Identify evidence that draws information directly and substantively from multiple sources to detect inconsistencies in evidence in order to revise or strengthen claims.

| D4.1.9-12 | Construct arguments using precise and knowledgeable claims, with evidence from multiple sources, while acknowledging counterclaims and evidentiary weaknesses. |

NCSS Core Themes and Description

Theme Number	Detailed Description of Each Aligned NCSS Theme
I Culture	Through the study of culture and cultural diversity, learners understand how human beings create, learn, share, and adapt to culture, and appreciate the role of culture in shaping their lives and society, as well the lives and societies of others. In schools, this theme typically appears in units and courses dealing with geography, history, sociology, and anthropology, as well as multicultural topics across the curricula.
II Time, Continuity, and Change	Through the study of the past and its legacy, learners examine the institutions, values, and beliefs of people in the past, acquire skills in historical inquiry and interpretation, and gain an understanding of how important historical events and developments have shaped the modern world. This theme appears in courses in history, as well as in other social studies courses for which knowledge of the past is important.
V Individuals, Groups and Institutions	Institutions such as families and civic, educational, governmental, and religious organizations, exert a major influence on people's lives. This theme allows students to understand how institutions are formed, maintained, and changed, and to examine their influence. In schools, this theme typically appears in units and courses dealing with sociology, anthropology, psychology, political science, and history.

Handouts/Materials/Web Links

Handout/Materials:
- "Hollywood or History?" graphic organizer
- "Hollywood or History? T-Chart" graphic organizer

Web Links:

A. Link to Film Clip(s):
- "Malcolm X. letter from mecca" (CaliStomp, 2008) [4:26 mins]
https://www.youtube.com/watch?v=K9bdYv8b-U
  - This clip depicts Malcolm X participating in the Hajj. After his departure from the Nation of Islam, Malcolm X participated in the Hajj, a mandatory part of the Islamic faith. He discusses what transpired during his Hajj and how it impacted his approach towards cvil rights and Whites.

– *Selma* (DuVernay, 2014): "Who Murdered Jimmie Lee Jackson" (for Part 2) [2:12 mins]
https://www.youtube.com/watch?v=EAwYHfKs-aE (Movieclips, 2020; Note: The full movie is available for free from FX Movies. The scene starts at the 55-min. mark.)
- *Selma* (DuVernay, 2014) is a film that could easily be watched in its entirety. This clip presents Dr. Martin Luther King Jr.'s eulogy of Jimmie Lee Jackson. In this clip, Dr. Martin Luther King Jr. is preaching in a church and discusses who killed Jackson. He does not stop with the police who murdered Jackson, but extends the blame throughout society to include the president and people who see what is happening but do nothing.

B. Primary Source(s):
– "Biden Pushes Faith as a Unifier at National Prayer Breakfast" (Kambhampaty, 2021) [for the Sparking Strategy/Warm-Up]
https://news.yahoo.com/biden-pushes-faith-unifier-national-104637577.html?guccounter=1&guce_referrer=aHR0cHM6Ly93d3cuZ29vZ2xlLmNvbS8&guce_referrer_sig=AQAAAKXnavK42O2HJWfF33C90zu3N8cVCe4k-YgrkxJXOtVne-0zXVJAA5oMjmy_EbnlMoIxFPm-9HYf-W8_pALx-ZP71gzIDKBG60R-E42zyJz24x-19HKAGXwbbkcJogh5x8iYza03PTaRUmQrdHqf218qVopC44E7pFTu8QEml-lGJ
- "Now, I have attended many of these prayer breakfasts over the years with a nation at war and struggle and strife, a nation of peace and prosperity, a nation though always in prayer. What we know this time is different. For so many in our nation, this is a dark, dark time. So, where do we turn? Faith." (President Biden, as quoted in Kambhampaty, 2021)

– "Malcolm and Martin" (Facing History and Ourselves, 2006) (for Part 1)
https://www.facinghistory.org/resource-library/eyes-prize-study-guide
- There are two excerpts from interviews, one with Coretta Scott King and one with James Cone, author of *Malcolm and Martin and America: A Dream or a Nightmare* (Cone, 1991). These brief excerpts introduce the differences between Malcolm X and Dr. Martin Luther King Jr.

– "Malcom X—Return From Mecca Interview—May 21, 1964" (Melaneyes Media, 2017; for Part 1) [14:57 min.], which may be cut down depending on time
https://www.youtube.com/watch?v=Hv80w3rCUC8
- In this interview, Malcolm X reflects on his time completing the Hajj and the impact it has had on his beliefs. There is also a transcript of a letter written by Malcom X about his experience after completing the Hajj available here: https://momentsintime.com/the-most-remarkable-revelatory-letter-ever-written-by-malcolm-x/#.YCwNdC2z3ow (Malcolm X, 1964)

– Dr. Martin Luther King Jr. Selma Speech ("Lyndon B. Johnson: The Road From Selma," n.d.; for Part 1) [3:40]
http://americanradioworks.publicradio.org/features/prestapes/c4.html
https://kinginstitute.stanford.edu/our-god-marching [transcript]
- Dr. Martin Luther King Jr's speech upon reaching Montgomery after the marches in Selma. Students can listen to the audio or read the transcript (King, 1965).

– "The Philosophy of Life Undergirding Christianity and the Christian Mission" (King, 1948–1951; for Part 1)
https://kinginstitute.stanford.edu/king-papers/documents/three-essays-religion

- This paper comes from Coretta Scott King's collection of Dr. Martin Luther King Jr's notes for sermons. It was written while King was a student at Crozer Theological Seminary and outlines his belief of what it means to be Christian.

C. Secondary Source(s):
  - *Malcolm X—Make It Plain* (7eventytimes7, 2016). Depending on time and the class, the teacher can choose to use multiple clips or shorten clips.
    https://www.youtube.com/watch?v=csWByunwVI8
    Transcript available at PBS (n.d.):
    https://www.pbs.org/wgbh/americanexperience/films/malcolmx/#transcript
    - (29:00–35:36, "Prison, 1946")
      - This clip focuses on Malcolm X's conversion to the Nation of Islam (NOI).
    - (1:11:23–1:13:15)
      - Malcolm X discusses the differences between him and Dr. Martin Luther King Jr.
  - "The People's Legs Are Not Praying—Why *Selma* Is not the Interfaith Movie I Was Hoping for" (Rosenhagen, 2015) [*Huffington Post* review: *Selma* (DuVernay, 2014)]
    https://www.huffpost.com/entry/the-peoples-legs-are-not-_b_6479070
    - In this review, Rosenhangen (2015) questions the portrayal of religion in *Selma* (DuVernay, 2014). He argues that while religion is a side part of the film, in actuality religion played a much more central role in the movement. While the speeches may take place in churches, very rarely is religion and religious belief is discussed.

Guiding Questions

What should students know or understand at the completion of the unit or lesson?

Primary Questions:
- How does religion shape the political philosophy of individuals?
- How did religion and religious beliefs impact various civil rights leaders?
- Is religion accurately portrayed in *Malcolm X* (Lee, 1992) and *Selma* (DuVernay, 2014)?

Additional Questions:
- What various approaches did Civil Rights leaders take?
  - In what ways were the approaches similar (or different)?
  - To what extent did they experience success (as they defined success)?

Important Vocabulary

List all of the important indicators of achievement (important people, places, and events) and vocabulary that students will need to know at the conclusion of the lesson.

Civil Rights Movement: The 1954–1968 civil rights movement in the United States was preceded by a decades-long campaign by African Americans and their like-minded allies to end legalized racial discrimination, disenfranchisement and racial segregation in the United States. The movement has its origins in the Reconstruction era during the late 19th century, although it made its largest legislative gains in the mid-1960s after years of direct actions and grassroots protests. The social movement's

major nonviolent resistance and civil disobedience campaigns eventually secured new protections in federal law for the human rights of all Americans. (Wikipedia)
Christianity: The religion based on the person and teachings of Jesus of Nazareth.
Islam: The religion based on the person and teachings of Muhammad.
Hajj: One of the Five Pillars of Islam where adherents to Islam make a pilgrimage to Mecca.
Malcolm X (1925–1965): an advocate for Black and human rights in the 1950s and 1960s. Member of the Nation of Islam before converting to Islam.
Dr. Martin Luther King, Jr. (1929–1968): civil rights leader of the 1950s and 1960s who preached nonviolence and civil disobedience to protest treatment of Blacks. One of the leaders of the marches at Selma. President of the Southern Christian Leadership Conference and a member of the Baptist religion (a sect of Christianity).
Nation of Islam (NOI): African American movement and organization, founded in 1930 and known for its teachings combining elements of traditional Islam with Black nationalist ideas. The Nation also promotes racial unity and self-help and maintains a strict code of discipline among members. (Britannica)
Selma: Site of three civil rights marches in 1965 held to protest against White citizens and governments denial of Black citizens' right to vote.

Assessment Strategies

Describe the assessments that will be used during the unit.

Formative Assessment:
- T-chart of King and Malcolm X
- Small group discussions
- "Hollywood or History?" graphic organizer

Summative Assessment:
- Whole group discussion
- Scene rewrite/addition (if time allows)

Teaching Strategies (Part 1)

5 min	Quote discussion	15 min	T-chart of King and Malcolm X's approach to civil rights	30 min	Group work on King or Malcolm X

Times are highly flexible and should be adjusted according to the number of sources used, length of introduction, period/block schedule, etc.

Teaching Strategies (Part 2)

5 min	Regroup (from previous day)	20 min	Whole group discussion	10 min	"Hollywood or History?" graphic organizer
10 min	Small group information sharing				

Times are highly flexible and should be adjusted according to the number of sources used, length of introduction, period/block schedule, etc.

Sparking Strategy/Warm-Up

Sparking Strategy (Lesson introduction)

The teacher will begin class by displaying a quote from President Biden at the 2021 National Prayer Breakfast (Kambhampaty, 2021; *Note:* This quote or opening activity may be updated based on current events).

The teacher will have the students write a response to the quote on what the students see as the role of faith and religion in politics. The teacher can ask students questions such as "What examples from history demonstrate the connection, or lack of, between religion and politics?" or "Do you think there should be a connection between religion and politics?"

After students have had a chance to write their response, the teacher can list the students' responses on the board.

Once students have shared their thoughts, the teacher can transition to the main question for the day: "How does religion shape the political philosophy of individuals?" The teacher will ask the students what they know about the two men (i.e., Dr. Martin Luther King Jr. and Malcolm X) and their philosophies towards Civil Rights before telling the students they will be learning more in-depth content about their religious beliefs and political philosophies through the lesson.

Lesson Procedures

In a numerical list, provide a step by step outline of what you plan to do in the lesson. Include questions you will ask the students and materials you will use.

Outline

Part 1

1. **Whole class work:** Based on students' prior exposure and work with sources, the teacher will model how to analyze sources using the interview with Coretta Scott King. Using the T-chart handout, the teacher will write notes based on C. S. King's interview. The teacher should note that C. S. King was married to Martin Luther King Jr., and while she certainly interacted with and knew Malcolm X, as with all sources, they need to consider the source. After modeling this interview source work for students, the teacher will have the students (either in groups or by themselves) analyze the interview from author James Cone, specifically how they approached/defined freedom, justice, and equality.

2. **Group Work:** After the students are comfortable with the similarities and differences between Malcolm X and Martin Luther King's approaches, the class will be broken into two groups to explore the civil rights activists in more depth.
   – The first group will focus on Malcolm X. Using the sources provided, the students should create a timeline for Malcolm X's life with particular attention to when he left the NOI and converted to Sunni Islam. The students will view clips from PBS's documentary on Malcolm X. These clips highlight the major events in Malcolm X's life; however, depending on time, the teacher can pick a few shorter clips. Students will also read or watch an interview with Malcolm X upon his return from the Hajj.

- The second group will focus on Martin Luther King Jr. The students will start by reading an excerpt from a paper King wrote while in college on what it means to be Christian and what being a Christian looks like in society. This paper, while written before King gained national and global attention, outlines his Christian beliefs and how he developed his political philosophy. Students can then choose to listen/read King's speech made after the Selma marches or view the clip from Selma (DuVernay, 2014). While listening/reading the two speeches, students will be asked to identify connections to King's religion and religious beliefs.

While the students are working in their groups, the students should focus on explicit connections to Christianity, Islam, and the NOI. Teachers may want to include a graphic organizer similar to below:

Source	Author	Historical Context	Connections to Religious Beliefs or Religion
Malcolm X's return from the Hajj	Malcolm X	In 1964, Malcolm X completed the Hajj to Mecca. He gave this interview upon his return to the United States.	Malcolm X discusses the impact of the Hajj and how the event itself impacted his views.

Part 2

1. **Regroup:** (i.e., if this takes place on a separate day of class). Students meet back up with their group members to answer any last minute questions and to ensure they have a strong understanding of the connections between their assigned individual and that individual's religious beliefs.
2. **Small group:** The teacher will then group the students in groups of four (two who researched Malcolm X and two who researched Martin Luther King Jr.). Each side will share their findings with the other group. The groups will then compare and contrast the two Civil Rights Leaders.
3. **Hollywood or History Scene Viewing:**
   - The teacher will first show the clip from *Malcolm X* (CaliStomp, 2008). After showing the clip, the teacher will ask the students to find parallels between the clip and the sources they analyzed the previous day.
   - The class will then view the scene from *Selma* (DuVernay, 2014). The teacher will again ask the students to find parallels between the clip and the sources they analyzed the previous day.
   - The teacher will ask the students how religion and religious belief is depicted in the movies. The class will answer the two overarching questions for the lesson: (a) "How did religion shape the philosophy of Malcolm X and Martin Luther King Jr.?" and (b) "Is religion accurately portrayed in *Malcolm X* and *Selma*?" The teacher can use the "Hollywood or History?" graphic organizer in order to help students answer these overarching questions.
4. **Extension:** As an extension activity, the students can rewrite or add a scene to the movie that they think accurately depicts the impact of religion on the political philosophy of either Malcolm X or Martin Luther King Jr. (or both). Another exten-

sion activity would be to have students respond to Rosenhagen's (2015) review of *Selma* (DuVernay, 2014) using what they learned from the sources.

Differentiation

Think about your students' skill levels, intelligences, and learning styles. How are you going to make this lesson meet the needs of all of your students?

- **Built in Scaffolds:** Allow students to work with scaffolds while analyzing sources. Teachers may want to model how to use the scaffolds. Assign heterogeneous groups and allow students to collaborate with each other.
- **ESL Interventions:** Distribute vocabulary list to students at the beginning of the lesson. Allow students to have textbooks or other resources for reference. Encourage students to turn on closed-captioning when playing videos or provide transcripts.
- **Extensions:** If time allows, assign one of the extension activities.

Summarizing Strategies/Synthesizing Activity

What strategies are you going to use to allow students to summarize what they learned in the lesson?

- "Hollywood or History?" graphic organizer
- "T-chart" graphic organizer
- Small group discussion
- Whole group discussion
- Source analysis

References

Are there any additional resources that might be relevant to your lesson? Are there sources that you need to reference? Please add any citations using APA.

7eventytimes7. (2016, June 8). *Malcolm X—Make it plain* (full PBS documentary) [YouTube video]. https://www.youtube.com/watch?v=csWByunwVI8

Biden Pushes Faith as a Unifier at National Prayer Breakfast. (2021, February 4). *Yahoo!News.* https://news.yahoo.com/biden-pushes-faith-unifier-national-104637577.html?guccounter=1&guce_referrer=aHR0cHM6Ly93d3cuZ29vZ2xlLmNvbS88&guce_referrer_sig=AQAAAKXnavK42O2HJWfF33C90zu3N8cVCc4k-YgrkxJXOtVne0zXVJAA5oMjmy_EbnlMoIxFPm-9HYf-W8_pALx-ZP-71gzIDKBG60R-E42zyJz24x-19HKAGXwbbkcJogh5x8iYza03PTaRUmQrdHqf218qVopC44E7pFTu8QEml-lGJ

CaliStomp. (2008, November 19). *Malcolm X. Letter from Mecca* [YouTube]. https://www.youtube.com/watch?v=K9bdYv8b–U

Cone, J. H. (1991). *Martin & Malcolm & America: A dream or a nightmare.* Orbis Books.

DuVernay, A. (Director). (2014). *Selma* [Film]. Paramount Pictures. Pathé; Harpo Films; Plan B Entertainment; Cloud Eight Films; Ingenious Media; Redgill Selma Productions.

Facing History and Ourselves. (2006). Malcolm and Martin. In *Eyes on the prize: America's civil rights movement 1954–1985* (p. 108) [A study guide to the television series]. Blackside.

Kambhampaty, A. (2021, February 4). Biden pushes faith as a unifier at National Prayer Breakfast. *Politico.* https://news.yahoo.com/biden-pushes-faith-unifier-national-104637577.html?guce_referrer=aHR0cHM6Ly93d3cuZ29vZ2xlLmNvbS88&guce_referrer_sig=AQAAAKXnavK42O2HJWfF33C90zu3N8cVCc4k-YgrkxJXOtVne0zXVJAA5oMjmy_EbnlMoIxFPm-9HYf-W8_pALx-ZP71gzIDKB

G60R-E42zyJz24x-19HKAGXwbbkcJogh5x8iYza03PTaRUmQrdHqf218qVopC44E7pFTu8QEml-lGJ&guccounter=2

King, M. L., Jr. (1948–1951). *Three essays on religion*. Stanford: The Martin Luther King, Jr. Research and Education Institute. https://kinginstitute.stanford.edu/king-papers/documents/three-essays-religion

King, M. L., Jr. (1965, March 25). *Our God Is Marching On!* [Speech transcript]. Stanford: The Martin Luther King, Jr. Research and Education Institute. https://kinginstitute.stanford.edu/our-god-marching

Lee, S. (Director). (1992). *Malcolm X* [Film]. Warner Bros.

Lyndon B. Johnson: The Road From Selma: Part 4. (n.d.). [Audio recording]. American Public Media. http://americanradioworks.publicradio.org/features/prestapes/c4.html

Malcolm X. (1964, April 26). *The most remarkable revelatory letter ever written by Malcolm X* [Letter]. Moments in Time. https://momentsintime.com/the-most-remarkable-revelatory-letter-ever-written-by-malcolm-x/#.YCwNdC2z3ow

Melaneyes Media. (2017, March 30). *Malcolm X—Return from Mecca interview—May 21, 1964* [YouTube]. https://www.youtube.com/watch?v=Hv80w3rCUC8

Movieclips. (2020, November 2). *Selma (2014)—Our lives are not fully lived scene (2/10) | Movieclips* [YouTube video]. https://www.youtube.com/watch?v=EAwYHfKs-aE

PBS. (n.d.). Malcolm X: Make it plain [Transcript]. *American Experience*. https://www.pbs.org/wgbh/americanexperience/films/malcolmx/#transcript

Rosenhagen, U. (2015, January 16). *The people's legs are not praying—Why* Selma *is not the interfaith movie I was hoping for* [Blog]. https://www.huffpost.com/entry/the-peoples-legs-are-not_b_6479070

Additional Resources

Roberts, S. L., & Elfer, C. J. (2019). *Hollywood or History? An inquiry-based strategy for using film to teach United States history*. Information Age Publishing.

Chapter 3: Religious Figures ▪ 113

Hollywood or History?
Malcolm X (1992) and Selma (2014)

Malcolm X (1992) and *Selma* (2014) are two films that depict the lives of various activists and events of the Civil Rights movement of the 1960s. *Malcolm X* is a biopic of Malcolm X and his relationship with the Nation of Islam (NOI) and how that impacted his political beliefs. *Selma* focuses specifically on the marches from Selma to Montgomery. While the movie is not a biopic of Dr. Martin Luther King, Jr, it does emphasize his perspective of the march. In this inquiry lesson students will investigate how Malcolm X and Dr. Martin Luther King Jr.'s religion and religious belief interacted with their political beliefs. Students will explore how each film portrays religion and religious belief and how that compares to various primary and secondary sources.

Evaluate each source provided and summarize your analysis below. In the section located at the bottom of the page, explain whether you think these scenes from *Malcolm X* (1992) and *Selma* (2014) should be considered as accurate accounts of history, pure Hollywood, or a mixture of both. Use examples from your sources/documents to explain your answer.

Primary Source	***Malcolm X* (1989)/ *Selma* (2014)**	**Secondary Source**

What do you think? Hollywood or History?

Hollywood or History?
Malcolm X (1992) and *Selma* (2014) T-Chart

Thoughts on or approaches to accomplishing:	Martin Luther King Jr.	Malcolm X
Freedom		
Justice		
Equality		

Of Gods and Men: On Hospitality and Interreligious Dialogue

Thomas E. Malewitz

FILM: *Of Gods and Men* (2010)

Grade	Subject	Topic
11–12	Christianity, Islam	• Interreligious Hospitality and Dialogue

Chapter Theme	Estimated Time Needed for Lesson
Historical Context: 20th century Interreligious History, Christian Monasticism, Islam, Martyrdom, Faith, Trappist	45 minutes; 4 days, if the full movie is used.

National Association for Media Literacy Education

Standard Number	Detailed Description of Each Standard You Are Discussing

Core Principles of Media Literacy Education in the United States	4. Media Literacy Education (MLE) develops informed, reflective, and engaged participants essential for a democratic society.
	
	Implications for Practice
	    4.1 MLE promotes student interest in news and current events as a dimension of citizenship, and can enhance student understanding of First Amendment rights and responsibilities.
	    4.4 MLE invites and respects diverse points of view.
	    4.5 MLE explores representations, misrepresentations, and lack of representation of cultures and countries in the global community.
	
	6. MLE affirms that people use their individual skills, beliefs, and experiences to construct their own meanings from media messages.
	
	Implications for Practice
	    6.1 MLE is not about teaching students what to think; it is about teaching them how they can arrive at informed choices that are most consistent with their own values.

State and Common Core Standard Description

State	Detailed Description of Each Standard You Are Discussing
Michigan Civics	C—6.4.3 Identify and describe a local, state, national, or international public policy issue; research and evaluate multiple solutions; analyze the consequences of each solution and propose, defend, and take relevant action to address or resolve the issue. *Considerations for research may include but are not limited to:* primary and secondary sources, legal documents, non-text based information, and other forms of political communication. *Considerations for analyzing credible sources may include but are not limited to:* logical validity, factual accuracy and/or omission, emotional appeal, unstated assumptions, logical fallacies, inconsistencies, distortions, appeals to bias or prejudice, and overall strength of argument.
New York Global History and Geography II	**10.8 Tensions between traditional cultures and modernization:** Tensions exist between traditional cultures and agents of modernization. Reactions for and against modernization depend on perspective and context. 10.8a Cultures and countries experience and view modernization differently. For some, it is a change from a traditional rural, agrarian condition to a secular, urban, industrial condition. Some see modernization as a potential threat and others as an opportunity to be met.
Virginia 11th grade	**VUS.13c** The student will apply social science skills to understand the social, political, and cultural movements and changes in the United States during the second half of the 20th century by explaining how the National Association for the Advancement of Colored People (NAACP), the 1963 March on Washington, the Civil Rights Act of 1964, the Voting Rights Act of 1965, and the Americans with Disabilities Act (ADA) had an impact on all Americans.
United States Conference of Catholic Bishops (USCCB) Curriculum Framework	
USCCB.IV— Jesus Christ's Mission Continues in the Church (The Church) III.A.6b	Ecumenism and Interreligious Dialogue. Jesus' prayer for unity (Jn 17:11; CCC, no. 820); Dialogue with interreligious communities and faiths, such as Islam.

NCSS C3 Framework

Dimension	Detailed Description of Each NCSS Dimension You Are Incorporating (should have all four).
D1.2.9-12	Explain points of agreement and disagreement experts have about interpretations and applications of disciplinary concepts and ideas associated with a compelling question.
D2.His.5.9-12.	Analyze how historical contexts shaped and continue to shape people's perspectives.
D3.3.9-12	Identify evidence that draws information directly and substantively from multiple sources to detect inconsistencies in evidence in order to revise or strengthen claims.
D4.1.9-12	Construct arguments using precise and knowledgeable claims, with evidence from multiple sources, while acknowledging counterclaims and evidentiary weaknesses.

NCSS Core Themes and Description

Theme Number	Detailed Description of Each Aligned NCSS Theme
II Time, Continuity, and Change	Studying the past makes it possible for us to understand the human story across time. Historical analysis enables us to identify continuities over time in core institutions, values, ideals, and traditions, as well as processes that lead to change within societies and institutions, and that result in innovation and the development of new ideas, values, and ways of life.
V Individuals, Groups and Institutions	Social studies programs should include experiences that provide for the study of interactions among individuals, groups, and institutions.
VI Power, Authority and Governance	Social studies programs should include experiences that provide for the study of how people create, interact with, and change structures of power, authority, and governance.

Handouts/Materials/Web Links

Handout/Materials:
- "Hollywood or History?" graphic organizer

Web Links:
A. Film Clip(s):
  – *Of Gods and Men* (Beauvois, 2010). [2 hrs]
    - *Of Gods and Men* #2 Movie CLIP—Nearest in Love (Movieclips, 2011a) [2 mins]
      https://www.youtube.com/watch?v=QRGusFszwdA
    - *Of Gods and Men* #3 Movie CLIP—Stubbornness (Movieclips, 2011b) [2 mins]
      https://www.youtube.com/watch?v=Tb6dbNhFk7I&list=PLZbXA4lyCtqp_QzmelrAKCktIyI0si96O&index=3
    - *Of Gods and Men* #4 Movie CLIP—Birds on a Branch (Movieclips, 2011c) [1 min]
      https://www.youtube.com/watch?v=iKw7Ndv4bRM

B. Primary Source(s):
  – "Chapter 53: The reception of guests—#1–15" (Lawrence, n.d.)
    https://christdesert.org/rule-of-st-benedict/chapter-53-the-reception-of-guests/

C. Secondary Source(s):
  – "Bishop Barron on *Of Gods and Men* [Spoilers]" (Bishop Robert Barron, 2011) [10 mins] https://www.youtube.com/watch?v=fWLTZqzK6XU
  – "Father James Marin, SJ: *Of Gods and Men* (Martin, 2011) [12 mins]
    https://www.pbs.org/wnet/religionandethics/2011/04/08/father-james-martin-sj-of-gods-and-men/8533/
  – "Algeria's Trappist Monk Massacre: The Case That Won't Go Away" (Prince, 2013)
    https://ips-dc.org/algerias_trappist_monk_massacre_the_case_that_wont_go_away/

Guiding Questions

What should students know or understand at the completion of the unit or lesson?

Primary Questions:
- What does authentic hospitality look like?
- What actions indicate interreligious dialogue?
- How can a dedication to hospitality create a dangerous situation in an unstable foreign country?
- Why do you think some people are willing to become a witness and sacrifice their time and lives for the betterment of others?

Important Vocabulary

List all of the important indicators of achievement (important people, places, and events) and vocabulary that students will need to know at the conclusion of the lesson.

Monasticism: a way of life in which one renounces worldly pursuits to devote oneself fully to spiritual work, usually lived out in community bound by an Order or Rule.

Rule of Saint Benedict: Originally written in 516, this monastic Rule lays out the guidelines of particular expectations for individuals within a Benedictine community, especially a duty of hospitality.

Trappist: a Cistercian monastic community founded in 1664, based on the Rule of St. Benedict. The Trappist lifestyle is based on three vows of: stability, fidelity to monastic life, and obedience.

Assessment Strategies

Describe the assessments that will be used during the unit.

Formative Assessment:
- Small group discussion, large group discussion

Summative Assessment:
- "Hollywood or History?" graphic organizer

Teaching Strategies

5 min	Warm-up activity	10 min	View/discuss *Of Gods and Men* (Beauvois, 2010) clips.	10 min	View/analyze/discuss Martin's review (Martin, 2011).
10 min	Read/discuss: "Chapter 53: The Reception of Guests (1–15)" (Lawrence n.d.).	10 min	View/analyze/discuss Barron's review (Bishop Robert Barron, 2011)	**Time Remaining/HMWK**	Read/compare/contrast Prince's (2013) critique in "Hollywood or History?" graphic organizer Conclusion/summary

Times are highly flexible and should be adjusted according to the number of sources used, length of introduction, period/block schedule, etc.

Sparking Strategy/Warm-Up

Sparking Strategy (Lesson introduction)

Introduce the concept of a monastic community and rule. Use the given lesson definitions to establish a foundation for the students. Explain that different communities have different expectations for community life (such as Benedictines, Dominicans, Franciscans, Trappists, etc.). Explain the life and choices of the founder of the Rule if needed.

Lesson Procedures

In a numerical list, provide a step by step outline of what you plan to do in the lesson. Include questions you will ask the students and materials you will use.

Outline
1. Have the students read a copy of "Chapter 53: The Reception of Guests (1–15)" (Lawrence, n.d.). Allow the students time to highlight chosen words or phrases regarding the importance of hospitality from the reading. On the board, make a list of the students' important words or phrases that the students highlighted. Allow students to briefly explain why they chose the word or phrase.
2. Transition the conversation to the context of the Trappist monks portrayed in *Of Gods and Men* (Beauvois, 2010). Show each of the three video clips from the film, while offering time for the students to reflect on the connection between the video clip and the concept of hospitality from the Rule of St. Benedict. Allow the students to connect the dialogue and action of the characters in the scenes to connect to the words or phrases written on the board.
3. View "Bishop Barron on *Of Gods and Men* [Spoilers]" (Bishop Robert Barron, 2011) [10 mins]. Separate students into small groups and have the students analyze and discuss Barron's critique of the film. Bring the students to a large class discussion back to the concept of hospitality on the board and the review of Barron.
4. View James Martin on *Of Gods and Men* (Martin, 2011) [12 mins]. Have students return into small groups and analyze and discuss Martin's critique of the film. Bring the students to a large class discussion back to the concept of hospitality on the board and the review of Martin.
5. Have students compare and contrast the film reviews of Barron and Martin in their small groups. What were the similarities? What were the differences?
6. Introduce or handout Prince (2013) "Algeria's Trappist Monk Massacre: The Case That Won't Go Away" or include a link for student access. Handout "Hollywood or History?" graphic organizer. Explain the worksheet expectations of comparing/contrasting the reviews of Barron, Martin, and Prince. Allow students to work on the assignment individually or in their group. Assign unfinished work for homework.

Differentiation

Think about your students' skill levels, intelligences, and learning styles. How are you going to make this lesson meet the needs of all of your students?

Scaffolds: Work with students individually if needed to answer questions and further explain any material. Make sure that the student table groups have mixed students so that higher achieving students are working with/helping their classmates.

ESL Interventions: Provide vocabulary terms pertaining to the Albanian Civil War of 1997 with useful synonyms and definitions/description in order to give students background knowledge and vocabulary helps as they move through the lesson itself. As a film that relies on the use of English subtitles to help students experience the mode of watching and reading a movie to create the full context of the story.

Extensions: Have students research the events surrounding the Albanian Civil War from 1997. Using their research, have the students create a poster project or academic essay explaining the connection of the life of the monks portrayed in *Of Gods and Men*

(Beauvoix, 2010) are bound within the surrounding civil unrest of Albanian during that historical time period.

Summarizing Strategies/Synthesizing Activity

What strategies are you going to use to allow students to summarize what they learned in the lesson?

- Analysis and critique of historical documents and film reviews
- Student-generated position statements with reference to documents/evidence
- Line of contention
- Small group discussion

References

Are there any additional resources that might be relevant to your lesson? Are there sources that you need to reference? Please add any citations using APA.

Beauvois, X. (Director). (2010). *Of gods and men* [Film]. Why Not Productions, Armada Films.

Bishop Robert Barron. (2011, April 4). Bishop Barron on *Of Gods and Men* (Spoilers) [YouTube video]. https://www.youtube.com/watch?v=fWLTZqzK6XU

Lawrence, P. (Trans.). (n.d.). Chapter 53: The reception of guests (1–15). Monastery of Christ in the Desert. https://christdesert.org/rule-of-st-benedict/chapter-53-the-reception-of-guests/

Martin, J. (2011, April 8). Father James Martin, SJ: *Of Gods and Men* [Video]. *Religion & Ethics Newsweekly*. https://www.pbs.org/wnet/religionandethics/2011/04/08/father-james-martin-sj-of-gods-and-men/8533/

Movieclips. (2011a, May 31). *Of gods and men* #2 movie CLIP—Nearest in love (2010) HD [YouTube video]. https://www.youtube.com/watch?v=QRGusFszwdA

Movieclips. (2011b, May 30). *Of gods and men* #3 movie CLIP—Stubbornness (2010) HD [YouTube video]. https://www.youtube.com/watch?v=Tb6dbNhFk7I&list=PLZbXA4lyCtqp_QzmelrAKCktIy I0si96O&index=4

Movieclips. (2011c, June 1). *Of gods and men* #4 movie CLIP—Birds on a branch (2010) HD [YouTube video]. https://www.youtube.com/watch?v=iKw7Ndv4bRM

Prince, R. (2013, June 27). *Algeria's trappist monk massacre: The case that won't go away*. Institute for Policy Studies. https://ips-dc.org/algerias_trappist_monk_massacre_the_case_that_wont_go_away/

Additional Resources

French, B. (n.d.). *Martyrs of peace—The monks of Tibhirine, Algeria: Preaching the Gospel of Christ with their lives*. The Word Among Us. https://wau.org/resources/article/re_martyrs_of_peace_the_monks_of_tibhirine_algeria/

Malewitz, T. E. (2020). True/false self: Refining the search for authenticity. In *Authenticity, passion, and advocacy: Approaching adolescent spirituality from the life and wisdom of Thomas Merton* (pp. 62–72). Wipf & Stock.

McGee, M. (2011). The monks of Tibhirine. *The Furrow, 62*(7/8), 418–422. http://www.jstor.org/stable/23046494

United States Conference of Catholic Bishops. (2000). *Catechism of the Catholic Church* (2nd ed.) Libreria Editrice Vaticana.

Hollywood or History?
Of Gods and Men (2010)

Of Gods and Men is a film that depicts a challenge of interreligious dialogue, hospitality, and the choice of faith and witness. Watch the reviews of Barron, Martin, and Prince

- "Bishop Barron on *Of Gods and Men* [Spoilers]" (Bishop Robert Barron, 2011) [10 mins] https://www.youtube.com/watch?v=fWLTZqzK6XU
- "Father James Martin, SJ: *Of Gods and Men*" (Martin, 2011) [12 mins] https://www.pbs.org/wnet/religionandethics/2011/04/08/father-james-martin-sj-of-gods-and-men/8533/
- "Algeria's Trappist Monk Massacre: The Case That Won't Go Away" (Prince, 2013) https://ips-dc.org/algerias_trappist_monk_massacre_the_case_that_wont_go_away/

What do you think of the film reviews (Bishop Robert Barron 2011; Martin 2011) and the critique of the historical event by Prince (2013)? Illustrate 5 similarities and/or differences between the critiques.

Barron (2011)	Martin (2011)	Prince (2013)
1	1	1
2	2	2
3	3	3
4	4	4
5	5	5
What do you think? Hollywood or History?		

CHAPTER 4

Rituals

What sacred practices give meaning to a culture or religion? Rituals, a repeated set of symbolic actions, activities, or gestures establish sacred meaning in a religion. Powerful actions and beliefs give meaning to past traditions, current spiritual relationships, and carry on the legacy for the future of a religious system. Essential rituals in religious practice are not always understood easily, as their meaning may not be found in the physical alone, while some rituals have a transcendent meaning that parallel the physical action. In Christianity, for example, the sacred ritual of Baptism involves the pouring of water or immersion into water of an individual being initiated in the church. This action of spiritual cleansing parallels a physical action of cleansing with water. In Judaism, many of the rituals are immediately bound in a communal experience of sharing stories and eating a meal, such as the Seder meal. Some rituals, though, can be opaque in their meaning. This chapter of *Hollywood or History? An Inquiry-Based Strategy for Teaching World Religions* uses four films to explore some rituals associated with world religions that offer engagement for secondary students that may not be familiar with the power of such sacred actions.

The first lesson plan explores the importance of music that defines a cultural identity. Trueba's (2000) *Calle 54* allows the viewer to experience the passion and power of music in the cultural identity of the Latin and American jazz scene. The blues, jazz, and gospel mediums have given a voice to underrepresented populations that history has often neglected. The songs of freedom and struggle have now become a legacy that teaches of America's past. The music itself serves as the protagonist of the musical and the melodies offer an invitation to a deeper reality and transcendent experience beyond language, through a history of African and Latino identity (Fern & Gonzalez, 2011).

The second lesson plan explores the mystical and odd rituals in Christian tradition, exorcism, healings, and prophecy. As a religious ritual that is often misunderstood and shrouded in mystery, exorcisms have recently become a theatrical horror device in films like *The Exorcist* (Friedkin, 1973) or *The Exorcism of Emily Rose* (Derrickson, 2005). Lungin's (2006) international award-winning film *The Island* offers a vision of the sacred and prophetic ritual not influenced by such Hollywood perspectives, but explores it from the perspective of an austere hermit prophet and healer in secluded Russia. This film does not over glamorize or trivialize ancient Christian ritual but focuses on the need for healing and wholeness of the human person, which is the heart of the ritual.

The third lesson plan explains an odd and recurring phrase during the Egyptian plague narrative in the Book of Exodus, "But the LORD hardened Pharaoh's heart" (Exodus 9:12). Although much scholarship has been devoted to the plagues from a Jewish perspective, this lesson explores Egyptian culture and rituals to give context and meaning to the story. Using DeMille's (1956) Academy award-winning masterpiece *The Ten Commandments*, the lesson allows the students to research the role of the Egyptian pharaoh and the rituals surrounding the judgment of the pharaoh within the Egyptian pantheon.

The final film in this section allows the students to research the devotion of pilgrimage. The sacred journey of a pilgrimage, essential to Islam and highly respected in Christianity, challenges a pilgrim to engage their beliefs and faith from unfamiliar locations culture perspectives in their relationship with the divine. Through Estevez's (2010) film, *The Way*, students will learn about the Camino de Santiago—an ancient Christian pilgrimage route, have an introduction to the concept of Hajj within Islam, and research how the ritual and power of pilgrimage open a devotee to a deeper cultural awareness and respect for the global realities of religious rituals.

REFERENCES

DeMille, C. B. (Director). (1956). *The Ten Commandments* [Film]. Paramount.
Derrickson, S. (2005). *The exorcism of Emily Rose* [Film]. Lakeshore Entertainment; Firm Films; Mist Entertainment.
Estevez, E. (Director). (2010). *The Way* [Film]. Filmax Entertainment.
Fern, & Gonzalez, O. (2011, May 11). *Calle 54*: A memorable love song to Latin Jazz. *The Washington Post*. https://www.washingtonpost.com/archive/lifestyle/2001/05/11/calle-54-a-memorable-love-song-to-latin-jazz/98a116e5-a726-49c4-aeef-13cf9413069a/
Friedkin, W. (1973). *The exorcist* [Film]. Hoya Productions.
Lungin, P. (Director). (2006). *The island* [Film]. Pavel Lungin's Studio.
Trueba, F. (Director). (2000). *Calle 54* [Film]. Buena Vista International.

The Relationship Between Music and Traditional African Religion

Miguel David Hernandez Paz

FILM: *Calle 54* (2000) [English Subtitled]

Grade	Subject	Topic
9–12	U.S. History, World Religions, Music Appreciation	Traditional African Religion

Chapter Theme	Estimated Time Needed for Lesson
Rituals: Culture, Heritage, Globalization, Music Appreciation	Part 1: 55 minutes Part 2: 55 minutes

National Association for Media Literacy Education

Standard Number	Detailed Description of Each Standard You Are Discussing

Core Principles of Media Literacy Education in the United States	3. Media Literacy Education (MLE) builds and reinforces skills for learners of all ages. Like print literacy, those skills necessitate integrated, interactive, and repeated practice.
	
	Implications for Practice
	    3.3 MLE engages students with varied learning styles.
	    3.4 MLE is most effective when used with co-learning pedagogies, in which teachers learn from students and students learn from teachers and from classmates.

State and Common Core Standard Description

State	Detailed Description of Each Standard You Are Discussing
National Standards in History (5th–12th grades) 5B – US ERA 6	Massive immigration after 1870 and how new social patterns, conflicts, and ideas of national unity developed amid growing cultural diversity. 2A. The student understands the sources and experiences of the new immigrants.

National Standards in History (5th–12th grades) 7th–12th Grade: 2A	Distinguish between the "old" and "new" immigration in terms of its volume and the immigrants' ethnicity, religion, language, place of origin, and motives for emigrating from their homelands. Trace patterns... how new immigrants helped produce a composite American culture that transcended group boundaries. Assess the challenges, opportunities, and contributions of different immigrant groups.
Alabama Grades 9–12 Human Geography	Identify the characteristics, distribution, and complexity of Earth's cultural mosaics. Explaining essential aspects of culture, including social structure, languages, belief systems, customs, religion, traditions, art, food, architecture, and technology.
Illinois Grades 9–12 Anthropology & Sociology	**SS.ANTH.2.9-12** Explain how cultures develop and vary in response to their physical and social environment, including local, national, regional, and global patterns. **SS.ANTH.5.9-12** Apply anthropological concepts and anthropological knowledge to a variety of everyday, real-world situations. **SS.SOC.2.9-12** Analyze the impact of social structure, including culture, institutions, and societies.
New York Grade 10 Global History and Geography	**10.8a** Cultures and countries experience and view modernization differently. For some, it is a change from a traditional rural, agrarian condition to a secular, urban, industrial condition. Some see modernization as a potential threat and others as an opportunity to be met. Students will investigate the extent to which urbanization and industrialization have modified the roles of social institutions such as family, religion, education, and government by examining one case study in each of these regions: Africa (e.g., Zimbabwe, Kenya, Nigeria, Sierra Leone), Latin America (e.g., Brazil, Argentina, Chile, Mexico), and Asia (e.g., China, India, Indonesia, South Korea).

Fine Arts/Music Appreciation

Dimension	
MHSMA.8	Understanding relationships between music, the other arts, and disciplines outside the arts.
MHSMA.9	Understanding music in relation to history and culture.

English Language/Reading in History/Social Studies

Dimension	
CCSS.ELA-Literacy. RH.9-10.10	By the end of Grade 10, read and comprehend history/social studies texts in the Grades 9–10 text complexity band independently and proficiently.
CCSS.ELA-Literacy. RH.6-8.9	Analyze the relationship between a Primary and Secondary Source on the same topic.
CCSS.ELA4RL1	Refer to details and examples in a text when explaining what the text says explicitly and when drawing inferences from the text.
CCSS.ELA-Literacy. RI.11-12.7	Integrate and evaluate multiple sources of information presented in different media or formats (e.g., visually, quantitatively) as well as in words in order to address a question or solve a problem.

NCSS Core Themes and Description

Theme Number	Detailed Description of Each Aligned NCSS Theme
I Culture	...the socially transmitted beliefs, values, institutions, behaviors, traditions and way of life of a group of people... Students come to understand to see themselves both as individuals and as members of a particular culture that shares similarities with other cultural groups, but is also distinctive. [And to understand] the multiple perspectives that derive from different cultural vantage points.
II Time, Continuity, and Change	...[Knowing how to read and reconstruct the past] to understand the human story across time [and] to identify continuities over time in core institutions, values, ideals, and traditions, as well as processes that lead to change within societies and institutions, and that result in innovation and the development of new ideas, values, and ways of life.
III People, Places, and Environments	...[Students] create their spatial views and geographic perspectives of the world beyond their personal locations... What do we mean by "region"?...
IV Individual Development and Identity	[Between social norms and emerging personal identities, the social processes that influence identity formation, and the ethical principles underlying individual action.] Personal identity is shaped by one's culture, by groups, and by institutional influences.

V Individuals, Groups, and Institutions	Institutions [core social—formal and informal—among individuals, groups, and institutions] play a variety of important roles in socializing individuals and meeting their needs, as well as in the promotion of societal continuity, the mediation of conflict, and the consideration of public issues.
VI Power, Authority, and Governance	Social studies programs should include experiences that provide for the study of how people create, interact with, and change structures of power, authority, and governance.
IX Global Connections	By interpreting [the costs and benefits of increased global connections] and its implications for different societies, cultures, and institutions... [and] through exposure to various media and first-hand experiences, young learners become aware of how things that happen in one part of the world impact [between national interests and global priorities] other parts of the world.
X Civic Ideas and Practices	All people have a stake in examining civic ideals and practices [critical to full participation in society] across time and in different societies.

The Cultural Approach Category/Description

Category	Description
Intellectual	Innovation in the social studies does not only refer to the methodological strategies (applied new technologies into geography and history teaching), but also to the conception and the didactic aspects of the discipline: What history to teach?
Aesthetic	Relates well-known global artistic disciplines, such as dance and music. The media arts create an environment for conversations of rich information between cultures.
Religious	Tradition African Religions have deep rooted connection to the arts. This Latin Jazz documentary explores that essential connection and context.
Social	The Social lens has the opportunity to offer a learned perspective of cultural history and geography to prepare students to join in the global conversation present in a 21st century diverse reality.

Film

Calle 54 (2000) is a film that uses Jazz as a pretext to present a sample of Latin American musicians. Each of them is casually interviewed and filmed while performing compositions of their repertory. These musical pieces—some of them elemental ones of the Latin musical folklore—are compiled in an original soundtrack, highly recommended to reach an idea of the Latin contribution to the global genre of Jazz. The intention of the documentary was to make a tribute to those musicians resulting in self-portraits that are harmonically supported on the most talented jazz performances that have ever been filmed. African culture and identity is consciously and unconsciously incorporated throughout the film. Rhythms and sounds arrived and were transmitted through generations to shape the expression of the African in the Americas.

Calle 54 (2000) is not a Hollywood production. This documentary offers a musical encounter that traces the Afro-Cuban cultural roots of the genre of Jazz to its modern expression.

Handouts/Materials/Web Links

Handout/Materials:
- "Hollywood or History?" graphic organizer
- "Hollywood or History?" questions workseet
- "Hollywood or History?" Appendix of readings

Web Links:

A. Link to Film Clip(s):
   Note: The attached weblinks are in Spanish without the availability of English subtitles. The documentary film itself does have the availability for English subtitles.
   - "Puntilla & Nueva Generación—Compa Galletano" (Don Quixote, 2019) [7 min]
     https://www.youtube.com/watch?v=sM4ExKI_j_8
   - "Aftro Cuban Jazz Suite—Chico O'Farrill" (Ronald Becerra Ronnie Beck, 2021) [9 mins]
     https://www.youtube.com/watch?v=bbJIYQErTHE

B. Primary Source(s):
   - "Louisiana's Code Noir (1724)/Black Code of Louisiana" (n.d.)
     https://www.blackpast.org/african-american-history/louisianas-code-noir-1724/
   - *El Sol de Jesús del Monte: Novela de Costumbres Cubanas* (Orihuela, 1852/2008, pp. 224–225)

C. Secondary Source(s):
   - *La Habana de Cecilia Valdés* (siglo XIX). (Torriente, 1946, pp. 91–93)
   - *The Creation of Jazz: Music, Race, and Culture in Urban America* (Peretti, 1992, pp. 12–38)

Guiding Questions

What should students know or understand at the completion of the unit or lesson?

Primary Questions:
- How does the background culture and narrative define Jazz as a musical genre?
  - Document the Latin contribution to the global genre of Jazz.
  - Explore how the rhythm and sounds of Africa arrived on the American continent.
  - Explain the unique artistic and cultural musical expression of the slave populations.
  - Explain how place is incorporated within a ritual atmosphere.
- Explain the Afro-American emergency in the colonies.
  - The activity and migrations between peoples of Caribe and the Southern United States.
  - Explore intercultural phenomena surrounding arts and music.
  - Regression of the classic European substrate and Afro-American emergency.
  - Explain how African musical culture survived from structures of the system of slavery.
  - Describe sacred art elements and inter-ethnical cohesion in Latin Jazz.
- How did Jazz music influence the progression of and in Latin culture and experience?
  - Explore how Jazz was developed and spread out of lived experiences.
  - Describe how Jazz varied in Louisiana's standard in the thirties and forties.

Additional Questions:
- Did the civil rights movement in the 1950s and 1960s achieve significant change? What role did the unique role of Latin and African roots in music influence that movement?

Important Vocabulary

List all of the important indicators of achievement (important people, places, and events) and vocabulary that students will need to know at the conclusion of the lesson.

Culture: the beliefs, customs, arts, etc. of a particular society, group, place or time.
Globalization: is a term used to describe the increasing connectedness and interdependence of world cultures and economies.
Heritage: something possessed as a result of one's natural situation or birth.

Assessment Strategies

Describe the assessments that will be used during the unit.

Formative Assessment: Roundtable discussion

Summative Assessment: Have students write a letter or make a video telling a younger student about the complexities, the potential biases, and inaccuracies found in Hollywood films and what they should do to be better informed about historical figures and events that are portrayed in movies.

Teaching Strategies (Part 1)

10 min	Roundtable Group—Questions Worksheet and graphic organizer delivery	15 min	Primary Sources and Secondary Source analysis	10 min	Line of Contention
7 min	Clip 1 viewing (Don Quixote, 2019)	10 min	Completion of graphic organizer/position statement	**Time Remaining/HMWK**	Deliver technical cards of sources (filmic and literary)

Times are highly flexible and should be adjusted according to the number of sources used, length of introduction, period/block schedule, etc.

- Roundtable Group—Worksheet Delivery
- Clip 1 watching: "Compa Galletano" (Don Quixote, 2019) [6:33 min.].
- Primary Source Reading: Orihuela (1852/2008).
- Secondary Source Reading: Torriente (1946).
- Completion of Graphic Organizer/Position Statement
- Line of Contention

Teaching Strategies (Part 2)

5 min	Review of Part 1 materials	9 min	Clip 2 viewing (Ronald Becerra Ronnie Beck, 2021)	10 min	Completion of graphic organizer/position statement
15 min	Secondary Source reading	10 min	Primary Source reading	**Time Remaining/HMWK**	Hollywood or history? Conclusion/summary

Times are highly flexible and should be adjusted according to the number of sources used, length of introduction, period/block schedule, etc.

- Secondary Source reading: Peretti (1992).
- View Clip 2: "Afro-Cuban Jazz Suite" (Ronald Becerra Ronnie Beck, 2021) [8:45 min.].
- Primary Source reading: "(1724) Black Code of Louisiana" (n.d.).
- Completion of graphic organizer/position statement
- Hollywood or history? conclusion/summary/extension

Sparking Strategy/Warm-Up

Sparking Strategy (Lesson introduction)

1. Deliver and discuss the context of the question on the Worksheet:
   – Define a *regional culture*.
   – Who am I? What happened in my past? How am I connected to my past?
   – Think about types of global connections. How do ideas spread between societies in today's interconnected world?
   – Does today's interconnected world result in change in societies?
   – How does culture accommodate new ideas and beliefs?
   – Reflect on the relation among benefits and problems of global interdependence and the likely perspective that people in different parts of the world might have on those benefits and problems.

Lesson Procedures

In a numerical list, provide a step by step outline of what you plan to do in the lesson. Include questions you will ask the students and materials you will use.

Outline

Part 1

1. Introduce "Hollywood or History?" graphic organizer and deliver worksheet. Students will be asked to read the Appendix sources to reach knowledge of the film wherein the clips are taken from. It is expected that this will provide fundamentals of the use of films in educative situations and of the nature (documentary, musical, European) of the film *Calle 54* (2000). Secondly, the questions included in the worksheet will prompt them into the kind of informational discussion that will help them to successfully accomplish the lesson tasks.

2. View Clip 1 (Don Quixote, 2019, 6:45 min.). It covers a picture of those singing, dancing, and handed-play drums. The scene is focused on migrated rhythm and harmonies that illustrate Afro-American religious immaterial patrimony. With the guides that students have obtained by means of the graphic organizer document and Questions Worksheet, it is expected this first clip will lead them into the religious element of the images and sounds they are up to culturally experience.

3. Allow the students to examine questions from the Questions Worksheet: Who am I? What happened in my past? How am I connected to those in my past?

4. Offer students time for primary source reading—Orihuela (1852/2008) [included in Appendix]. It is extracted from the first anti-slavery novel that paid attention to the existence of free Black people in the colonial Caribbean society. Explore the historical account the leisure-time slaves participated in.

5. Allow the students to examine question from the Questions Worksheet: How do ideas spread between societies in today's interconnected world?

6. Offer students time for secondary source reading—Torriente (1946) [included in Appendix of Readings]. This secondary source is included as a bridge between the previous historical information and establishes a relation between the previous societies that had lived at least one century ago in the Caribbean.

7. Completion of graphic organizer. Have the students compare and contrast the sources complemented by the Appendix and the graphic organizer questions. This is to examine the three selected sources competence for teaching and learning History of World Religions in their respective textboxes.
8. Line of Contention. The line of contention will present a discussion that will put all the materials together regarding their connection to contemporary cultural expectations.

Part 2

1. Pose question to the students, review from Part 1: "What do we mean by the phrase *regional culture?*" Continue to use the Questions Worksheet. Have students focus again on the topic of the importance of art, dance, and music to a culture.
2. Offer students time for Secondary Source reading—Peretti (1992). This second Secondary Source comes to introduce that meeting of elements to students. It is expected to also prepare them to better understand the context of Clip 2 (Ronald Becerra Ronnie Beck, 2021).
3. Clip 2 (Ronald Becerra Ronnie Beck, 2021, 8:45 min.) showcases a big band that demonstrates common instrumentation and interpretative musical style of Latin-American and North American continental Jazz. Orchestral formation like this successfully introduced White audiences—in the decades of the thirties and forties—into an African hybrid atmosphere at performing in dancing halls. This clip will help students appreciate the common instrumental and interpretative corpus of Jazz, in order to rightly accomplish a concept that resulted in the consolidation of the *Latin thing* in the sixties.
4. Offer students time for Primary Source reading—*(1724) Black Code of Louisiana* (n.d.). The regulation on treatment of the slavery was widespread. The code brought here in the lesson goes back to the colonial period of North America, when the French Empire stated this normativity to rule over Caribbean colonies and New Orleans. Explore with students how the language of the code treated the slaves.
5. Continue with the Questions Worksheet question: "How does today's interconnected world result in change in societies?" Allow students to research and explore how art, dance, and music have shaped the way cultural intersections created regional cultures and cultural identities.
6. Allow students time to complete the graphic organizer/position statement.
7. Hollywood or History? conclusion. Allow the students time to reflect on the "Hollywood or History?" graphic organizer: "What historic aspects are reflected in the sources?"; "Does the source accurately reflect the reality that it claims to be a portrait of?"

Differentiation

Think about your students' skill levels, intelligences, and learning styles. How are you going to make this lesson meet the needs of all of your students?

Scaffolds: Work with students individually, if needed, to answer questions and further explain any material. Make sure that the student table groups have mixed students so that higher achieving students are working with/helping their classmates.

ESL Interventions: Provide vocabulary terms pertaining to the cultural regions explored with African cultures with useful synonyms and definitions/description in order to give students background knowledge and vocabulary help as they move through the lesson itself. Consider selecting among the sources with images, or finding additional documents, from the source collections provided.

Extensions: Have students write a letter or make a video telling a younger student about the complexities, the potential biases and inaccuracies found in history and films and what they should do to be better informed about historical figures and events that are portrayed in movies regarding slavery and cultural arts and music.

Summarizing Strategies/Synthesizing Activity

What strategies are you going to use to allow students to summarize what they learned in the lesson?

- Line of Contention
- Roundtable Discussion (Part 1)
- "Hollywood or History?" graphic organizer and worksheets

References

Are there any additional resources that might be relevant to your lesson? Are there sources that you need to reference? Please add any citations using APA.

Don Quixote. (2019, January 13). *Puntilla & Nueva Generación—Compa Galletano* [YouTube video]. https://www.youtube.com/watch?v=sM4ExKI_j_8

Hernández, M. (2008). *El sol de Jesús del Monte. Novela de costumbres Cubanas.* Ediciones Idea.

(1724) Louisiana's Code Noir | (1724) Black Code of Louisiana (n.d.). [Primary documents]. https://www.blackpast.org/african-american-history/louisianas-code-noir-1724/

Orihuela, A. A. (2008). *El Sol de Jesús del Monte: Novela de Costumbres Cubanas.* Editores J. Boix y Cª. (Original work published 1852)

Peretti, B. W. (1992). *The creation of Jazz: Music, race, and culture in urban America.* University of Illinois Press.

Ronald Becerra Ronnie Beck. (2021, September 6). *Aftro Cuban jazz suite—Chico O'Farrill* [YouTube video]. https://www.youtube.com/watch?v=bbJIYQErTHE

Torriente, L. (1946). *La Habana de Cecilia Valdés (siglo XIX).* Habana: J. Montero.

Additional Resources

Brodd, J. (2015). *World religions: A voyage of discovery, 4th ed.* Saint Mary's Press.

Chiorazzi, A. (2015). The spirituality of Africa. *Harvard Gazette.* https://news.harvard.edu/gazette/story/2015/10/the-spirituality-of-africa/

New World Encyclopedia. (n.d.). *Music of Africa.* https://www.newworldencyclopedia.org/entry/Music_of_Africa

Hollywood or History?
Calle 54 (2000)

Calle 54 (2000) is a film that explores the genre of music called jazz. Jazz finds its cultural roots from the African experience of global struggle. Students will explore how the film portrays historical cultural identity and how that compares to various Primary and Secondary Sources from the similar historical context.

Evaluate each source provided and summarize your analysis below. In the section located at the bottom of the page, explain whether you think these scenes from *Calle 54* (2000) should be considered as accurate accounts of history, pure Hollywood, or a mixture of both. Use examples from your sources/documents to explain your answer.

Primary Source	*Calle 54* (2000)	Secondary Source
What Do You Think? Hollywood or History?		

Hollywood or History?
Calle 54 (2000) Questions Worksheet

Name: _____

Class: _____

Date: _____

Due: _____

Questions for Individual Reflection

1. Define a regional culture.

2. Who am I?

3. What happened in my past?

4. How am I connected to events in my past?

Questions for Reflection on Global Connections and Identities

5. How do ideas spread between societies in today's interconnected world?

6. Does today's interconnected world result in change in societies?

7. How does culture accommodate new ideas and beliefs?

8. Reflect on the relation among benefits and problems of global interdependence and the likely perspective that people in different parts of the world might have on those benefits and problems.

Hollywood or History?
Calle 54 (2000) Appendix of Readings

Part 1

Primary Source (Orihuela, 1852/2008):

> The scene I never missed was that one that the blacks performed every evening Sundays near their sleeping-place; that wild dance they focus to, by the rhythm of a kind of drum, which they produce a grey rhythmic from, accompanied by an instrument called *marino bola*, or by another one based-on a bow and a tight string, whose extreme get close the mouth as they hit the string with a stick that produces a sad and monotone sound, which they usually chorus in the language of the nation of musician belong to, and scandal they broke through-in and the strange movements of dancers look more the meeting of hungry haunting animals at the time of competing for the capture, than rational beings. And so they get such a psycho-alibi, that they forget their misfortune existence at the time they enjoy what is their only allowed leisure time.
>
> Same instruments are played by *mandingas, congos, carabalíes papá,* the *carabalíes viví, lucumíes,* next to many other nations they belong to; with their characteristic dancing, with their gesture and non-politic mimics that are impossible to describe, with their mocking music, hell noisy; and as the leisure time is up with the sundown, fatigued and sweaty, they go into sleeping-place and lay down, awaiting a new dawn, to go on with the hard working stuff of every non festive days..." (pp. 224–225)
>
> **Texto original:** A la escena que no faltaba nunca, era a la que ofrecía la negrada en las tardes de los domingos cerca de sus barracones, en esa clase de baile salvaje a que se entregan a compás de una especie de tambora, de la que sacan una cadencia fúnebre que acompañan con un instrumento que llaman *marino bola*, o con otro que se compone de un arco y una cuerda tirante, del que un extremo se acercan a la boca, mientras hieren la cuerda con una varita y da un sonido triste y monótono que suelen corear en la lengua de la nación a que pertenecen los músicos, y la algazara en que prorrumpen y los movimientos extraños de los que danzan, visto a distancia, más parece una reunión de fieras en el momento de disputarse la presa, en que van a saciar el hambre que las devora, que seres racionales. Y esa diversión favorita de los negros, los embriaga de tal manera, que en los momentos en que la gozan olvidan todas las penalidades de la miserable existencia que arrastran. En los mismos instrumentos alternan los mandingas, los congos, los carabalíes papá, y los carabalíes viví, los lucumíes, y otra multitud de naciones distintas a que pertenecen; con sus bailes característicos, con sus gestos y pantomimas groseras e imposibles de describir, con sus músicas grotescas, ruidosas e infernales; y cuando suena la campaña del batey, puesto ya el sol, entrasen fatigados y llenos de sudor en sus respectivas habitaciones para levantarse con la aurora y volver a la pesada faena de los días no festivos...

Secondary Source (Torriente, 1946):

> Hours of labour and rest of the slaves were regulated, as well as days off and joy. If the former were unavoidable duties for them, the latter had also an obligatory character, so to owners as to slaves, who had to celebrate Sundays and religious festivities by dancing and drums. These days were called "días de table.
>
> [...]
>
> Dancing and "días de table" were consequently the only joy allowed to slaves. Nevertheless, this spiritual relief was not discovered by blacks in America, but it was an imported costume by

them..." Power of music—Israel Castellanos says (1927)—and inspired dancing on African spirit in captivity were a costume well known by slavers, who permitted to affected and nostalgic—even compelled them by mean of the whip—to sing and dance on board [during the trip]. Favourite entertainment of blacks—singing and rhythm—was this way ratified both in the sea as in land.

[...]

From their African land they brought the language, the fetishism, the plastic arts, the dance, music, instruments they used in parties and in other traditions. This was that the music of drums took root in Cuba and that all their parties are expressed by these instruments, and dance got the sensual frenzy that has been the heritage of characteristic Cuban dance: la Rumba.

The blacks used different musical instruments in their festivities, such as drums, maracas, marimbula, and others. But drums—very primitive and their preferred one—were the symbol of the "día de table." (pp. 91–93)

Texto original: Los esclavos tenían reglamentadas las horas de labor y descanso, así como los días de recreo y diversión. Si los unos eran deberes ineludibles para las dotaciones, los otros tenían también carácter obligatorio, tanto para los amos, como para los esclavos, quienes debían celebrar con baile e tambores los domingos y las festividades religiosas. Estos días eran conocidos por *días de tabla*... Era, pues, la única diversión lícita que tenía el esclavo, la del baile y los días de tabla. No fue, sin embargo, esta una expansión espiritual que los negros encontraron en América, sino que por el contrario fue una costumbre por ellos importada... "El poder de la música—dice Israel Castellanos—y el baile sobre el espíritu de los africanos cautivos, fue tan conocido por los esclavistas, que a los afligidos, a los nostálgicos, se les permitía cantar y bailar o se les constreñía—por medio del látigo—a hacerlo sobre cubierta. Así la diversión favorita de los negros, la música vocal y el ritmo, se sancionó en el mar como en la tierra... Importaron los negros desde su tierra africana, el lenguaje, el fetichismo, las artes plásticas, el baile, la música, los instrumentos que usaban en las fiestas y otras tradiciones. Fue por esto que la música de tambores enraizó en el suelo cubano y que las fiestas todas de la negrada se expresaban por medio de estos instrumentos, a cuyo compás el baile alcanzó ese frenesí sensual que ha sido la herencia del baile típico cubano: la rumba. Los negros, en sus festividades, hacían uso de variados instrumentos musicales, como los tambores, las maracas, la *marímbula* y otros. Pero el verdadero símbolo del día de tabla eran los tambores, instrumento muy primitivo y el preferido por los negros."

Part 2

Secondary Source (Peretti, 1992):

Music and dance were interwoven with African religion and its American adaptations. West African religions integrated spirit love, possession rites, communal gathering, singing, dancing and the playing of instruments elements impossible to disassociate from another. Drums housed specific spirits and dances represented them... Most distinctly, the music was highly rhythmic, the contribution of the drums and of its symbiotic relation to dance. As dance brought all kinds of villagers together, this diversity was represented in the polyrhythms of drummers and clappers, the complex interviewing of pulses which Western listeners characterized as extreme 'syncopation'... The New Orleans experience presented challenges deriving from slavery, plantation life, racial classification, and the Afro-Caribbean heritage, which especially stimulated the growth of the instrumental blues... By 1917, New Orleans signified, among other things, a conjunction of rural and urban culture, Africa and Europe, individual skill and communal fraternizing, Protestant and Creole sensibilities and the violent past and an encouraging future. Jazz's meaning as the art of the urbanizing African American would become even more significant as large numbers of Southern blacks moved North, during the Great Migration of the coming decade. (Peretti, 1992, pp. 12–38)

Primary Source (1724) Black Code of Louisiana (n.d.):

   I. Decrees the expulsion of Jews from the colony.
   II. Makes it imperative on masters to impart religious instruction to their slaves.
   III. Permits the exercise of the Roman Catholic creed only. Every other mode of worship is prohibited.
   IV. Negroes placed under the direction or supervision of any other person than a Catholic are liable to confiscation.
   V. Sundays and holidays are to be strictly observed. All negroes found at work on these days are to be confiscated.

[. . .]

In the name of the King,

Bienville, De la Chaise.

Fazende, Bruslé, Perry, March, 1724.

Exorcism, Healings, and Mercy: The Role of the Holy Fool and Prophet in *The Island*

Thomas E. Malewitz

FILM: *The Island* (2006) [English subtitled]

Grade	Subject	Topic
11–12	Orthodox Christianity; Judaism	Understanding Prophetic Healing and Exorcisms

Chapter Theme	Estimated Time Needed for Lesson
Rituals: Prophecy, Exorcism, Miracles, Healing	45 minutes

National Association for Media Literacy Education

Standard Number	Detailed Description of Each Standard You Are Discussing

Core Principles of Media Literacy Education in the United States	4. Media Literacy Education (MLE) develops informed, reflective, and engaged participants essential for a democratic society.
	
	Implications for Practice
	    4.4 MLE invites and respects diverse points of view.
	    4.5 MLE explores representations, misrepresentations, and lack of representation of cultures and countries in the global community.
	
	6. MLE affirms that people use their individual skills, beliefs, and experiences to construct their own meanings from media messages.
	
	Implications for Practice
	    6.1 MLE is not about teaching students what to think; it is about teaching them how they can arrive at informed choices that are most consistent with their own values.

State and USCCB Standard Description

State	Detailed Description of Each Standard You Are Discussing
Michigan Civics	**C—6.4.3** Identify and describe a local, state, national, or international public policy issue; research and evaluate multiple solutions; analyze the consequences of each solution and propose, defend, and take relevant action to address or resolve the issue. *Considerations for analyzing credible sources may include but are not limited to:* logical validity, factual accuracy and/or omission, emotional appeal, unstated assumptions, logical fallacies, inconsistencies, distortions, appeals to bias or prejudice, and overall strength of argument.
New York Global History and Geography II	**10.8 Tensions Between Traditional Cultures and Modernization:** Tensions exist between traditional cultures and agents of modernization. Reactions for and against modernization depend on perspective and context. 10.8a Cultures and countries experience and view modernization differently. For some, it is a change from a traditional rural, agrarian condition to a secular, urban, industrial condition. Some see modernization as a potential threat and others as an opportunity to be met.
United States Conference of Catholic Bishops (USCCB) Curriculum Framework	
USCCB.V Sacraments— III.B.1c.1-6	Understanding the role and theology of healing in the Church: 1) Illness (CCC, nos. 1500–1502) 2) Christ the physician (CCC, no. 1503) 3) Faith and healing (CCC, no. 1504) 4) Christ's suffering (CCC, no. 1505) 5) Disciples carry cross (CCC, no. 1506) 6) Holy Spirit's gift of healing (CCC, no. 1509)
USCCB.Option V Ecumenical and Interreligious Issues V.B.1-4	*Interreligious Dialogue* There are many forms of interreligious dialogue. The dialogue of shared spiritual experience. Such dialogue requires mutual search for truth among those learned in their own religious traditions. Requires respect and understanding of differences in culture as well as in belief. Requires training in accurate knowledge of other religions.

NCSS C3 Framework

Dimension	Detailed Description of Each NCSS Dimension You Are Incorporating (should have all four).
D1.2.9-12	Explain points of agreement and disagreement experts have about interpretations and applications of disciplinary concepts and ideas associated with a compelling question.
D2.His.5.9-12	Analyze how historical contexts shaped and continue to shape people's perspectives.
D3.3.9-12	Identify evidence that draws information directly and substantively from multiple sources to detect inconsistencies in evidence in order to revise or strengthen claims.
D4.1.9-12	Construct arguments using precise and knowledgeable claims, with evidence from multiple sources, while acknowledging counterclaims and evidentiary weaknesses.

NCSS Core Themes and Description

Theme Number	Detailed Description of Each Aligned NCSS Theme
II Time, Continuity, and Change	Studying the past makes it possible for us to understand the human story across time. Historical analysis enables us to identify continuities over time in core institutions, values, ideals, and traditions, as well as processes that lead to change within societies and institutions, and that result in innovation and the development of new ideas, values, and ways of life.
V Individuals, Groups and Institutions	Social studies programs should include experiences that provide for the study of interactions among individuals, groups, and institutions.
VI Power, Authority and Governance	Social studies programs should include experiences that provide for the study of how people create, interact with, and change structures of power, authority, and governance.

Chapter 4: Rituals ■ **143**

Handouts/Materials/Web Links

Handout/Materials:

- "Hollywood or History?" graphic organizer

Web Links:

A. Film Clip(s):
   - *The Island* (Lungin, 2006).
     A full version of the film can be found at:
     https://www.youtube.com/watch?v=Wz-vegualMg (Sergey Korsakov, 2016)
     - Clip to be used for this lesson: "The Exorcism Scene" (1:24:45–1:38:05)
B. Primary Source(s):
   - Mark 9:14–29
C. Secondary Source(s):
   - "The Holy Fool as a TV Hero: About Pavel Lungin's Film *The Island* and the Problem of Authenticity" (Bodin, 2011).

Guiding Questions

What should students know or understand at the completion of the unit or lesson?

Primary Questions:

- How can the notion of spiritual healing extend beyond the physical healings?
- Why can Jesus of Nazareth be identified as a divine healer?
- Why is it important to understand the wholeness of healing in a faith context?
- How does faith connect with healing in Scripture and prophetic actions?
- Why is mercy and forgiveness an important aspect of spiritual healing?

Important Vocabulary

List all of the important indicators of achievement (important people, places, and events) and vocabulary that students will need to know at the conclusion of the lesson.

Exorcism: the religious or spiritual practice of removing a demon from an individual.
Healing (religious context): restoring wholeness of body, mind, and spirit.
Holy Fool: A title or type applied to an individual who has given up all worldly possessions in severe dedication to following God. The term derives from Paul of Tarsus, "we are fools for Christ's sake…" (1 Corinthians 4:10).

Assessment Strategies

Describe the assessments that will be used during the unit.

Formative Assessment: Small group discussion, large group discussion

Summative Assessment: "Hollywood or History?" graphic organizer

Teaching Strategies

5 min	Warm-Up Activity	15 min	View/notes *The Island* (Lungin, 2006) clip	5 min	Read/compare/contrast/reflection essay
10 min	Read/discuss Mark 9:14–29	10 min	Small group discussion	Time Remaining/ HMWK	

Times are highly flexible and should be adjusted according to the number of sources used, length of introduction, period/block schedule, etc.

Sparking Strategy/Warm-Up

Sparking Strategy (Lesson introduction)

Introduce the concept of healing in contemporary culture. Ask the students to list types of doctors and the field of medicine/health care they work with. List the responses on the board. Help the students understand the difference between a general practitioner and specialist. Ask the students why medical specialists are needed. Allow students time to reflect and discuss. Offer students examples of medical specialists, if needed, to spark the conversation. Guide the students to think of specialists beyond physical medicine to include specialists for the mind, like psychologists and psychiatrists.

Lesson Procedures

In a numerical list, provide a step by step outline of what you plan to do in the lesson. Include questions you will ask the students and materials you will use.

Outline

1. Ask the students, "What type of specialists might individuals go to for spiritual needs or healing?" Allow students time to reflect and answer with supporting evidence (some answers might include a counselor or priest). Include ways in which the given examples would help the spiritual healing of an individual.
2. Have the students read Mark 9:14–29, and analyze the story to explore and explain why Jesus of Nazareth could be identified as a divine healer. Use questions such as: "How was the individual healed?"; "How did it make him whole?"; "Why was the individual healed?"; and "What role did faith play in the story?"
3. Define the term "exorcism" for the students. Ask students to share what they might know, or have heard, about the term (many students will be familiar with Hollywood portrayals such as in Horror films). Assist the students to understand that the concept of exorcism is not as theatrical as Horror films portray.
4. Explain and give context that the following film clip from *The Island* (Sergey Korsakov, 2016), offers a portrayal of an exorcism. The character, Father Anatoly, is depicted as a prophet in the film, or as Russian Othordox Christianity often labels a Holy Fool. Define "holy fool" for the students.
5. Play the film clip from *The Island* (Sergey Korsakov, 2016, 1:24:45–1:38:05 [15 mins]). Have the students take notes on the words or actions that occur in the film throughout the exorcism scene.

6. After the film clip, have the students compare their notes, in small groups. What did they see occur in the film? How did it relate to prayer or faith? What did Father Anatoly do? How did the young woman respond during and after the exorcism?
7. With the remaining time in class bring the discussion back to the large group. Have a student representative share some of the discussion points from their small group for the class as a whole.
8. For homework, have the students read Per-Arne Bodin's (2011) "The Holy Fool as a TV Hero: About Pavel Lungin's Film *The Island* and the Problem of Authenticity." Have the students analyze the article and compare with the notes that they had between the film clip and their small group discussion. Have the students write a reflection paper or article critique for their formative assessment on the topic.

Differentiation

Think about your students' skill levels, intelligences, and learning styles. How are you going to make this lesson meet the needs of all of your students?

Scaffolds: Work with students individually if needed to answer questions and further explain any material. Make sure that the student table groups have mixed students so that higher achieving students are working with/helping their classmates.

ESL Interventions: Provide vocabulary terms for students. The teacher should also stop the film clip periodically as the film is subtitled, to allow students the opportunity to ask questions or follow-up with the dialogue and context of the story.

Extensions: Have students research a project on additional exorcism miracles from the New Testament by Jesus, Paul, or Peter. Allow students to investigate the prayers associated with exorcisms and the importance of faith in the ritual.

Summarizing Strategies/Synthesizing Activity

What strategies are you going to use to allow students to summarize what they learned in the lesson?

- Analysis and critique of historical documents (Scripture) and film review
- Notetaking and small group discussion
- Large group discussion

References

Are there any additional resources that might be relevant to your lesson? Are there sources that you need to reference? Please add any citations using APA.

Lungin, P. (Director). (2006). *The Island* [Film]. Pavel Lungin's Studio. [Russia]
Bodin, P.-A. (2011). The holy fool as a TV hero: About Pavel Lungin's film *The Island* and the problem of authenticity. *Journal of Aesthetics & Culture, 3*(1), 63–65. https://doi.org/10.3402/jac.v3i0.6365
Sergey Korsakov. (2016, June 5). *The Island* (Russian movie with English subtitles) [YouTube video]. https://www.youtube.com/watch?v=Wz-vegualMg

Additional Resource

United States Conference of Catholic Bishops. (2000). *Catechism of the Catholic Church* (2nd ed.) Libreria Editrice Vaticana.

Hollywood or History?
The Island (2006)

The Island (2006) focuses on events surrounding a hermit, Father Anatoly, who lives in seclusion on an island in Russia. Over the course of the film, Father Anatoly is depicted as an exorcist, healer, and mysterious prophet.

Evaluate each source provided and summarize your observations and analysis in corresponding spaces provided. In the section located at the bottom of the page, explain whether you think *The Island* (2006) portrays an accurate account of a prophet and exorcist within the context of the given resources. Use examples from your primary and secondary sources to explain your answer.

Primary Source(s)	*The Island* (2006)	Secondary Source

What do you think? Hollywood or History?

Exploring the Egyptian Book of the Dead: Weighing of the Heart Ceremony

Thomas E. Malewitz

FILM: *The Ten Commandments* (1956)

Grade	Subject	Topic
7–12	Judaism; Egyptian mythology	Weighing of the Heart Ceremony: Comparing the Egyptian Book of the Dead and the Exodus Narrative

Chapter Theme	Estimated Time Needed for Lesson
Rituals: Egyptian, Exodus Narrative, Faith	Two class periods Part 1 (Introduce Topic/Start Project [55 minutes]) Part 2 (Complete Project/Discussion [55 minutes])

National Association for Media Literacy Education

Standard Number	Detailed Description of Each Standard You Are Discussing

Core Principles of Media Literacy Education in the United States	3. Media Literacy Education (MLE) builds and reinforces skills for learners of all ages. Like print literacy, those skills necessitate integrated, interactive, and repeated practice.
	
	Implications for Practice
	    3.3 MLE engages students with varied learning styles.
	    3.4 MLE is most effective when used with co-learning pedagogies, in which teachers learn from students and students learn from teachers and from classmates.

State and USCCB Standard Description

State	Detailed Description of Each Standard You Are Discussing
Kentucky (Grade 6) Development of Civilizations	**6.I.CC.3** Evaluate how individuals and groups addressed local, regional, and global problems throughout the development of civilizations.
Civics	**6.C.PR.1** Analyze the purposes and effects of laws in River Valley Civilizations and Classical Empires between 3500 BCE–600 CE.
Michigan (Grade 7) Growth and Development of World Religions	**W3.2.1** Identify and describe the core beliefs of major world religions and belief systems, including Hinduism, Judaism, Buddhism, Christianity, Confucianism, Sikhism, and Islam. *Examples may include, but are not limited to:* comparing major figures, sacred texts, and basic beliefs (ethnic vs. universalizing; monotheistic vs. polytheistic) among religions; case studies of continuity of local indigenous belief systems or animistic religions; comparisons with religious traditions that developed after 1500 CE such as Protestantism.
Illinois High School Social Studies	**SS.H.1.9-12** Evaluate how historical developments were shaped by time and place as well as broader historical contexts
	SS.H.2.9-12 Analyze change and continuity within and across historical eras
	SS.H.3.9-12 Evaluate the methods utilized by people and institutions to promote change
United States Conference of Catholic Bishops (USCCB) Curriculum Framework	*Doctrinal Elements of a Curriculum Framework for the Development of Catechetical Materials for Young People of High School Age* (2008)
USCCB.I Revelation of God—VI.C.2	The Bible has a definite historic basis for events recounted in both the Old and the New Testaments
USCCB.Option A Sacred Scripture— II.C.1-3	Analyze the Book of Exodus: Prominence and the call of Moses; divine liberation from slavery to freedom.
USCCB.Option A Sacred Scripture— VI.A.1-3	Recognize the purpose of a prophet: To interpret signs of the times in light of covenant; Afflict the comfortable and comfort the afflicted; Understand that prophesies (and works) were medicinal, meant to convert listeners to God.

NCSS C3 Framework

Dimension	Detailed Description of Each NCSS Dimension You Are Incorporating (should have all four).
D1.2.9-12	Explain points of agreement and disagreement experts have about interpretations and applications of disciplinary concepts and ideas associated with a compelling question.
D2.His.5.9-12	Analyze how historical contexts shaped and continue to shape people's perspectives.
D3.3.9-12	Identify evidence that draws information directly and substantively from multiple sources to detect inconsistencies in evidence in order to revise or strengthen claims.
D4.1.9-12	Construct arguments using precise and knowledgeable claims, with evidence from multiple sources, while acknowledging counterclaims and evidentiary weaknesses.

NCSS Core Themes and Description

Theme Number	Detailed Description of Each Aligned NCSS Theme
II Time, Continuity, and Change	Studying the past makes it possible for us to understand the human story across time. Historical analysis enables us to identify continuities over time in core institutions, values, ideals, and traditions, as well as processes that lead to change within societies and institutions, and that result in innovation and the development of new ideas, values, and ways of life.
V Individuals, Groups and Institutions	Social studies programs should include experiences that provide for the study of interactions among individuals, groups, and institutions.
VI Power, Authority and Governance	Social studies programs should include experiences that provide for the study of how people create, interact with, and change structures of power, authority, and governance.

Handouts/Materials/Web Links

Handout/Materials:
- "Hollywood or History?" graphic organizer
- "Hollywood or History?" project directions/rubric

Web Links:

A. Link to Film Clip(s):
   - *The Ten Commandments* (DeMille, 1956) [~10 mins total]
     Disc 2: 17:00–23:30 & 37:52–39:06
   - "The Weighing of the Heart" (n.d.) [2 mins]
     https://www.metmuseum.org/metmedia/video/collections/egyptian/weighing-of-the-heart

B. Primary Source(s):
   - Exodus 7:13–11:10 (the section is of interest as the language switches from Pharaoh hardening his heart to the LORD hardening Pharaoh's heart beginning in Exodus 9:12)

C. Secondary Source(s):
   - "Ancient Egyptian Burial" (Mark, 2013)
     https://www.worldhistory.org/Egyptian_Burial/
   - "The Egyptian Afterlife & the Feather of Truth (Mark, 2018)
     https://www.worldhistory.org/article/42/the-egyptian-afterlife--the-feather-of-truth
   - *Book of the Dead: Becoming God in Ancient Egypt* (Scarf, 2017)
     https://oi.uchicago.edu/museum-exhibits/book-dead

Guiding Questions

What should students know or understand at the completion of the unit or lesson?

Primary Questions:

- Explain ways of interpreting the phrase "God hardened Pharaoh's heart," as stated in passages like: Exodus 9:12, 10:20, 10:27, and 11:10.
- How might the Weighing of the Heart ceremony from the *Egyptian Book of the Dead* (Scarf, 2017) have connection to the narrative of the 10 plagues from the Book of Exodus?
- How does the phrase "God hardened Pharaoh's heart" illustrate to the Israelites that the LORD has spiritual power over the Egyptian gods?

Important Vocabulary

List all of the important indicators of achievement (important people, places, and events) and vocabulary that students will need to know at the conclusion of the lesson.

Egyptian Book of the Dead: An Egyptian ceremonial book that contains rituals/spells used as funerary rites in Egypt.

Imhotep: A priest of Egypt from the 27th BC, who later was worshiped as a deity by the Egyptian people.

Weighing of the Heart: An Egyptian ceremony to determine if an Egyptian will live with the gods after their death.

Assessment Strategies

Describe the assessments that will be used during the unit.

Formative Assessment: Video clips, lecture, and group discussion

Summative Assessment: Project and/or presentation of group project

Teaching Strategies (Day 1)

15 min	Discussion/ introduce Egyptian funerary rituals (Mark, 2013, 2018)	15 min	Primary Sources and Secondary Source analysis	Time Remaining/ HMWK	Group Project
5 min	Discuss/view clips from: "Weighing of the Heart" (n.d.)	10 min	Discuss/view clips from: *Ten Commandments* (DeMille, 1956)		

Times are highly flexible and should be adjusted according to the number of sources used, length of introduction, period/block schedule, etc.

Teaching Strategies (Day 2)

35 min	Group work on project
15 min	Discussion of project and/or presentations of projects

Times are highly flexible and should be adjusted according to the number of sources used, length of introduction, period/block schedule, etc.

Lesson Procedures

In a numerical list, provide a step by step outline of what you plan to do in the lesson. Include questions you will ask the students and materials you will use.

Outline

1. Introduce the unit by discussing Egyptian funerary rituals/mummification, using Mark's (2013, 2018) articles for description, as needed.
2. View the "Weighing of the Heart" (n.d.) clip (5 min).
3. Briefly discuss the weighing of the heart process with time for student questions.
4. Explain the context of the Pharaoh, Moses, and the 10 Plagues.
5. Read passages from Exodus 7:13–11:10; especially the context of Exodus 9:12, Exodus 10:20, Exodus 10:27, and Exodus 11:10.
6. View the *Ten Commandments* (DeMille, 1956).

7. Discuss how in the *Ten Commandments* (DeMille, 1956) Pharaoh blames Nefertiti (his wife) for his stubbornness and hardened heart.
8. Transition the conversation to the group project assignment.
9. Introduce the expectations of the project.
10. After students are in groups, allow students to use their iPad/device to research information on the weighing of the heart ceremony and the Egyptian gods associated with the ceremony.
11. Check on the progress of the group projects and answer any questions.
12. After the projects are completed (on Day 2), collect the projects through email/uploaded file or have the students present their research findings for the class.

Differentiation

Think about your students' skill levels, intelligences, and learning styles. How are you going to make this lesson meet the needs of all of your students?

Extensions: The project could be presented by the student-groups as a presentation for a written and verbal assessment of research and knowledge of the topic.

Summarizing Strategies/Synthesizing Activity

What strategies are you going to use to allow students to summarize what they learned in the lesson?

- Research project
- Group presentation (optional)

References

Are there any additional resources that might be relevant to your lesson? Are there sources that you need to reference? Please add any citations using APA.

DeMille, C. B. (Director). (1956). *The Ten Commandments* [Film]. Paramount.
Kay, K., & Greenhill, V. (2012). *Leader's guide to 21st century education: 7 steps for schools and districts.* Pearson.
Mark, J. J. (2013, January 19). Ancient Egyptian burial. *World History Encyclopedia.* https://www.worldhistory.org/Egyptian_Burial/
Mark, J. J. (2018, March 30). The Egyptian afterlife & the feather of truth. *World History Encyclopedia.* https://www.worldhistory.org/article/42/the-egyptian-afterlife-the-feather-of-truth/
Scarf, F. (Ed.). (2017). *Book of the dead: Becoming god in ancient Egypt.* University of Chicago.
The Weighing of the Heart. (n.d.). *Visiting the Met?* https://www.metmuseum.org/metmedia/video/collections/egyptian/weighing-of-the-heart

Additional Resources

Currid, J. D. (1993). Why did God harden Pharaoh's heart? *The Bible Review, 9*(6), 46–47. https://www.baslibrary.org/bible-review/9/6/13
Monreal, T., & Varga, B. A. (2021). Representing ancient Egypt(ians)/visual mediums and public perception. In S. Roberts & C. Elfer (Eds.), *Hollywood or history?: An inquiry-based strategy for using film to teach World History* (pp. 67–79). Information Age Publishing.

Hollywood or History?
The Ten Commandments (1956)

The Ten Commandments (1956) focuses on the events surrounding the Book of Exodus and the life of Moses. Over the course of the film, Egyptian culture is portrayed and explored as a contrast to the developing Jewish religion.

Evaluate each source provided and summarize your observations and analysis in corresponding spaces provided. In the section located at the bottom of the page, explain whether you think scenes from *The Ten Commandments* (1956) should be evaluated as an accurate account of Egyptian culture within the context of the given resources. Use examples from your primary and secondary sources to explain your answer.

Primary Source(s)	*The Ten Commandments* (1956)	Secondary Source(s)

What do you think? Hollywood or History?

Hollywood or History?
The Ten Commandments (1956) Weighing the Heart Ceremony

Name(s): _____
_____
_____
_____

Due:
80 points (slides/information)

Your quest is:

Create a 10 slide Powerpoint/Keynote/Google Slides to explore the Weighing of the Heart ceremony of Ancient Egypt

Use your notes, Powerpoints and/or book, and internet to research and offer information about the Weighing of the Heart Ceremony in Ancient Egypt. Include information about the following Egyptian gods in your presentation: Osiris, Horus, Ma'at, Anubis, Thoth, and Ammut/Ammit.

Expectations:

Context: List, define, and explain the process of the weighing of the heart ceremony and all 6 of the Egyptian gods mentioned above

References: 5 credible references in MLA Style

Evidence: (at least) 3 direct quotations about the ceremony

Creativity: (at least) 6 to 8 pictures in context and description.

(*Hint:* Be sure to include a title and works-cited slide which includes Scripture citations and all references.)

Here are a few places to start your research:
- Exodus 9:2–11:10
- https://www.metmuseum.org/metmedia/video/collections/egyptian/weighing-of-the-heart
- https://www.egyptian-scarabs.co.uk/weighing_of_the_heart.htm
- https://www.ancient.eu/article/42/the-egyptian-afterlife–the-feather-of-truth/

Project Rubric

Grade: _____ / 80   Name(s)

1. Context				
Biographical information: clear information about the ceremony and the Egyptian gods	A—20 points	B—15 points	C—10 points	D—5 points

2. Scriptural connections				
Synthesize and *make connections* between the ceremony and Scripture	A—20 points	B—15 points	C—10 points	D—5 points

3. Evidence				
Clear supporting evidence about the ceremony	A—20 points	B—15 points	C—10 points	D—5 points
Adhered to stated Expectations: as stated above	A—10 points	B—7 points	C—5 points	D—2 points

4. Organization for presentation				
Mechanics—spelling, proper designations, clear	A—5 points	B—4 points	C—3 points	D—2 points

5. References				
Proper references, not just copy/pasting ULRs	A—5 points	B—4 points	C—3 points	D—2 points

Adapted from essay rubric template resources Kay, K. and Greenhill, V. Pearson Education, Inc. 2012.

The Camino de Santiago: Pilgrimage as a Devotion of Cultural Awareness and Personal Renewal

Thomas E. Malewitz

FILM: *The Way* (2010)

Grade	Subject	Topic
9–12	Christianity; Islam	Understanding the Purpose and Power of Pilgrimage

Chapter Theme	Estimated Time Needed for Lesson
Rituals: Pilgrimage, Devotions	45 mins.

National Association for Media Literacy Education

Standard Number	Detailed Description of Each Standard You Are Discussing
Core Principles of Media Literacy Education in the United States	4. Media Literacy Education (MLE) develops informed, reflective, and engaged participants essential for a democratic society. *Implications for Practice* 4.4 MLE invites and respects diverse points of view. 4.5 MLE explores representations, misrepresentations, and lack of representation of cultures and countries in the global community. 6. MLE affirms that people use their individual skills, beliefs, and experiences to construct their own meanings from media messages. *Implications for Practice* 6.1 MLE is not about teaching students what to think; it is about teaching them how they can arrive at informed choices that are most consistent with their own values.

State and USCCB Standard Description

State	Detailed Description of Each Standard You Are Discussing
Illinois High School Social Studies: Geography	**SS.G.9.9-12** Describe and explain the characteristics that constitute a particular culture. **SS.G.10.9-12** Explain how and why culture shapes worldview.
Michigan High School World History and Geography	**F1 World Historical and Geographical Inquiry and Literacy Practices** Explain and use disciplinary processes and tools from world history. These processes and tools include but are not limited to: contextualizing evidence and historical phenomena under study; explaining and applying different periodization schemes; using and connecting different spatial frames (examples may include but are not limited to global, interregional, regional); recognizing that perspectives are shaped by different experiences across time and space; sourcing, analyzing, and corroborating multiple sources of evidence (examples may include but are not limited to primary and secondary; verbal and visual; in print, three-dimensional, and digital); and using spatial reasoning to evaluate the role of human–environment interactions in history.
New York Global History and Geography II	**10.8 Tensions Between Traditional Cultures and Modernization:** Tensions exist between traditional cultures and agents of modernization. Reactions for and against modernization depend on perspective and context. 10.8a Cultures and countries experience and view modernization differently. For some, it is a change from a traditional rural, agrarian condition to a secular, urban, industrial condition. Some see modernization as a potential threat and others as an opportunity to be met.
United States Conference of Catholic Bishops (USCCB) Curriculum Framework	*Doctrinal Elements of a Curriculum Framework for the Development of Catechetical Materials for Young People of High School Age* (2008)
USCCB.OptionB History of the Catholic Church— II.9.C.2	Understanding the role of pilgrimage as devotion for spiritual reflection and personal renewal.

158 ▪ Hollywood or History?

USCCB.Option V Ecumenical and Interreligious Issues—V.B.1-4	Interreligious Dialogue There are many forms of interreligious dialogue. The dialogue of shared spiritual experience. Such dialogue requires mutual search for truth among those learned in their own religious traditions. Requires respect and understanding of differences in culture as well as in belief. Requires training in accurate knowledge of other religions.

NCSS C3 Framework

Dimension	Detailed Description of Each NCSS Dimension You Are Incorporating (should have all four).
D1.2.9-12	Explain points of agreement and disagreement experts have about interpretations and applications of disciplinary concepts and ideas associated with a compelling question.
D2.His.5.9-12	Analyze how historical contexts shaped and continue to shape people's perspectives.
D3.3.9-12	Identify evidence that draws information directly and substantively from multiple sources to detect inconsistencies in evidence in order to revise or strengthen claims.
D4.1.9-12	Construct arguments using precise and knowledgeable claims, with evidence from multiple sources, while acknowledging counterclaims and evidentiary weaknesses.

NCSS Core Themes and Description

Theme Number	Detailed Description of Each Aligned NCSS Theme
II Time, Continuity, and Change	Studying the past makes it possible for us to understand the human story across time. Historical analysis enables us to identify continuities over time in core institutions, values, ideals, and traditions, as well as processes that lead to change within societies and institutions, and that result in innovation and the development of new ideas, values, and ways of life.
V Individuals, Groups and Institutions	Social studies programs should include experiences that provide for the study of interactions among individuals, groups, and institutions.

Handouts/Materials/Web Links

Handout/Materials:
- "Hollywood or History?" graphic organizer
- "Hollywood or History?" project directions/rubric

Web Links:
A. Link to Film Clip(s):
   - *The Way* (Estevez, 2010)
   - "The Way—Movie Trailer (2011) HD" (Rotten Tomatoes Trailers, 2011) [3 mins]
     https://www.youtube.com/watch?v=o5VZKWcgw6c
   - "The Way—Martin Sheen Interview" (Umbrella Entertainment, 2012) [9 mins]
     https://www.youtube.com/watch?v=PH077E5FAfQ
   - "The Hajj: Islamic Sacred Pilgrimage" (n.d.) [5 mins]
     https://ket.pbslearningmedia.org/resource/sj14-soc-hajj/the-hajj-islamic-sacred-pilgrimage/

B. Secondary Source(s):
   - "How Has Camino Developed? Geographical and Historical Factors Behind the Creation and Development of the Way of St. James in Poland" (Mróz, 2017)
     https://www.researchgate.net/publication/319008252_How_Has_Camino_Developed_Geographical_and_Historical_Factors_behind_the_Creation_and_Development_of_the_Way_of_St_James_in_Poland

Guiding Questions

What should students know or understand at the completion of the unit or lesson?

Primary Questions:
- What is the purpose of a pilgrimage?
- What can an individual learn about their faith from a different culture?
- Why is travel important to broaden one's view of the world and global beliefs?
- How can a pilgrimage be a personal journey of change?

Important Vocabulary

List all of the important indicators of achievement (important people, places, and events) and vocabulary that students will need to know at the conclusion of the lesson.

El Camino de Santiago (the Way of St. James): a series of ancient pilgrimage networks leading to the shrine of St. James the Great in Spain.

Hajj: an annual pilgrimage to Mecca. A mandatory religious duty that Muslims must fulfill at least once in their lifetime, who are financially and physically capable.

Pilgrimage: a purposeful journey to a foreign land, usually for religious devotion or spiritual discipline or development.

Assessment Strategies

Describe the assessments that will be used during the unit.

Formative Assessment: Small group discussion and individual research

Summative Assessment: Research project

Teaching Strategies (Day 1)

5 min	Warm-Up Activity	15 min	View/notes/discuss: "*The Way*—Movie Trailer" (Rotten Tomatoes Trailers, 2011) and "The Way—Martin Sheen Interview" (Umbrella Entertainment, 2012) clip	5 min	Research project work until the conclusion of class and into homework
10 min	View/notes/discuss "The Hajj: Islamic Sacred Pilgrimage" (n.d.)	10 min	Small group discussion	Time Remaining/ HMWK	

Times are highly flexible and should be adjusted according to the number of sources used, length of introduction, period/block schedule, etc.

Sparking Strategy/Warm-Up

Sparking Strategy (Lesson introduction)

Ask the students about their favorite trip, or places that they have traveled. Have the student support why the chosen experiences were so important for them. List student answers on the board. Compare and contrast the student answers.

Lesson Procedures

In a numerical list, provide a step by step outline of what you plan to do in the lesson. Include questions you will ask the students and materials you will use.

Outline

1. Introduce the concept and spiritual devotion of pilgrimage. Define the term for the students. Explain that the concept of pilgrimage as devotion is an important aspect of major religions such as Christianity and Islam.
2. Introduce and define Hajj as one of the tenets of faith in Islam. Divide students into small groups and have them discuss why it would be important for a religion to have a law for pilgrimage.
3. Have the student groups take notes on the video clip "The Hajj: Islamic Sacred Pilgrimage" (n.d.) [5 mins]. Ask the students questions about the video clip and the

previous definition of pilgrimage and Hajj, such as "What reason do the pilgrims give for going on Hajj?" and "Do you think that the experience changed their perspective on their life or beliefs?"

4. Have the student groups take notes on the video clip "*The Way*—Movie Trailer (Rotten Tomatoes Trailers, 2011)" and "*The Way*—Martin Sheen Interview" (Umbrella Entertainment, 2012) clip [12 mins total].
5. Ask the students what similarities or differences were present between the video clips. Have the students work in groups to support the answers from their group work.
6. Introduce the research project assignment. Read the directions for the students and allow the students time to research materials for the project during the remaining class time.
7. Have the student-groups present their project for the class at the conclusion of the set time frame for their research, as assigned by the teacher.

Differentiation

Think about your students' skill levels, intelligences, and learning styles. How are you going to make this lesson meet the needs of all of your students?

Scaffolds: Work with students individually if needed to answer questions and further explain any material. Make sure that the student table groups have mixed students so that higher achieving students are working with/helping their classmates.

ESL Interventions: Provide vocabulary terms for students. The teacher should also stop the film clip periodically as the film is subtitled, to allow students the opportunity to ask questions or follow-up with the dialogue and context of the story.

Differentiation: Allow the students to write a research paper or record a video travel log for the research project instead of a presentation.

Summarizing Strategies/Synthesizing Activity

What strategies are you going to use to allow students to summarize what they learned in the lesson?

- Analysis and critique of video clips and film
- Notetaking and small group discussion
- Research project

References

Are there any additional resources that might be relevant to your lesson? Are there sources that you need to reference? Please add any citations using APA.

Estevez, E. (Director). (2010). *The Way*. Filmax Entertainment.

Kay, K., & Greenhill, V. (2012). *Leader's guide to 21st century education: 7 steps for schools and districts*. Pearson.

Mróz, F. (2017). How has Camino developed? Geographical and historical factors behind the creation and development of the way of St. James in Poland. In E. Alarcón & P. Roszak (Eds.), *The way of St. James: Renewing insights* (pp. 29–58). https://www.researchgate.net/publication/

319008252_How_Has_Camino_Developed_Geographical_and_Historical_Factors_behind_the_Creation_and_Development_of_the_Way_of_St_James_in_Poland

Rotten Tomatoes Trailers. (2011, August 22). *The way*—Movie trailer (2011) HD [YouTube video]. https://www.youtube.com/watch?v=o5VZKWcgw6c

The Hajj: Islamic Sacred Pilgrimage. (n.d.). PBS Learning Media. https://florida.pbslearningmedia.org/resource/sj14-soc-hajj/the-hajj-islamic-sacred-pilgrimage/

Umbrella Entertainment. (2012, February 12). *The way*—Martin Sheen interview [YouTube video]. https://www.youtube.com/watch?v=PH077E5FAfQ

Additional References

Bartholomew, C., & Hughes, F. (Eds.) (2016). *Explorations in a Christian theology of pilgrimage*. Routledge.

Caidi, N. (2019). Pilgrimage to Hajj: An information journey. *The International Journal of Information, Diversity, and Inclusion, 3*(1). https://doi.org/10.33137/ijidi.v3i1.32267

Oviedo, L., de Courcier, S., & Farias, M. (2014). Rise of pilgrims on the "Camino" to Santiago: Sign of change or religious revival? *Review of Religious Research, 56*(3), 433–442. https://www.jstor.org/stable/43186237

Chapter 4: Rituals ▪ **163**

Hollywood or History?
The Way (2010)

Directed by Emilio Esteves, *The Way* (2010) focused on the spiritual journey of pilgrimage. This film focused on the journey of Thomas Avery with his pain and emotional distress. Over the course of his experience the Camino de Santiago Mr. Avery experiences a passion that ends in a renewal of mind and spirit.

Evaluate each source provided and summarize your observations and analysis in corresponding spaces provided. In the section located at the bottom of the page, explain whether you think scenes from *The Way* (2010) should be evaluated as an accurate account of what it means to depict a pilgrimage, or spiritual journey, within the context of the given resources. Use examples from your primary and secondary sources to explain your answer.

Primary Source(s)	***The Way* (2010)**	**Secondary Source(s)**
What do you think? Hollywood or History?		

Hollywood or History?
The Way (2010)
Research Project

Name(s): _____
_____
_____
_____

Due:

80 points (slides/information)

Research and create a 10-slide Powerpoint/Keynote/Google Slides to explore the Camino de Santiago (the Way of St. James).

Use your notes, resources and/or textbook, and internet to research and offer information about the Camino de Santiago (the Way of St. James). Include information that explores, explains, and offers information about the one of the following ancient routes of the Camino:

- Camino Coastal
- Camino Frances
- Camino Norte
- Via de la Plata

Expectations:

Context: List, define, and explain the process of the Camino, including the number of days for the route, an estimated travel log between stops, and a rough itinerary of the pilgrimage (What would you expect to see? How much might it cost to travel? What types of food or lodging would be available?)

References: 5 credible references in MLA Style

Evidence: (at least) 3 direct quotations about the chosen Camino route

Creativity: (at least) 6 to 8 pictures in context and description

(*Hint:* Be sure to include a title and works-cited slide which includes all citations and references.)

Here are a few places to start your research:
- https://www.caminodesantiago.gal/en/inicio
- https://caminoways.com/the-ways-of-saint-james
- https://www.pilgrimagetraveler.com/way-of-st-james.html
- http://santiago-compostela.net/

Project Rubric

Grade: _____ / 80   Name(s)

1. Context				
Biographical information: clear information about the Camino route	A—20 points	B—15 points	C—10 points	D—5 points

2. Scriptural connections				
Synthesize and *make connections* between the concept of pilgrimage and the Camino	A—20 points	B—15 points	C—10 points	D—5 points

3. Evidence				
Clear supporting evidence	A—20 points	B—15 points	C—10 points	D—5 points
Adhered to stated Expectations: as stated above	A—10 points	B—7 points	C—5 points	D—2 points

4. Organization for presentation				
Mechanics—spelling, proper designations, clear	A—5 points	B—4 points	C—3 points	D—2 points

5. References				
Proper references, not just copy/pasting ULRs	A—5 points	B—4 points	C—3 points	D—2 points

Adapted from essay rubric template resources Kay, K. and Greenhill, V. Pearson Education, Inc. 2012.

CHAPTER 5

Wisdom Literature

Wisdom literature serves as a practical guide for living a good and sacred life. Many religions have a collection of writings to help believers live well and in the moral code of the religious expectation. Some of the wisdom literature seeks questions to the human condition like the books of Ecclesiastes and Job in Judaism, while other collections of wisdom writings search for peace and detachment such as the writing of the Buddha. This final chapter of *Hollywood or History? An Inquiry-Based Strategy for Teaching World Religions* explores three films that examine the importance of wisdom literature in the modern media context of storytelling through film.

The first lesson plan included in this chapter uses the multiple international award-winning short film *Admissions* (Kakatsakis, 2011)—starring James Cromwell—to raise thought provoking questions about heaven and the afterlife. Who will you meet in heaven? What is judgment in the afterlife based on? What limitations do our biases have during our life? Although these questions are easy for secondary students to reflect upon, these types of questions are found throughout religious canons. This film offers a conversation starter for a complicated topic from a tangible and real-life perspective to start a poignant conversation about who we really are, and who we label as our enemy.

The second lesson plan in this section is the comedy *Groundhog Day* (Ramis, 1993) starring Bill Murray. Buddhism teaches that in order to escape the wheel of rebirth known as samsara, following the Dharma of the Buddha is essential. The teachings focus on detachment from suffering and prescribing to the Noble Eightfold Path. Directed by the late Harold Ramis, *Groundhog Day* (Ramis, 1993) centers around the egotistical Phil Connors and how his irreverent speech and actions play a role in trapping him in the cycle of samsara as he is living Groundhog Day over and over again.

The final film included in this section is the international award-winning Iranian short film *Thursday Appointment* (Kheradmandan, 2019). Although only roughly 3 minutes in length, this beautiful and touching example of human charity exemplifies the challenge of bringing peace to a broken and violent world. Using the context of a Sufi poem by Hafez, the actions in the short film illustrate an open heart and willingness to offer that love to others. Much like stanzas from Proverbs or the challenge of finding serenity between one and nature in the writings of Rumi this film creates a conversation starter for secondary students to analyze human behaviors and compare and contrast their own responses in similar situations.

REFERENCES

Kakatsakis, H. (Director). (2011). *Admissions* [Film]. One Film Company. http://www.admissionsfilm.com

Kheradmandan, M. R. (Director). (2019). *Thursday Appointment* [Film]. Soureh.

Ramis, H. (Director). (1993). *Groundhog Day* [Film]. Columbia Pictures.

The Truth of Salvation Is Reconciliation

Adam P. Zoeller

FILM: *Admissions* (2011)

Grade	Subject	Topic
12	Judaism; Islam	Israel–Palestine Conflict and Inter-Religious Dialogue

Chapter Theme	Estimated Time Needed for Lesson
Wisdom Literature: Conflict, Reconciliation, Salvation, Terrorism	45 minutes

National Association for Media Literacy Education

Standard Number	Detailed Description of Each Standard You Are Discussing
Core Principles of Media Literacy Education in the United States	3. Media Literacy Education (MLE) builds and reinforces skills for learners of all ages. Like print literacy, those skills necessitate integrated, interactive, and repeated practice. *Implications for Practice* 3.3 MLE engages students with varied learning styles. 3.4 MLE is most effective when used with co-learning pedagogies, in which teachers learn from students and students learn from teachers and from classmates.

State and Common Core Standard Description

State	Detailed Description of Each Standard You Are Discussing
California State Board of Education Grade 12 History—Social Science Content Standards	12.3 Students evaluate and take and defend positions on what the fundamental values and principles of civil society are (i.e., the autonomous sphere of voluntary personal, social, and economic relations that are not part of government), their interdependence, and the meaning and importance of those values and principles for a free society. 1. Explain how civil society provides opportunities for individuals to associate for social, cultural, religious, economic, and political purposes. 3. Discuss the historical role of religion and religious diversity.

Kentucky High School: Geography Standards	G: Human Interactions and Interconnections **HS.G.HI.1** Analyze how the forces of cooperation and conflict within and among people, nations, and empires influence the division and control of Earth's surface and resources. **HS.G.I.UE.1** Evaluate the credibility of multiple sources representing a variety of perspectives relevant to compelling and/or supporting questions in geography. **HS.G.I.UE.2** Gather information and evidence from credible sources representing a variety of perspectives relevant to compelling and/or supporting questions in geography. **HS.G.I.UE.3** Use appropriate evidence to construct and revise claims and counterclaims relevant to compelling and/or supporting questions in geography.

Massachusetts *Curriculum Framework* English Language Arts and Literacy Grades 9–10 Writing Standards	1. Write arguments (e.g., essays, letters to the editor, advocacy speeches) to support claims in an analysis of substantive topics or texts, using valid reasoning and relevant and sufficient evidence.
	   a. Introduce precise claim(s), distinguish the claim(s) from alternate or opposing claims, and create an organization that establishes clear relationships among claim(s), counterclaims, reasons, and evidence.
	   b. Develop claim(s) and counterclaims fairly, supplying evidence for each while pointing out the strengths and limitations of both in a manner that anticipates the audience's knowledge level and concerns.
	   c. Use words, phrases, and clauses to link the major sections of the text, create cohesion, and clarify the relationships between claim(s) and reasons, between reasons and evidence, and between claim(s) and counterclaims.
	   d. Establish and maintain a style appropriate to audience and purpose (e.g., formal for academic writing) while attending to the norms and conventions of the discipline in which they are writing.
	   e. Provide a concluding statement or section that follows from and supports the argument presented.

USCCB Curriculum Framework	
Elective Option E Ecumenical and Interreligious Issues	III. The Relationship of the Catholic Church to the Jewish People A2. The Jewish people were God's special choice to be the instrument for the salvation of the world. They were the first to hear the Word of God, that is, Divine Revelation (CCC, no. 839).

Elective Option E Ecumenical and Interreligious Issues	IV. The Church and Other Non-Christians A2. The Catholic Church and Muslims acknowledge God as the Creator and claim ties to the faith of Abraham.

Elective Option E Ecumenical and Interreligious Issues	V. Proclamation and Dialogue
	  A2. "Those who, through no fault of their own, do not know the Gospel of Christ or his Church, but who nevertheless seek God with a sincere heart, and, moved by grace, try in their actions to do his will as they know it through the dictates of their conscience—those too may achieve eternal salvation" (CCC, no. 847; LG, no. 16)
	V. Proclamation and Dialogue
	  B2. Such dialogue requires mutual search for truth among those learned in their own religious traditions.
	  B3. Requires respect and understanding of differences in culture as well as in belief.
	  B4. Requires training in accurate knowledge of other religions.

NCSS C3 Framework

Dimension	Detailed Description of Each NCSS Dimension You Are Incorporating (should have all four).
D1.2.9-12	Explain points of agreement and disagreement experts have about interpretations and applications of disciplinary concepts and ideas associated with a compelling question.
D2.His.5.9-12	Analyze how historical contexts shaped and continue to shape people's perspectives.
D3.3.9-12	Identify evidence that draws information directly and substantively from multiple sources to detect inconsistencies in evidence in order to revise or strengthen claims.
D4.1.9-12	Construct arguments using precise and knowledgeable claims, with evidence from multiple sources, while acknowledging counterclaims and evidentiary weaknesses.

NCSS Core Themes and Description

Theme Number	Detailed Description of Each Aligned NCSS Theme
I Culture	The study of culture examines the socially transmitted beliefs, values, institutions, behaviors, traditions, and way of life of a group of people; it also encompasses other cultural attributes and products, such as language, literature, music, arts and artifacts, and foods. Students come to understand that human cultures exhibit both similarities and differences, and they learn to see themselves both as individuals and as members of a particular culture that shares similarities with other cultural groups, but is also distinctive. In a multicultural, democratic society and globally connected world, students need to understand the multiple perspectives that derive from different cultural vantage points.
IV Individual Development and Identity	The study of individual development and identity will help students to describe factors important to the development of personal identity. They will explore the influence of peoples, places, and environments on personal development. Students will hone personal skills such as demonstrating self-direction when working towards and accomplishing personal goals, and making an effort to understand others and their beliefs, feelings, and convictions.

Handouts/Materials/Web Links

Handout/Materials:
- "Hollywood or History?" graphic organizer
- Appendix A

Web Links:
  A. Link to Film Clip(s):
  – *Admissions* (Kakatsakis, 2011)
    https://itunes.apple.com/us/movie/admissions/id562773627
  B. Primary Source(s):
  – "Nostra Aetate: Declaration on the Relation of the Church with Non-Christian Religions" (Vatican II Council, 1965).
    https://www.vatican.va/archive/hist_councils/ii_vatican_council/documents/vat-ii_decl_19651028_nostra-aetate_en.html
  C. Secondary Source(s):
  – "Universal Declaration of Human Rights" (United Nations, 1948/2015)
    https://www.un.org/en/udhrbook/pdf/udhr_booklet_en_web.pdf

Guiding Questions

What should students know or understand at the completion of the unit or lesson?

Primary Questions:
- How does confirmation bias impede conflict resolution?
- Why is empathy a valuable strategy for interreligious dialogue?
- Does the existence of various major world religions contradict monotheism?
- How does reconciliation affect admittance into the afterlife?

Important Vocabulary

List all of the important indicators of achievement (important people, places, and events) and vocabulary that students will need to know at the conclusion of the lesson.

Comparative Methodology: studying other religions provides the opportunity to understand our own religion more fully.
Empathy: the capacity for seeing things from another person's perspective.
Ethnocentric Monoculturalism: the belief that one's race or nation is superior to another.
Heaven: the abode of God, the angels, and the spirits of the righteous after death; the place or state of existence of the blessed after the mortal life.
Hell: the place or state of punishment of the wicked after death; the abode of evil and condemned spirits.
Israeli: a native or inhabitant of modern Israel.
Jerusalem: ancient holy city and center of pilgrimage for Jew, Christians, and Muslims.
Palestinian: a native or inhabitant of Palestine.
Reconciliation: the state of being reconciled, as when someone becomes resigned to something not.
Terrorism: the unlawful use of violence or threats to intimidate or coerce a civilian population or government, with the goal of furthering political, social, or ideological objectives.

Assessment Strategies

Describe the assessments that will be used during the unit.

Formative Assessment: Class discussion, journal Reflective Questions, Socratic Seminar
Summative Assessment: Essay Topic—"Can anyone go to Heaven?"

Teaching Strategies

10 min	Sparking Strategy	10 min	Provide time to complete questions	5 min	Conclusion of the Socratic Seminar
10 min	Introduce the short film and begin watching the film.	10 min	Completion in the Socratic Seminar	Time Remaining/ HMWK	
Times are highly flexible and should be adjusted according to the number of sources used, length of introduction, period/ block schedule, etc.					

Sparking Strategy/Warm-Up

Sparking Strategy (Lesson introduction)

Invite students to define the following vocabulary terms covered from the introduction to the course: empathy, comparative methodology, and ethnocentric monoculturalism. Allow students to defend why empathy is vital for understanding world religions.

Lesson Procedures

In a numerical list, provide a step by step outline of what you plan to do in the lesson. Include questions you will ask the students and materials you will use.

Outline

Please Note: It is recommended that the placement of this lesson coincides with teaching the religions of Judaism and Islam.

1. Invite students to view the United Nations "Universal Declaration of Human Rights" (United Nations, 1948/2015; https://www.un.org/en/udhrbook/pdf/udhr_booklet_en_web.pdf). Request a volunteer to read Article 10:

   > Everyone is entitled in full equality to a fair and public hearing by an independent and impartial tribunal, in the determination of his rights and obligations and of any criminal charges against him.

   Use the information in Article 10 to explain public trials in this world, but also to rhetorically ask the students to consider how and who judges our actions in the next life.

2. Introduce the premise of the short film that students are about to view in class. Winners of eightAwards including the New York International Independent Film and Video Festival (2012) and the International Film Festival for Peace, Inspiration, and Equality (2012), *Admissions* is a short film directed by Harry Kakatsakis (2011) "that tells a transformational tale about what it takes to find lasting peace, even in war-torn places like the Middle East. Featuring an Israeli couple and a Palestinian man, this modern parable is set in the Admissions Room for the afterlife. Its purpose is to start a conversation that heals" (IMDb, n.d.).

3. In light of the description of the short film and Article 10, describe why the feature is called Admissions.

4. Clip to video *Admissions* (Kakatsakis, 2011) https://itunes.apple.com/us/movie/admissions/id562773627. Please note the length of this short film is approximately 21 minutes.

5. Solicit initial feedback from the class in regards to their immediate reactions to the video. Invite students to share their reactions in one word or a phrase. Once students share these reactions verbally, invite the students to write these reactions on the board.

6. Provide an opportunity for students to answer the following reflective questions:
   a. Can anyone go to Heaven?
   b. Did the Israeli couple and the Palestinian man get a fair trial? Refer to Article 10 of the UN "Universal Declaration of Human Rights" (United Nations, 2015).

c. How can Article 1 of the United Nations (1948/2015) "Universal Declaration of Human Rights" be applied to the scenario in this short film?
      i. *All human beings are born free and equal in dignity and rights.*
   d. How can Article 13 of the United Nations (1948/2015) "Universal Declaration of Human Rights" be applied to the scenario in this short film?
      i. Everyone has the right to freedom of movement and residence within the border of each state.
      ii. Everyone has the right to leave any country, including his own, and to return to his country.
7. Transition the class from reflective journaling questions to participation in a Socratic Seminar. Divide the class in half. Create two circles in class with the desks. There needs to be an outer circle and an inner circle. The inner circle is tasked with answering the following higher level thinking questions in light of the short film. This student-centered approach should be led by and conducted by the students. The outer circle should listen and take notes based upon what they heard. After approximately 10 minutes, have the participants in both circles switch. Students not only switch physical positions but also responsibilities of the seminar.

   Questions for Socratic Seminar
   - How does confirmation bias impede conflict resolution?
   - Why is empathy a valuable strategy for interreligious dialogue?
   - Does the existence of various major world religions contradict monotheism?
   - How does reconciliation affect admittance into the afterlife?

8. At the conclusion of class, explain the Catholic church belief about the value of interfaith dialogue:

   > [The Church] looks with sincere respect upon those ways of conduct and of life, those rules and teachings which, though differing in many particulars from what she holds and sets forth, nevertheless often reflect a ray of that Truth which enlightens all men. (Vatican Council II, 1965, p. 2)

Differentiation

Think about your students' skill levels, intelligences, and learning styles. How are you going to make this lesson meet the needs of all of your students?

Introverts: the opportunity to journal and answer reflective questions quietly and independently as well as to listen during the Socratic Seminar prior to participation in the discussion.
Extraverts: the opportunity to share their immediate reactions post video as well as lead discussion during the student-centered Socratic Seminar.
Visual Learners: the opportunity to engage in media literacy by watching the short film.
Auditory Learners: the opportunity to listen during the Socratic Seminar.

Summarizing Strategies/Synthesizing Activity

What strategies are you going to use to allow students to summarize what they learned in the lesson?

- Journaling responses to reflective questions and completing an essay on the topic of admittance to the afterlife.

References

Are there any additional resources that might be relevant to your lesson? Are there sources that you need to reference? Please add any citations using APA.

IMDb. (n.d.). *Admissions: Plot.* https://www.imdb.com/title/tt2066826/plotsummary

Kakatsakis, H. (Director). (2011). *Admissions* [Film]. One Film Company. https://itunes.apple.com/us/movie/admissions/id562773627

United Nations. (2015). *Universal declaration of human rights* [Web booklet]. https://www.un.org/en/udhrbook/pdf/udhr_booklet_en_web.pdf (Original work published 1948)

United States Conference of Catholic Bishops. (2000). *Catechism of the Catholic Church* (2nd ed.) Libreria Editrice Vaticana.

Vatican Council II. (1965). *Nostra Aetate: Declaration on the relation of the Church with non-Christian religions.* https://www.vatican.va/archive/hist_councils/ii_vatican_council/documents/vat-ii_decl_19651028_nostra-aetate_en.html

Additional Resources

Center for Media Literacy. (n.d.). *What is media literacy? NAMLE's short answer and a longer thought.* National Association for Media Literacy Education. http://www.medialit.org/reading-room/what-media-literacy-namles-short-answer-and-longer-thought

Chapter 5: Wisdom Literature ■ **177**

Hollywood or History?
Admissions **(2012)**

Winner of 8 awards including the New York International Independent Film & Video Festival (2012) and the International Film Festival for Peace, Inspiration, and Equality (2012), *Admissions* (2012) is a short film directed by Harry Kakatsakis "that tells a transformational tale about what it takes to find lasting peace, even in war-torn places like the Middle East. Featuring an Israeli couple and a Palestinian man, this modern parable is set in the Admissions Room for the afterlife. Its purpose is to start a conversation that heals" (IMDB, n.d., para. 1).

Evaluate each source provided and summarize your observations and analysis in corresponding spaces provided. In the section located at the bottom of the page, explain whether you think the scenes from *Admissions* (2011) should be evaluated as an accurate account of the main theme of Vatican II Document *Nostra Aetate* (1965) or the United Nations Universal Declaration of Human Rights (1948), or both. Use examples from your sources/documents to explain your answer.

Primary Source	***Admissions* (2012)**	**Secondary Source**
What Do You Think? Hollywood or History?		

Hollywood or History?
Admissions (2012)
Appendix A: Socratic Seminar

Winner of 8 awards including the New York International Independent Film & Video Festival (2012) and the International Film Festival for Peace, Inspiration and Equality (2012), *Admissions* (2011) is a short film directed by Harry Kakatsakis "that tells a transformational tale about what it takes to find lasting peace, even in war-torn places like the Middle East. Featuring an Israeli couple and a Palestinian man, this modern parable is set in the Admissions Room for the afterlife. Its purpose is to start a conversation that heals" (IMDB, n.d., para. 1).

Directions Part 1: Introduce the UN Universal Declaration of Human Rights (1948) to the class focusing specifically on the following articles:

Article 1: All human beings are born free and equal in dignity and rights.

Article 10: Everyone is entitled in full equality to a fair and public hearing by an independent and impartial tribunal, in the determination of his rights and obligations and of any criminal charges against him.

Article 13: Everyone has the right to freedom of movement and residence within the border of each state. Everyone has the right to leave any country, including his own, and to return to his country.

Allow students to work independently or with a partner to answer these questions in light of the Articles from the UN Universal Declaration of Human Rights. Did the Israeli couple and the Palestinian man get a fair trial? How can Article 1 of the UN Universal Declaration of Human Rights be applied to the scenario in this short film? How can Article 13 of the UN Universal Declaration of Human Rights be applied to the scenario in this short film?

Directions Part 2: Divide the class in half. Create two circles in class with the desks. There needs to be an outer circle and an inner circle. The inner circle is tasked with answering the following higher level thinking questions in light of the short film. This student-centered approach should be led by and conducted by the students. The outer circle should listen and take notes based upon what they heard. After approximately 10–15 minutes, have the participants in both circles switch. Students not only switch physical positions but also responsibilities of leading the discussion and taking notes during the seminar.

Questions for Socratic Seminar:
1. How does confirmation bias impede conflict resolution?
2. Why is empathy a valuable strategy for interreligious dialogue?
3. Does the existence of various major world religions contradict monotheism?
4. How does reconciliation affect admittance into the afterlife?

Escaping the Cycle of Groundhog Day

Adam P. Zoeller

FILM: *Groundhog Day* (1993)

Grade	Subject	Topic
12	Buddhism	Dharma (Samsara and Noble Eightfold Path)

Chapter Theme	Estimated Time Needed for Lesson
Wisdom Literature: Attachment Reincarnation, Suffering, Transcendence	Part 1: 30 minutes (Dharma of the Buddha) Part 2: 1:41 minutes for the film *Groundhog Day* (Comparing and contrasting themes such as temptation, desires, attachment, and the Eightfold Path, specifically Right Speech and Right Action.

National Association for Media Literacy Education

Standard Number	Detailed Description of Each Standard You Are Discussing

Core Principles of Media Literacy Education in the United States	3. Media Literacy Education (MLE) builds and reinforces skills for learners of all ages. Like print literacy, those skills necessitate integrated, interactive, and repeated practice.
	
	Implications for Practice
	    3.3 MLE engages students with varied learning styles.
	    3.4 MLE is most effective when used with co-learning pedagogies, in which teachers learn from students and students learn from teachers and from classmates.

State and Common Core Standard Description

State	Detailed Description of Each Standard You Are Discussing
Massachusetts English Language Arts and Literacy (Grades 9–10 Writing Standards)	1. Write arguments (e.g., essays, letters to the editor, advocacy speeches) to support claims in an analysis of substantive topics or texts, using valid reasoning and relevant and sufficient evidence. a. Introduce precise claim(s), distinguish the claim(s) from alternate or opposing claims, and create an organization that establishes clear relationships among claim(s), counterclaims, reasons, and evidence. b. Develop claim(s) and counterclaims fairly, supplying evidence for each while pointing out the strengths and limitations of both in a manner that anticipates the audience's knowledge level and concerns. c. Use words, phrases, and clauses to link the major sections of the text, create cohesion, and clarify the relationships between claim(s) and reasons, between reasons and evidence, and between claim(s) and counterclaims. d. Establish and maintain a style appropriate to audience and purpose (e.g., formal for academic writing) while attending to the norms and conventions of the discipline in which they are writing. e. Provide a concluding statement or section that follows from and supports the argument presented.
New York Common Core Social Studies 9–12 Framework Reading Standards for Literacy in History/Social Studies Integration of Knowledge and Ideas	7. Integrate and evaluate multiple sources of information presented in diverse formats and media (e.g., visually, quantitatively, and in words) in order to address a question or solve a problem. Distinguish between fact, opinion, and reasoned judgment in a text. 8. Evaluate an author's premises, claims, and evidence by corroborating or challenging them with other information. 9. Integrate information from diverse sources, both primary and secondary, into a coherent understanding of an idea or event, noting discrepancies between sources.

North Carolina Standards for World History Inquiry 9–12	Apply the inquiry models to analyze and evaluate social studies topics and issues in order to communicate conclusions and take informed actions.
	    I.1.3 Summarize the central ideas and meaning of primary and secondary sources through the use of literacy strategies.
	    I.1.4 Analyze causes, effects, and correlations.
	    I.1.4 Determine the relevance of a source in relation to the compelling and supporting questions.

USCCB Curriculum Framework	

Elective Option E: Ecumenical and Interreligious Issues	IV. The Church and other non-Christians.
	  B. There are non-Christian religions common in the United States, including major world religions such as Hinduism and Buddhism, and others such as Sikhs, Mormons, and Bahai.
	    1. Common elements with Christianity.
	      a. As human beings we share a common origin and end.
	      b. Many of these religions teach to some degree compassionate action, moral restraint, spiritual discipline, and respect for human dignity.
	      c. These religions contain elements of truth and virtue, which can help orient their members toward reception of the Gospel.
	    2. Those who do not know Christ but who still strive to know and live in truth and holiness can be saved.

NCSS C3 Framework

Dimension	Detailed Description of Each NCSS Dimension You Are Incorporating (should have all four).
D1.2.9-12	Explain points of agreement and disagreement experts have about interpretations and applications of disciplinary concepts and ideas associated with a compelling question.
D2.His.5.9-12	Analyze how historical contexts shaped and continue to shape people's perspectives.
D3.3.9-12	Identify evidence that draws information directly and substantively from multiple sources to detect inconsistencies in evidence in order to revise or strengthen claims.
D4.1.9-12	Construct arguments using precise and knowledgeable claims, with evidence from multiple sources, while acknowledging counterclaims and evidentiary weaknesses.

NCSS Core Themes and Description

Theme Number	Detailed Description of Each Aligned NCSS Theme
IV Individual Development and Identity	The study of individual development and identity will help students to describe factors important to the development of personal identity. They will explore the influence of peoples, places, and environments on personal development. Students will hone personal skills such as demonstrating self-direction when working towards and accomplishing personal goals, and making an effort to understand others and their beliefs, feelings, and convictions.

Handouts/Materials/Web Links

Handout/Materials:
- "Hollywood or History?" graphic organizer
- Appendix A: Guided Questions

Web Links:

A. Film(s):
  - *Groundhog Day* (Ramis, 1993)
B. Primary Source(s):
  - "The Buddha's 'First Sermon,' Delivered at the Deer Park in Benares" (n.d.) http://www.columbia.edu/itc/religion/f2001/edit/docs/buddhas_first_sermon.htm
C. Secondary Source(s):
  - "Groundhog Day,' The Buddhist Lifehacker Movie" (Allan, 2017) https://www.cnn.com/2016/02/01/health/groundhog-day-movie-wisdom-project/index.html
  - "A religious Scholar's View on the Buddhist Themes Behind Groundhog Day" (Bauld, 2018) https://news.uchicago.edu/story/religious-scholars-view-buddhist-themes-behind-groundhog-day
  - "The Life of the Buddha [Documentary]" (Kishubhai, 2012) https://www.youtube.com/watch?v=Heho8bXXLi4

Guiding Questions

What should students know or understand at the completion of the unit or lesson?

Primary Questions:
1. What would the Buddha say about the cause of Phil's suffering?
2. How does Phil's suffering relate to the concept of samsara/cycle of rebirth?
3. What is symbolic about Phil seeing his shadow?
4. How does Phil's character develop in light of the demon Marra tempting him within his own psyche. Provide examples to support.
5. Apply the Eightfold Path (Right Speech) to the development of Phil's character.

6. Apply the Eightfold Path (Right Action) to the development of Phil's character.
7. At what moment in the film does Phil become enlightened about the true meaning of living the same day over and over again?
8. Provide examples from the film where you witnessed the concepts of anatta and/or annica being present for Phil.

Important Vocabulary

List all of the important indicators of achievement (important people, places, and events) and vocabulary that students will need to know at the conclusion of the lesson.

Buddha: to wake up, an awakened one, an enlightened being.
Demon Marra: psychological temptation during the Buddha's meditation.
Dharma: the teachings of the Buddha.
Eightfold Path: goals to be mastered in life in order to escape suffering. It includes, but is not limited to right speech and right action.
Four Noble Truths: essential teachings of the Buddha that include: (a) to live is to suffer, (b) suffering is caused by attachment or desires, (c) suffering can end, and (d) suffering can end using the Eightfold Path.
Samsara: the cycle of reincarnation.
Siddhartha Gautama (2500 BCE): The Buddha.

Assessment Strategies

Describe the assessments that will be used during the unit.

Formative Assessment: Guided questions to the film; classroom discussions, and reflective journaling

Summative Assessment: Essay topic—Compare and contrast the journeys of Phil and Siddhartha focusing on their temptation, attachment, suffering, and enlightenment.

Teaching Strategies Part 1

10 min	Sparking Strategy	10 min	Introduce the Buddha's Eightfold Path	5 min	Questions and answers.
10 min	Read "The Buddha's 'First Sermon,' Delivered at the Deer Park in Benares" (n.d.) and relate this to themes of the Buddha's Dharma.	10 min	Invite students to discuss which societal temptation impede living the Eightfold Path	**Time Remaining/ HMWK**	

Times are highly flexible and should be adjusted according to the number of sources used, length of introduction, period/block schedule, etc.

Teaching Strategies Part 2

10 min	Review themes of Buddhism from previous class	10 min	Watching Groundhog Day (Ramis, 1993) will take more than one class period. Students will complete guided questions to film while watching.	5 min	Students will evaluate how the main character's thoughts and actions affecting his reincarnation.
10 min	Begin watching film *Groundhog Day* (Ramis, 1993)	10 min		Time Remaining/ HMWK	

Times are highly flexible and should be adjusted according to the number of sources used, length of introduction, period/block schedule, etc.

Sparking Strategy/Warm-Up

Sparking Strategy (Lesson introduction)

Have students list characters (protagonists and antagonists) from literature and/or film whose words and actions support the respective character's knowledge, wisdom, or enlightenment of the world or their place in it.

Lesson Procedures

In a numerical list, provide a step by step outline of what you plan to do in the lesson. Include questions you will ask the students and materials you will use.

Outline

Part 1: Exploring the Buddha's Dharma
1. Invite students to get into groups of 2–3 people and share examples of the Buddha's Dharma based on his first sermon at Deer Park. Possible answers could include the Four Noble Truths and the 3 Marks of Existence.
2. Invite students to share the results of their group work. Focus on the Eightfold Path: right views, right intentions, right speech, right action, right livelihood, right effort, right meditation, and right conduct. Reinforce the teaching of how the Eightfold Path are not steps to be achieved, but continuous and are ways to live a life of moderation and balance.
3. In a classroom discussion, invite students to share which societal or personal temptations prohibit or impede successful application of the Eightfold Path in a person's life.

Part 2: Comparing and contrasting themes such as temptation, desires, attachment, and the Eightfold Path (specifically right speech and right action).
1. Introducing the film *Groundhog Day* by Harold Ramis (1993), explains how the themes of Buddhism will be present. Provide guided questions to the film:
   – What would the Buddha say about the cause of Phil's suffering?
   – How does Phil's suffering relate to the concept of samsara/cycle of rebirth?
   – What is symbolic about Phil seeing his shadow?

- How does Phil's character develop in light of the demon Marra tempting him within his own psyche. Provide examples to support.
- Apply the Eightfold Path (right speech) to the development of Phil's character.
- Apply the Eightfold Path (right action) to the development of Phil's character.
- At what moment in the film does Phil become enlightened about the true meaning of living the same day over and over again?
- Provide examples from the film where you witnessed the concepts of anatta and/or annica being present for Phil.

2. Students will be asked to answer these questions by the end of the film.
3. At the conclusion of the film, review right speech and right action and ask students when Phil transitioned from his selfish ways to become unselfish. How did his mindset help grant him salvation from Groundhog Day?
4. Lastly, students are invited to work in collaborative learning groups to complete the following activity: During the festival of Groundhog Day, Punxsutawney Phil may or may not see his shadow. This legend determines the length of winter. What is symbolic about the director naming the name character and the groundhog both Phil? What is symbolic about Phil Connors being trapped in Punxsutawney during winter? When does Phil Connors metaphorically see his shadow? How does this affect his actions? Explain.

Differentiation

Think about your students' skill levels, intelligences, and learning styles. How are you going to make this lesson meet the needs of all of your students?

Guided Questions: Students will complete guided questions to the film that chronologically and thematically invite students to grasp the primary intended concepts.

Collaborative Learning Groups: Students will work with partners or groups to share results of the guided questions and to offer any assistance to students needing additional help.

Classroom Discussion: Teacher will pose higher level thinking questions in light of the guided questions to challenge the class to make relevant connections between the main character in the film to that of the Dharma of the Buddha.

Introverts: students may independently work on guided questions to the film.

Summarizing Strategies/Synthesizing Activity

What strategies are you going to use to allow students to summarize what they learned in the lesson?

- Students will be asked to complete guided questions to the film which focus on the application and analysis of the plot, primary themes, and character development in light of the Dharma of the Buddha.
- Students will complete an essay on the film.

References

Are there any additional resources that might be relevant to your lesson? Are there sources that you need to reference? Please add any citations using APA.

Allan, D. G. (2017). *Groundhog day, the Buddhist lifehacker movie.* CNN. https://www.cnn.com/2016/02/01/health/groundhog-day-movie-wisdom-project/index.html

Bauld, A. (2018). *A religious scholar's view on the Buddhist themes behind Groundhog Day.* University of Chicago. https://news.uchicago.edu/story/religious-scholars-view-buddhist-themes-behind-groundhog-day

Kishubhai. (2012, January 29). The life of the Buddha [BBC documentary] [YouTube video]. https://www.youtube.com/watch?v=Heho8bXXLi4

Ramis, H. (1993). *Groundhog Day* [Motion Picture]. Columbia Pictures.

The Buddha's 'First Sermon,' Delivered at the Deer Park in Benares. (n.d.). Columbia University. http://www.columbia.edu/itc/religion/f2001/edit/docs/buddhas_first_sermon.htm

Additional Resources

Center for Media Literacy. (2001). *National Association for Media Literacy Education.* http://www.medialit.org/reading-room/what-media-literacy-namles-short-answer-and-longer-thought

Chapter 5: Wisdom Literature ■ 187

Hollywood or History?
Groundhog Day (1993)

Buddhism teaches that in order to escape the wheel of rebirth known as samsara, following the Dharma of the Buddha is essential. The teachings focus on detachment from suffering and prescribing to the Noble Eightfold Path. Directed by the late Harold Ramis, *Groundhog Day* (1993) centers around the egotistical Phil Connors and how his irreverent speech and actions play a role in trapping him in the cycle of samsara as he is living Groundhog Day over and over again.

Evaluate each source provided and summarize your observations and analysis in corresponding spaces provided. In the section located at the bottom of the page, explain whether you think the scenes from *Groundhog Day* (1993) should be evaluated as an accurate representation of the Dharma of Buddha from the "First Sermon at Deer Park" or *A religious scholar's View on the Buddhist Themes Behind Groundhog Day* (2018) or a mixture of both. Use examples from your sources/documents to explain your answer.

Primary Source	***Groundhog Day* (1993)**	**Secondary Source**

What Do You Think? Hollywood or History?

Hollywood or History?
Groundhog Day (1993)
Appendix A: Guided Questions

Directed by Harold Ramis, *Groundhog Day* (1993) is about a weatherman named Phil Connors who finds himself reliving the same day over and over again. The main character Phil, played by Bill Murray, is trapped in Punxsutawney, Pennsylvania unable to escape February 2nd. The movie centers around the egotistical Phil Connors and how his irreverent speech and actions play a role in trapping him in the cycle of living Groundhog Day. As each day unfolds for Phil, he slowly begins to recognize his affect on others and eventually finds a way to escape.

Directions: During the festival of Groundhog Day, Punxsutawney Phil may or may not see his shadow. This legend determines the length of winter. Using your knowledge of this tradition, answer the following questions by analyzing the symbolism of the film in light of the Eightfold Path and Samsara.

1. What is symbolic about the director naming the main character after the actual groundhog from Punxsutawney, Pennsylvania?
2. What is symbolic about Phil Connors being trapped in Punxsutawney during winter?
3. When does Phil Connors metaphorically see his shadow? How does this affect his speech and his actions? Explain.
4. How does the amount of time it takes Phil to begin living a better life with his words and actions indicative of the Buddha's teaching that the Eightfold Path is not steps to be mastered and move on, but instead continuously living according to these guidelines.

Wisdom Literature and the Power of the Poetic Word

Thomas Malewitz

FILM: *Thursday Appointment* (2019) [English subtitles]

Grade	Subject	Topic
7–12	Judaism; Sufism	Wisdom Literature, Poetry, and the Power of Symbolic Language in Religion

Chapter Theme	Estimated Time Needed for Lesson
Wisdom Literature: poetry, symbolic language, wisdom, happiness, grief	45 minutes

National Association for Media Literacy Education

Standard Number	Detailed Description of Each Standard You Are Discussing

Core Principles of Media Literacy Education in the United States	1. Media Literacy Education (MLE) requires active inquiry and critical thinking about the messages we receive and create.
	
	Implications for Practice
	  1.3 MLE emphasizes strong sense critical thinking, that is, asking questions about all media messages, not just those with which we may disagree.
	  1.4 MLE trains students to use document-based evidence and well-reasoned arguments to support their conclusions.

State and USCCB Standard Description

State	Detailed Description of Each Standard You Are Discussing
Kentucky High School Reading Standards for Informational Texts	RI.11-12.9 Analyze documents of historical and literary significance, including how they address related themes and concepts.

Michigan (Grade 7) Growth and Development of World Religions	**W3.2.1** Identify and describe the core beliefs of major world religions and belief systems, including Hinduism, Judaism, Buddhism, Christianity, Confucianism, Sikhism, and Islam. *Examples may include, but are not limited to:* comparing major figures, sacred texts, and basic beliefs (ethnic vs. universalizing; monotheistic vs. polytheistic) among religions; case studies of continuity of local indigenous belief systems or animistic religions; comparisons with religious traditions that developed after 1500 CE such as Protestantism.
New York (Grade 9) High School Global History	**9.2a** Belief systems developed beliefs and practices to address questions of origin, the requirements to live a good life, and the nature of the afterlife. Students will identify the place of origin, compare and contrast the core beliefs and practices, and explore the sacred texts and ethical codes for Hinduism, Buddhism, Judaism, Christianity, Islam, Confucianism, and Daoism.
United States Conference of Catholic Bishops (USCCB) Curriculum Framework	
USCCB.Option A Sacred Scripture— V.A, C, & D	Analyze wisdom literature as a collection of practical guides to human problems and questions, including sections of: Psalms, Proverbs, Ecclesiastes, Song of Songs, Wisdom, and Sirach.

NCSS Core Themes and Description

Theme Number	Detailed Description of Each Aligned NCSS Theme
II Time, Continuity, and Change	Studying the past makes it possible for us to understand the human story across time. Historical analysis enables us to identify continuities over time in core institutions, values, ideals, and traditions, as well as processes that lead to change within societies and institutions, and that result in innovation and the development of new ideas, values, and ways of life.
V Individuals, Groups and Institutions	Social studies programs should include experiences that provide for the study of interactions among individuals, groups, and institutions

Handouts/Materials/Web Links

Handout/Materials:
- "Hollywood or History?" graphic organizer

Web Links:
A. Link to Clip(s):
   - *Thursday Appointment* [Short Film] (Kheradmandan, 2019) [3 mins]
     https://www.youtube.com/watch?v=XXx_Hw34V-Q (Barr Pictures Media, 2019)
B. Primary Source(s):
   - "For Years My Heart Inquired of Me" (Hafez, 2008)
     https://www.poetryfoundation.org/poetrymagazine/poems/50967/for-years-my-heart-inquired-of-me
   - Psalm 23
   - Proverbs 10:12
C. Secondary Source(s):
   - Leonard Cohen/The Webb Sisters (LeonardCohen, 2019) [5 mins]
     https://www.youtube.com/watch?v=O_XcMAGZjuY

Guiding Questions

What should students know or understand at the completion of the unit or lesson?

Primary Questions:
- How can sacred poetry offer wisdom to everyday life?
- How can a personal sacrifice illustrate a gesture of love?
- How does digital media bring ancient sacred poetic writings new meaning and connection to life in the digital age?

Important Vocabulary

List all of the important indicators of achievement (important people, places, and events) and vocabulary that students will need to know at the conclusion of the lesson.

Hafez: Khāwje Shams-od-Dīn Moḥammad Ḥāfeẓ-e Shīrāzī (1315–1390) was an Iranian Sufi poet. His writings are regarded as the pinnacle of Iranian poetry. Much of his poetry focuses on faith and divine love.

Psalms: 150 sacred poetic ritual prayers tracing elements and emotions from the history of Judaism.

Proverbs: practical life lessons within Judaism to live based on wisdom.

Assessment Strategies

Describe the assessments that will be used during the unit.

Formative Assessment: reflection on the meditative uses of sacred poetry and wisdom literature for personal growth and healthily shared emotion in community.

Summative Assessment: Write a poem to express a prayer or belief, as a way to offer hope and optimism for a challenge.

Teaching Strategies

10 min	Sparking Strategy	10 min	Read Psalm 23 with followed discussion	5 min	Reflect on the actions and poetry of the clip
10 min	View "The Webb Sisters—If It Be Your Will" (Leonard Cohen, 2019)/discussion	10 min	Introduce Proverbs 10:12 and view *Thursday Appointment* (Kheradmandan, 2019)	**Time Remaining/ HMWK**	Poetry assignment

Times are highly flexible and should be adjusted according to the number of sources used, length of introduction, period/ block schedule, etc.

Sparking Strategy/Warm-Up

Sparking Strategy (Lesson introduction)

Have the students bring to class and analyze some of the lyrics to one of their favorite songs. Be sure that the lyrics are appropriate to share in class. Have the students examine the emotions, challenges, and/or the symbolism in the lyrics. Ask the students: "What struggles is the artist describing?"; "Why might they write lyrics based on such an event?"; and "Why do the lyrics connect with you (the student)?"

Lesson Procedures

In a numerical list, provide a step by step outline of what you plan to do in the lesson. Include questions you will ask the students and materials you will use.

Outline
1. After the Warm-Up briefly explain that poetry has been an essential part of humanity to share emotion, and open one's heart through art to find wisdom in how to live a meaningful and happy life.
2. Play Cohen/Webb's "If It Be Your Will" (LeonardCohen, 2019) [5 mins]. Supply the students with the lyrics [optional]
3. Supply students with copies of Psalm 23
4. Compare and contrast "If It Be Your Will" (LeonardCohen, 2019) and Psalm 23. What similar words or themes exist between the words of the two poems? What differences are present between the poems? What do you think is the focal theme of the two examples?
5. Explain that sacred poetry is not just in the form of songs, but can also be in brief wisdom for life. Use Proverbs 10:12 as an example.
6. Show *Thursday Appointment* (Kheradmandan, 2019) [3 mins]
7. Compare Proverbs 10:12 and the actions of the old man in *Thursday's Appointment* (Kheradmandan, 2019). Ask questions such as: "How does the sacred poetry of Hafiz (2008) influence the old man's actions?" and "How is Proverbs 10:12 demonstrated in *Thursday Appointment* (Kheradmandan, 2019)?"

8. Reflect on the video clip. Explain the tradition that on Thursdays in Iran many individuals visit their deceased loved ones. They bring gifts of candies and flowers to the cemetery. In the final scene the wife was not in the car, but only candies and flowers. What did the old man sacrifice by giving away the flowers? How did that sacrifice affect the other family?
9. Assign the poetry assignment for the students to complete for the next class. Challenge the students to create a poem based on the themes of sacred poetry, on themes of love, sacrifice, and hope. Use Hafiz's (2008) "For Years My Heart Inquired of Me," a Psalm, and Proverbs as an example.

Differentiation

Think about your students' skill levels, intelligences, and learning styles. How are you going to make this lesson meet the needs of all of your students?

Scaffolds: Work with students individually if needed to answer questions and further explain any material.

Language Interventions: Provide closed captions on the video clip. Include lyrics of the poetry for the students to follow along when the poem is used in class.

Extensions: Have students examine themes found in works of a favorite musician that parallels the examples of the sacred poetry. Allow the students to research the context of the song and find any connections to struggles in the life of the musician to give deeper meaning to the lyrics. Have the student create a report or presentation to present their findings to the class.

Summarizing Strategies/Synthesizing Activity

What strategies are you going to use to allow students to summarize what they learned in the lesson?

- Roundtable discussion
- Personal reflection
- Analyze sacred texts
- Create poetry

References

Are there any additional resources that might be relevant to your lesson? Are there sources that you need to reference? Please add any citations using APA.

Barr Pictures Media. (2019, December 28). *Beautiful Iranian short film 2 MILLION views award winning winner film festival Thursday Appointment* [YouTube video]. https://www.youtube.com/watch?v=XXx_Hw34V-Q

Hafez. (2008, April). For years my heart inquired of me [D. Davis, Trans.]. *Poetry.* https://www.poetryfoundation.org/poetrymagazine/poems/50967/for-years-my-heart-inquired-of-me

Kheradmandan, M. R. (Director). (2019). *Thursday Appointment* [Film]. Soureh.

LeonardCohen. (2019, March 29). *The Webb sisters—If it be your will (live in London) ft. Leonard Cohen* [YouTube video]. https://www.youtube.com/watch?v=O_XcMAGZjuY

Additional Resources

Barton, S. (2011) The power of the Psalms in the lives of urban teenagers. *Leaven: A Journal of Christian Ministry, 19*(3), 6. https://digitalcommons.pepperdine.edu/leaven/vol19/iss3/6

Carroll, R. (2005). Finding the words to say it: The healing power of poetry. *Evidence-Based Complementary and Alternative Medicine, 2*, 161–172. https://doi.org/10.1093/ecam/neh096

Childs, M. (2016). Reflecting on translanguaging in multilingual classrooms: Harnessing the power of poetry and photography. *Educational Research for Social Change, 5*(1), 22–40. https://www.researchgate.net/publication/305714574_Reflecting_on_translanguaging_in_multilingual_classrooms_Harnessing_the_power_of_poetry_and_photography

Landman, C. (2020). Healing the wounded: The Psalms and therapy. *Old Testament Essays, 33*(3), 663–673. https://dx.doi.org/10.17159/2312-3621/2020/v33n3a17

Hollywood or History?
Thursday Appointment (2019)

Thursday Appointment (2019) is an Iranian short film that reminds the viewer of the importance of generosity, sacrifice, and how our actions affect the lives of others. Within the context of a Hafez love poem, an elderly gentleman becomes a witness of hope, through a simple gift.

Evaluate each source provided and summarize your observations and analysis in corresponding spaces provided. In the section located at the bottom of the page, explain whether you think the scenes from *Thursday Appointment* (2019) should be evaluated as an accurate account of a wise life in comparison to the primary sources, secondary source, or both. Use examples from your sources/documents to explain your answer.

Primary Source	***Thursday Appointment* (2019)**	**Secondary Source**

What Do You Think? Hollywood or History?

About the Contributors

Ariel Cornett is an assistant professor in the Department of Elementary and Special Education at Georgia Southern University. She teaches undergraduate and graduate elementary social studies methods courses. She received her doctorate from the University of Virginia in curriculum and instruction with a focus on social studies education in 2020. Her research interests focus on the teaching and learning of social studies in elementary classrooms and communities. She has presented her work at several conferences such as the College and University Faculty Assembly (CUFA), National Council for the Social Studies (NCSS), and American Educational Research Association (AERA). She has coauthored publications in the following journals: *Social Studies and the Young Learner* (SSYL), *Journal of Social Studies Research* (JSSR), *Social Studies Research and Practice* (SSRP), and *School Community Journal* (SCJ).

Charles Elfer (series coeditor) currently serves as associate professor of history education at Columbus State University (GA), where he teaches courses pertaining to history, social studies education, and educational foundations. Charles also serves as coordinator of history and social studies education for all graduate and undergraduate programs, as a board member for the Georgia Council for the Social Studies, and as the coeditor of *History Matters!* (e-journal). In addition to his ongoing coeditorial contributions to the Hollywood or History? strategy and book series, he is closely affiliated with The The Ivey Center for the Cultural Approach to History. A former high school teacher, Charles received his PhD from the University of Georgia in social studies education in 2011, with an emphasis in curriculum history, place-based education, and history/social studies methods.

Colleen Fitzpatrick is an assistant professor in the Department of Teacher Education at the Judith C. Herb College of Education at the University of Toledo. Her research interests focus on the complex and interactional role the context of a classroom, school, district, or state plays in how teachers and students experience teaching and learning social studies. Prior to coming to the University of Toledo, Dr. Fitzpatrick was a teacher scholar postdoctoral fellow at Wake Forest University and a middle and high school social studies teacher.

Stephanie Garrone-Shufran is an assistant professor of education in the Winston School of Education and Social Policy at Merrimack College in North Andover, Massachusetts. She teaches courses on educating emergent bilinguals and developing language and literacy skills for all students in both the undergraduate and graduate teacher education programs. Her research focuses on methods for preparing preservice English as a second language (ESL) teachers to advocate for their students and the motivations behind choosing ESL teaching as a career. Prior to entering higher education, she was a sheltered content and ESL teacher of middle school emergent bilinguals in Massachusetts.

Miguel David Hernández Paz is a historian and musicologist. His research interests involve the interconnectivity of the history of America and the arts, particularly through a lens of journalism, cultural anthropology, and music as it has shaped and defined cultural identities. Miguel possesses a master's degree in museology and cultural management from the University of La Laguna, where he also pursued a doctorate in information sciences. He has served in various scientific events, including the *I Congreso de Historia del Periodismo Canario*, which his latest book chapter "De Museología y enfoques museísticos, a propósito de las funciones de las hemerotecas canarias" explored.

Thomas E. Malewitz (volume coeditor) is assistant professor and the director of the EdD leadership program at Spalding University. He possesses a MTS, graduate certificate in Scripture, and a PhD in education and social change. Tom worked over a decade as a theology teacher in Catholic secondary education. He has presented national workshops and papers on 21st century pedagogical practices, adolescent formation, and spirituality, and has served as a textbook assessment developer for Ave Maria Press. Tom is a CMA book award-winning author for *Authenticity, Passion, and Advocacy* (Wipf & Stock, 2020) in the category of youth and young adult pastoral ministry. He has peer-reviewed articles published in *The Journal of Catholic Education* and *The Merton Annual*. Tom is an active member of the American Educational Research Association (AERA), Catholic Theological Society of America (CTSA), College English Association (CEA), International Thomas Merton Society (ITMS), and Thomas Merton Society of Great Britain and Ireland (TMS-GBI).

Daniel E. Martin is a secondary school theology teacher with 18 years of teaching experience. He earned his PhD in theology from the University of Dayton. His dissertation focused on the influence of Roman Catholicism on Sargent Shriver's contributions to public policy and international development. His areas of expertise include Catholic social teaching, social ethics, religion and film, religion and politics, and religion and science. He has contributed to theological texts from Continuum and Lit Verlag. Dr. Martin has articles published by *The Maronite Voice, The Covington Messenger,* and *Louisville's Eccentric Observer*. He has presented at academic conferences sponsored by the College Theology Society, the Upper Midwest Chapter of the American Academy of Religion, the Sisters of Notre Dame USA, the Archdiocese of Louisville, the University of Dayton, and Dominican University of Illinois. Dan is currently involved in diversity, equity, and inclusion work at both a local and regional level.

Scott L. Roberts (series coeditor) currently serves as associate professor of social studies education at Central Michigan University. He teaches courses in elementary social studies education, current educational issues, and research methods. He has served as a board member of the Michigan Council for Social Studies, on several committees for the National Council for the Social Studies, on the editorial board of Social Studies and the Young Learner, and was named the Georgia Council for the Social Studies' Gwen Hutchinson Outstanding Social Studies Educator (2012). A former middle school teacher, he received his doctorate from the University of

Georgia in social studies education in 2009. He is the author of multiple publications concerning history education and is the coeditor *Hollywood or History? An Inquiry-Based Strategy for Using Film to Teach United States History* (Information Age Publishing, 2018), *Hollywood or History? An Inquiry-Based Strategy for Using Film to Teach World History* (Information Age Publishing, 2021) and the coauthor of *Teaching Middle Level Social Studies: A Practical Guide for 4th–8th Grade* (Information Age Publishing, 2022). His research interests include state history, discussion-based strategies, history education, and educational technology.

Rory P. Tannebaum is an associate professor of education at Merrimack College in North Andover, Massachusetts. His research interests focus on developing preservice social studies teachers who are capable of facilitating meaningful dialogue on controversial issues and events. He currently teaches undergraduate and graduate-level courses to preservice teachers hoping to teach in the K–12 school system. Prior to becoming part of higher education, he was a middle school social studies teacher who taught South Carolina history in North Charleston, South Carolina.

Adam P. Zoeller (volume coeditor) is a secondary school theology teacher with 20 years experience in Carmelite and Xaverian traditions teaching Scripture, Christology, and World Religions. He earned his MEd in educational leadership from the University of Cincinnati. He has been published in *The Journal of Catholic Education*, has led webinars for the National Catholic Educational Association, and has served as an educational consultant for Journey Films. In addition, Adam has also served as an educational consultant for Ave Maria Press for the development of their World Religions teacher's manual. He has presented nationally on the topics of adolescent spirituality, athletics, media literacy, and Catholic identity. He is a member of the National Catholic Educational Association (NCEA).

Printed in the United States
by Baker & Taylor Publisher Services